AFRICAN AMERICANS AND WHITES

Changing Relationships on College Campuses

Edited by
Robert M. Moore III

Center for the Study of Higher Education
The Pennsylvania State University
400 Rackley Building
University Park, PA 16802-3203
(814) 865-6346; FAX: (814) 865-3638

University Press of America,® Inc.
Lanham · Boulder · New York · Toronto · Oxford

Copyright © 2006 by
University Press of America,® Inc.
4501 Forbes Boulevard
Suite 200
Lanham, Maryland 20706
UPA Acquisitions Department (301) 459-3366

PO Box 317
Oxford
OX2 9RU, UK

All rights reserved
Printed in the United States of America
British Library Cataloging in Publication Information Available

Library of Congress Control Number: 2006929005
ISBN-13: 978-0-7618-3500-4 (paperback : alk. paper)
ISBN-10: 0-7618-3500-8 (paperback : alk. paper)

∞™ The paper used in this publication meets the minimum
requirements of American National Standard for Information
Sciences—Permanence of Paper for Printed Library Materials,
ANSI Z39.48—1984

Contents

Preface   vii

Acknowledgements   ix

Introduction   xi

Part I. Teaching

    Chapter 1   **Teaching Region, Learning Humility**   3
                               Larry J. Griffin

    Chapter 2   **Too White to Teach Race?**   19
                               Andrea Malkin Brenner

    Chapter 3   **Beyond the Veil: Black and White Perspectives**   37
                               on Teaching about Racial Inequality
                               Wanda Rushing and Zandria Robinson

Part II. Student Groups

    Chapter 4   **Black and Gay Identity Selection**   57
                               Tim Baylor

| Chapter 5 | **Facilitating Student Involvement and Cross-Race Contact: The Impact of Membership in a Black Greek Organization**
Stephanie M. McClure | 77 |
| Chapter 6 | **History of a BSU at a Professional Health Science University**
Joseph W. Ruane | 89 |

Part III. Social Distance

Chapter 7	**Racial Divides on a Diverse Campus: An Exploration of Social Distance at a State Liberal Art University** Erica Chito Childs and Eunice Matthews-Armstead	103
Chapter 8	**Self-Segregation, Friendship Formation and the College Experience: Separate but Equal?** Bette J. Dickerson and Kianda Bell	117
Chapter 9	**"Let's Talk about *The Simpsons* or Something"** Todd Schoepflin	129
Chapter 10	**Interracial Dating and Marriage: Fact, Fantasy and the Problem of Survey Data** Charles A. Gallagher	141
Chapter 11	**Social Distance and the "Tipping Effect" Among College Students at a Northern New Jersey University** Kathleen Korgen, Gabe T. Wang, and James Mahon	155

Part IV. Marginality and Policy

| Chapter 12 | **Exploring Black Identity Via Marginality Theory**
Jeffrey R. Breese and Kathleen Grant | 173 |
| Chapter 13 | **Is Diversity Policy Inherently Contradictory?**
Frank Ridzi and Joshua G. McIntosh | 193 |

| Chapter 14 | **An Old Journey in a New Direction: The Two Faces of Desegregation**
F. Erik Brooks | 207 |
| Chapter 15 | **Activism Scholarship: Answering 'the question'**
Marybeth Gasman | 223 |

About the Contributors   233

Preface

I remember my first days away from home at college. My dormitory was huge, about 800 people, a living small city with late-night cafes and numerous comfortable lounges used to relax and talk with others. I had experienced and expected racial segregation in some social situations. I had the distinction of being the only African American in my built-for-the baby boom elementary school in the mid 1960's. The school was later turned into a YMCA as the subsequent generation was much smaller.

I learned to navigate beneath the radar screen of others who attended my school to avoid controversy. I learned what whites felt about African Americans. Although I counted most of my classmates as my friends, I still felt a sense of difference. I didn't dare go to the same swim clubs they attended during the summer out of fear that those who did not know me would be openly hostile.

My classmates' parents were newcomers to the suburbs. Many had grown up inside the city limits of Philadelphia, sons and daughters of the working class, and had moved to the suburbs as adults to live a more middle class lifestyle in the 50's. At the same time the migration of African Americans from rural America to urban America occurred. The movement of whites to the suburbs during this time period is commonly referred to as "white flight."

Although millions of African Americans were moving to the cities after World War II, my father's family, his grandfather, had arrived in Philadelphia, with perhaps a stopover in Baltimore from rural Virginia, near the very early years of the 20th century. He owned a moving company. My father told me that my middle name was taken from the surname of a white doctor who had befriended my great grandfather.

When I attended a large junior high school in the late 1960's, about 1500 kids, I was one of two African Americans. There were days that were frightening. I was aware of the other individual who was African American but I did not know him. Near the end of 9th grade, I asked my parents if I could attend a different school. My social life just did not seem complete where I was. Both of my parents worked, rather unusual for that time period especially for middle class families.

My new school was affiliated with the Quakers, a Friends school. It was a private institution on the Philadelphia mainline. For the first time I had African American friends, not many, ten or so, a substantial number for me. I attended African American parties on the weekends throughout Philadelphia, and had my first girlfriend in tenth grade, African American.

Had I attended the public high school and not the private school, I would have been, again, one out of less than five African Americans out of nearly a couple thousand students. This period was consonant with the airing of, All in the Family, when crossing the racial divide still brought attention and required a rethinking of one's "quality of life." I had many close friends when I attended the public schools who accepted me for who I was. But this was a time period of social turbulence and social change. Many individuals who I was unable to get to know one-on-one were not as accepting. Parents, especially fathers, frequently showed disdain for my presence and contact with their children. There were less than 60 students in my graduating class at my private high school.

Although I have very fair skin, I have never wavered from identifying as African American. Although, there were days in my youth when I kept rather quiet. To this day I hold a fascination and deep interest in the changing relationship between African Americans and whites on college campuses. I felt those changes quite intimately when I was in college over a couple decades ago - the sense of having to choose sides, caught in between, the warmth and camaraderie of being with and identifying as African American, and the sense of confusion whites had at this time at the dawn of a multicultural push, on the heals of the Black Power movement.

The following pages are about the contemporary relationship between African Americans and whites on college campuses. Perhaps one day this book will fade into antiquity, be obscure, unintelligible in meaning to a future reader who may happen to stumble upon it. The "racial" nuisances will become unknown. I am told that the public high school that I feared so deeply now has 47 languages spoken by its students. What a wonderful experience it would have been for me to have experienced such diversity. But overall the social distance felt between many African Americans and whites today is still great, a reflection of the overall inequality still experienced by each relative to the other in our society as well as the historical legacies of race relations in America.

Acknowledgments

I dedicate this edition to my students. The quest to learn from them is great, more so than what I possibly can give. Hopefully the articles in this book will inspire as well as shed light on an ever changing sociological phenomenon, the relationship between African Americans and whites on college campuses.

Introduction

I sometimes tell my students not to worry about trying to express a politically correct opinion or vision about issues related to race. I casually mention throughout the semester that if you feel confused at the end of the course then I have done my job to encourage and foster students to think more deeply about the making and maintenance of racial categories, the production of stereotypes and the existence of inequalities that exist in our society. There is less emphasis on factual material in my class and more on the presentation of perspectives or paradigms in an effort to teach lifelong learning skills, ways of seeing the changing relationships between African Americans and whites long after the semester and one's college career have ended.

The following book places emphasis on everyday life circumstances on our nation's college campuses. I have created and listed a very short set of questions at the end of each chapter, not to turn the book into a text that can be used in a classroom course, but with an eye to challenge the reader to think more deeply, to connect the dots in ways most Americans are unable to do, to deepen one's sociological imagination.

Twenty-three authors affiliated with a variety of institutions such as Georgia State, American University, University of North Carolina, University of Memphis, William and Paterson University, Niagara University and Lemoyne University have been included in this book. The book is divided into four parts: Teaching, Student Groups, Social Distance, and Marginality and Policy.

As indicated in the table of contents numerous facets of the college experience have been included. The book can be used as a resource for those who are interested in examining the everyday nuances of race relations on college and university campuses as well as a reference for those engaged in research. Although many articles have been written from the perspective of personal experience, numerous references to relevant research are included in most articles. The authors have attempted to present to the reader in a meaningful, responsible and scholarly way what they believe to be the changing relationships between African Americans and whites on college campuses.

I

Teaching

Chapter 1

Teaching Region, Learning Humility[1]

Larry J. Griffin

Part One

After graduating from a whites-only public high school in Mississippi in 1965, I entered a small public college in the state--Delta State College (now University)--in its last year of segregated existence. I graduated with a degree in accounting and worked as an auditor for ten months for the U.S. Navy. Because so much was happening in American university and public life in the mid- to late 1960s, and so much was changing in the South, I'll never know exactly why accountancy so quickly escaped my unhappy presence. But I am pretty sure that a man named William Pennington was very much responsible. Bill Pennington was a Methodist minister, a part-time philosophy instructor (later department chair) at Delta State, and the teacher who, in a very gentle but wholly compelling way, led me to open my eyes, look around, and think about the world around me--my world, Mississippi of the 1960s. And in doing that, Bill Pennington also irreversibly changed my life.

Though Pennington taught me many things of value, the most important was that college teaching itself is a profoundly moral act. By "moral," I do not mean

---

[1] Portions of this essay were first presented at talks at Vanderbilt University and the Southern Sociological Society. I am grateful to the following for their insightful comments on earlier drafts: Karen E. Campbell, Marshall Eakin, Allison Pingree, and Peggy A. Thoits. This essay is dedicated to William A. Pennington.

that it is necessarily "good" or has "good" results, only that teaching, "good" or "bad," is rooted in a framework of moral values about self and others, that it is motivated by moral understandings of educational goals, that it is performed with pedagogical practices moral in nature, and thus that it, teaching, inevitably entails moral choice and exerts moral consequence. Because college teachers are culturally and institutionally empowered to impart to students new knowledge and critical perspectives, we are also empowered to alter their moral outlook and standards, to open their eyes, and thereby change forever their lives. College teachers should be humbled by this knowledge, humbled, paradoxically, because most of us both know too well our own intellectual and performative limitations ("was I too simplistic?" "flat wrong?" "boring?"), and, at the same time, know too little about how consequential, even perilous, our classrooms can be for our students. Teaching binds our weaknesses, biases, defensiveness, and egotism to our institutional and interpersonal power, and then it makes us confront this fact, just as it forces many of us to acknowledge that our own accomplishments are as much a matter of luck as merit. Though teaching, then, we learn humility.

All of this was way beyond my comprehension when I graduated from Delta State in 1969. I knew only that I wanted to do for others what Bill Pennington had done for me, and that to do that I had to teach. And teach I have, for almost a quarter of a century in four institutions of higher education, public and private. Though teaching of any sort is inescapably moral in its context and consequence, if not always in its content, college courses about race, gender, sexuality, class, religion, and, for reasons that will become clear, region--to name some of the politically sensitive topics often taught in the social sciences and humanities--deal with issues that are by their very nature moral; that is, with the "rightness" or "wrongness" of the way social arrangements are or were constituted and with the conflictual or challenging strategies advanced to change or perpetuate group relations and privilege. Such courses therefore are more likely to be morally upsetting, even emotionally wrenching, for students and faculty alike.[2] Probing, difficult questions about our purposes in teaching such courses, and about how we should and do teach them, are therefore almost fated to--and indeed, ought--to arise. Those of us who teach such classes should occasionally examine our motives for doing so, reflect on the utility of our procedures in doing so, and

---

[2] There is a vast literature in sociology and other disciplines on teaching culturally sensitive/controversial material. See, for example, the following articles from the journal Teaching Sociology, published by the American Sociological Association: Susanne Bohmer and Joyce L. Briggs, "Teaching Privileged Students About Gender, Race, and Class Oppression" 19 (April, 1991): 154-63; Amy B. Lusk and Adam S. Weinberg, "Discussing Controversial Topics in the Classroom: Creating a Context for Learning" 22 (October 1994): 301-08; Mark Beeman and Robert W. Volk, "Challenging Ethnic Stereotypes: A Classroom Exercise" 24 (July, 1996): 299-304; Frances V. Moulder, "Teaching About Race and Ethnicity: A Message of Despair or a Message of Hope?" 25 (April, 1997): 120-27.

worry--worry as a dog "worries" a bone, and also "worry" as in the experience of anxiety--about the consequences, for us and our students, of having done so. Through such worry, we learn humility.

Part Two

My teaching cannot be reduced to the facts of my personal biography--political and religious beliefs matter, as do intellectual tastes and institutional needs--but why, how and what I teach nonetheless do significantly reflect biographical experience. Born and reared in what historian James Cobb has called "the most Southern place on earth," the Mississippi Delta, at just about the time Strom Thurmond and the Dixiecrats bolted the Democratic party in 1948, I am the grandson of hardscrabble Mississippi hill farmers/ sharecroppers, and the son of non-unionized, small-town New South factory and office workers who often labored at minimum wages and suffered periodic bouts of unemployment.[3] I have argued elsewhere that for Jim Crow-era southerners of my parents' and grandparents' generations, race was the basis of their personal and group identities, channeling their ambitions for themselves and their children, establishing their patterns of sociability, defining their "duty," their moral sensibility, and their legal and cultural "place," and privileging whiteness with a degree of political presence, economic advantage, and honorific obeisance unparalleled by all else that socially constituted women and men in the South at the time. I suppose this is true also of my generation, those of us who came of age in the region in the 1950s and 1960s: race was the window through which we saw our world, the ground upon which we walked, the air we breathed. Past, present, and possibility were all interwoven with race, and all were interpreted, vitally if not exclusively, in racial terms. In a culture premised on and organized by racial meanings and practices, in which literally no facet of human existence escaped profound racial coloration, explanation, and trajectory, race became the primary way southerners, black and white, knew our selves and our situations, articulated our hopes, and envisioned our futures.[4]

Given the confluence of biography, history, and disciplinary endorsement, then, I have always taught race (and class, to an extent), whether my course happened to be introductory sociology, or social problems, the sociology of work or education or one explicitly designed around race relations. After leaving Indiana University

---

[3] James Cobb, *The Most Southern Place on Earth: The Mississippi Delta and the Roots of Southern Identity* (New York: Oxford University Press, 1992).

[4] Larry J. Griffin, "How Do We Disentangle Race and Class? Or Should We Even Try?" Work and Occupations 22 (February, 1995): 85-93.

for Vanderbilt in 1990, a move motivated in part by a desire to return to the South, I continued to teach race, now combined, though, with teaching region. To teach is to learn, and committed college teachers are always learning--learning about the topics we teach, about our students, about what higher education can and cannot do, about ourselves--but I took a crash course in learning-by-teaching in all of these ways by having to prepare a public lecture on teaching I was required, as a recipient of a teaching award, to deliver to interested Vanderbilt faculty in 1997. What happened was that I had to acknowledge in my teaching what "the South" was and what the region meant to the world, to America, to my students, and to myself. What I learned was humility.

For the public lecture, I chose to speak on "Teaching Controversial Material" because my award was in part based on the perception of the awards committee that though I usually taught such material, and did so from a frank, if not dogmatic, political stance, I did not unduly offend or anger most students. To get a better sense of what the students thought of my presentation of such material and to learn, from their perspective, how it might be improved, I read in a single sitting all of my Vanderbilt course evaluations, about six years worth of commentary. Despite their well-publicized weaknesses and abuses, student course/instructor evaluations do indicate something of import about courses and those who teach them, so I have always taken them seriously. But I have never read so many at one time, or read them so single-mindedly fixated on the criticisms of my teaching. And there were criticisms aplenty: I seemed too anxious to defend liberal "preconceptions" from conservative attack; did not warn students of the emotional weight of the reading/discussion early enough in the semester for them to drop the class; harked too much on the problems of racism and spoke too little about its solutions; used books (especially Andrew Hacker's pointed *Two Nations: Black and White, Separate, Hostile, Unequal*, 1992) that were unfair and unbalanced.

Having taught similar material for years, and having heard many of the complaints before, I was somewhat dispirited, though not particularly surprised. What I read from an anonymous student about my first "Sociology of the South" course, however, shocked me. It read, verbatim: "Blacks, slavery and CR [civil rights; my insert] are important but not total. What about our culture?" Because every student in that inaugural "South" offering was white and most from the South, the word "our" in the student's course evaluation could have had only one meaning. Simply put, a student had left my class on the South believing, despite what were then my best efforts, in the reality of segregated black and white histories that most certainly did not converge in the American South, believing in the existence of a white regional culture having nothing to do with—and therefore innocent of--African Americans, or slavery, or the black freedom struggle.

Teaching about the region to the region's own was one reason I had moved to Vanderbilt, and the "South" course already elicited more investment of self and emotion than any I had ever taught. So what I read hurt, humbled. That only one student out of twenty or so openly voiced the complaint did not matter: to my mind, the statement painfully signified my failure and that of the course, failure as judged not by some abstract or external standard but in the very terms and language I held dearest. Whatever my success as a teacher, it was obvious in that class that I had done things I should not have and left undone things I should have attended to. I had little reason for hubris.

My failure on this signal point was not really due to the materials I used in that first class, wonderful books and essays by C. Vann Woodward, Jacquelyn Hall, Michael Schwartz, Doug McAdam, James Oakes, and others.[5] True, each of these scholars is white, but the fault did not rest with excessively racialized reading on my part. I had, independent of class, read and grieved over Richard Wright's *Black Boy*, understood and agreed with Martin Luther King, Jr's impatience in *Why We Can't Wait*, and devoured and passed along to many Anne Moody's searing autobiography, *Coming of Age in Mississippi*. Instead, the problem was that despite such reading my comprehension of what the region really was--its ontological being, as it were--was filtered through a racial lens so profoundly and subtly distorting that I evoked in class, and thereby gave license to others to evoke, an implicit identity between "the South," on the one hand, and "the white South," on the other, between "southerners," on the one hand, and "white southerners," on the other. Referring to Woodward's still important but deeply flawed interpretation of "southern identity," for example, I would say (or, what is worse, triumphantly lead my students to conclude) that its basis lay in "the South's" defeat in the Civil War and its guilt for racial crimes. As an inference about white southerners, or the white South, such a claim offers genuine purchase: as a valid statement about "southerners," or about "the South," it is absurd. As I have come to realize, and since written about in a different venue, "southerners," generally speaking, could not have been guilty of racial tyranny because *black southerners* were its victims, not its perpetrators. "Southerners," moreover, did not lose the Civil War: the Confederacy lost the War, even as some southerners, *black southerners*, won it and thus their legal freedom.[6] At the time of the award,

---

[5] C. Vann Woodward, "The Search for Southern Identity," pp. 3-25 in Woodward, *The Burden of Southern History*, rev. ed. (Louisiana State University Press, 1968); Jacqueline Hall, "Disorderly Women: Gender and Labor Militancy in the Appalachian South" Journal of American History, 73 (September, 1986): 354-382; Michael Schwartz, *Radical Protest and Social Structure: The Southern Farmers' Alliance and Cotton Tenancy, 1880-1890* (New York, Academic Press, 1976); Doug McAdam, *Political Process and the Development of Black Insurgency* (Chicago: University of Chicago Press, 1982); James Oakesci (New York: Alfred A. Knopf, 1990).

[6] Larry J. Griffin, "Southern Distinctiveness, Yet Again, or, Why America Needs the South" Southern Cultures 6 (Fall, 2000): 47-72. Roger Cunningham, "Appalachianism and Orientalism: Reflections on Reading Edward Said," Journal of the Appalachian Studies Association 1: 125-32. On southern cultures and a bi-racial southern culture, see, for example, Richard Gray, "Negotiating Differences:

though, I "knew" this only intellectually; I did not *know* it as an existential, orienting truth.

Such formulations of "southern identity," reproduced and valorized in my course, are similar in their logic to the mode of thought Roger Cunningham called "Appalachianism" (and before him Edward Said labeled "Orientism"), a way of thinking about Appalachia (or the "Orient") that is "a discourse of power, a way of seeing and talking about things which is conditioned by domination and which tends both to perpetuate itself and to perpetuate that domination. It is a way of organizing perceptions into a closed self-referential system which takes on a life of its own, shaping assumptions and perceptions even among those who are unaware of any motivation to oppress." Coming back to discussions of the South, the consequences of thinking and teaching thusly are harsh indeed: by defining and framing the South largely, if unknowingly, in terms of *whiteness*, this and similar interpretations make--conceptually, semantically, morally--racially plural southern *cultures* unimaginable, make a bi-racial South impossible, make a syncretic southern culture arising from black and white together inconceivable.[7]

By uncritically parroting the formulations of Woodward and others, I had rendered myself incapable of thinking not only about what "the South" was, or who a "southerner" was, but also about why these questions mattered, intellectually and morally.[8] My white students could hardly be expected to open their eyes under my tutelage, as Bill Pennington had helped me do under his, if I myself was unable to open my own and search for this undetected and unwanted cynosure implicitly structuring the entire course. My failure to absorb and digest the elemental truth that black southerners were *southerners* and, consequently, that "the South" belonged as much to them as to whites· was a failure of vision and empathy, an act of moral blindness more troubling still because my student critic's easy, seemingly natural use of the phrase "our culture" implicated me as a member of his or her whites-only southern culture. All of these realizations--cognitive epiphanies, and perhaps moral ones as well--one after another in a tightly

---

Southern Culture(s) Now," Pp. 218-27 in *Dixie Debates: Perspectives on Southern Cultures*, Richard H. King and Helen Taylor, eds. (New York: New York University Press, 1996), and Mechal Sobel, *The World They Made Together: Black and White Values in Eighteenth-Century Virginia* (Princeton: Princeton University Press, 1987).

[7] My Vanderbilt colleague, and fellow Mississippian, Jimmie Lewis Franklin insightfully explored this theme in his 1993 Presidential address to the Southern Historical Association. See his "Black Southerners, Shared Experience, and Place: A Reflection," Journal of Southern History 59 (February 1994): 3-18.

[8] The most influential sociologist of the U.S. South, John Shelton Reed, has an uncanny knack for doing this with humor and great intelligence. For an appreciation of Reed's accomplishments and a discussion of the sociological relevance of the region, see Larry Griffin, "The Promise of a Sociology of a South," Southern Cultures 7 (Spring, 2001): 50-75.

sequenced pattern were humbling indeed. They also spurred change, both in how I thought and in what I taught.

Part Three

In the spring of 2002, I teach the "South" course for the seventh time, and I am, finally, reasonably satisfied with it. The course continues to draw on southern history to raise questions about power, inequality, race, protest, and stereotyping that transcend any particular place or time. Because I believe that by obsessing about regional particularity we put human flesh on the sociologically general, and, simultaneously, that by wrestling with the general we grasp more firmly that particularity. Fittingly for a course now titled "The South in American Culture" and cross-listed with African American Studies and American/Southern Studies, however, it is now framed as much by the region's conflicted, and too often sorrowful, relationship to America as by overtly "sociological" concepts. It has become much more interdisciplinary over the years, now extensively employing fiction, music, film, and autobiography created by blacks and whites, women and men. The course increasingly draws minority students, so it is now much more multi-hued than when I first taught it. All of this is exactly right, I think: the South is too big, too contradictory, and too diverse to teach aided by only one or two disciplines, mediums, perspectives, representations, or voices.

To the extent that the course works as it should, it resembles in important ways a conversation of sorts between the South and America, a dialogue in which the region's meaning to and significance for the nation are the primary subjects. Rather than view the region as something exotic and separate from nation, the course presumes precisely the opposite, namely that the South, even in its peculiarity and distinctiveness, historically has been tightly bound to "America," and that the definitions of region and nation have always been co-dependent, each making and remaking the other.[9] This is made clear to students in their very first assignment: fitting the region into the "America" so powerfully evoked by Gunnar Myrdal in the introductory chapter ("American Ideals and the American Conscience") of his *An American Dilemma* (1944), and analyzing how the South might have thwarted, or paradoxically furthered, what Myrdal defined as "The American Creed." Though such readings, hearing (not reading, not watching, but *hearing*) speeches such as Martin Luther King's "I Have A Dream," and through confronting texts such as King's magisterial "Letter from the Birmingham Jail," in

---

[9] One of most insightful discussions of how "the South" has repeatedly altered the course of U.S. history is Carl Degler, "Thesis, Antithesis, Synthesis: The South, the North, and the Nation." Journal of Southern History 53 (February, 1987).

which he evinces a South with no place in a morally just United States, my students learn that in studying the South, one also inevitably studies America.[10]

The conversation between nation and region is the course's scaffolding, so to speak, sometimes deliberately left bare, more often woven into considerations of how race, gender, and class made the South what it has become today. Through the late C. Vann Woodward's influential history, *The Strange Career of Jim Crow* (3rd rev. ed., 1974), students come to see that race has largely defined the South as something separate from the nation. First published in the mid-1950s, *Strange Career* was described by Martin Luther King, Jr. as the "bible of the Civil Rights Movement" because it argued that Jim Crow, as a relatively recent (i.e., post-Reconstruction), deliberately created "invented tradition" rather than what was euphemistically called a "time-honored practice," could be undone by moral agency. The novelty of this has probably faded with time, but Woodward's corollary, that white southerners could have organized a humane racial order in the 1890s but instead *chose* the path of white supremacy in part because of the class interests and power of the region's so-called "better elements," remains an eye-opener.

Seeing how children learn of the rules and restrictions of Jim Crow, and then observing what they do with this information and what it does to them, is quite instructive for students who, themselves, may be encountering the South's racial apartheid for the first time as a serious topic of study. So by using the hurt or angry or puzzled or arrogant voices of southerners close in age to those of the students in the course, several of the assigned books on race and region have a "coming of age," eye-opening feel to them. The story in Harper Lee's still poignant *To Kill a Mockingbird* (1960) is, of course, told in Scout Finch's young white (and increasingly horrified) voice, and much of Anne Moody's *Coming of Age in Mississippi* (1968) powerfully recounts Anne's childhood and teen years in the 1940s and 1950s, when she suffered from lacerating poverty and grew to know and despise its main cause for black Mississippians, white supremacy. Though one is fiction, the other autobiography, both texts deal with how young girls, one black and one white, experienced the Jim Crow South in the pre-*Brown* days. There are some commonalties deriving from a shared southern culture, gender, and rurality, but mostly students see that differences in class and race gave rise to vast, unignorable differences in what it meant to be southern.

Anne Moody's experience, moreover, can be very usefully contrasted with that of Melton McLaurin. In his memoir of growing up in a very small town in North Carolina, *Separate Pasts: Growing Up White in the Segregated South* (1987), McLaurin, today a historian of the region (see below) and almost exactly Moody's age, describes a "South" that is about as racist as Moody's Mississippi, but one lived, through the double privilege of white skin color and economic comfort, as

---

[10] Pp. 76-95 in Martin Luther King, Jr., *Why We Can't Wait* (New York: Mentor, 1964).

its opposite. It is also an obviously conflicted South, and McLaurin has his grandfather, "Lonnie Mac," serve as the repository of the racial contradictions of many southern whites--racist, paternalistic, and oddly egalitarian, all at the same time. *Separate Pasts* is especially illuminating when McLaurin uses the rituals of adolescent males to demonstrate how unfathomably insecure whites' were in their dominance and how truly captive they were to their self-created constructions of African Americans. These and other points are driven home, I think, by having students read a portion of Moody and then a chunk of McLaurin, returning again to Moody, then back to McLaurin. Black and white together, though separate: the South before the Second Reconstruction.

By demonstrating just limited and ineffective white liberalism in the region was, Lee's *To Kill a Mockingbird* also offers painful lessons in how white southerners were imprisoned by jails of their own making. The question of whether Atticus Finch was a racial paternalist--well-meaning, perhaps, but hardly a friend of racial equality--sparks a lively (and unresolvable) class debate.[11] but what is clear is that for all his undoubted personal decency and devotion to law, Atticus could not save Tom Robinson. The very best the white South had to offer in the mid-1930s, then, was not good enough. Nor, frankly, was it ever good enough. Southern whites did not, en mass, "rescue" or "save" African Americans in the region. Blacks, of course, "saved" themselves through sustained, non-violent collective militancy a generation later. My students learn a good bit about the Civil Rights Movement from Woodward's *Strange Career*, from the documentary series "Eyes on the Prize," and from a number of essays analyzing the Movement in such communities as Nashville and Birmingham.[12] but they encounter it most directly and richly in Moody's *Coming of Age*. Much of Moody's autobiography describes her years as a dedicated activist in Mississippi. *Coming of Age* is especially good on the always tense, often harrowing, day-to-day experiences of African Americans immersed in the Movement and on what intransigent white resistance to freedom cost Moody personally. Students in the course thus learn that "southern heritage" is more complex, both for worse and for better, than they might have thought, including, as it does, both another, less honorable, "southern" tradition and its exact opposite, a marvelous emancipatory gift from the region to the world, the Civil Rights Movement.

---

[11] This is the argument of Joseph Crespino in is article "The Strange Career of Atticus Finch," Southern Cultures 6 (Summer, 2000): 9-29.

[12] Linda Wynn, "The Dawning of a New Day: The Nashville Sit-Ins, February 13-May 10, 1960." Tennessee Historical Quarterly 50 (Spring, 1991): 42-54. Martin Luther King, Jr., "Letter from the Birmingham Jail." Aldon D. Morris, "Birmingham Confrontation Reconsidered: An Analysis of the Dynamics and Tactics of Mobilization." American Sociological Review 58 (October, 1993): 621-636.

Emancipatory collective action did end Jim Crow in the region--at least as a system of state-sanctioned, state-mandated segregation--but it only set the stage for, rather than guaranteed, real racial equality. After the Movement's initial legal successes in the mid-1960s, the South's meaning was even more contested, more uncertain, more in flux than ever, with black southerners continuing to struggle to make their voices heard and to secure in daily practice what was theirs in law. Ernest Gaines's absorbing novel, *A Gathering of Old Men*, about a 1970s killing on a Louisiana sugarcane plantation and its galvanizing effect on a group of elderly African American men, wonderfully captures this sense of new world hesitantly, painfully coming into existence with no template as to what it will become. Initially, the text is confusing, opaque, even-off-putting: readers must process page after page before they have a handle on what's going on, or who the characters are and how they are related, a narrative device I suspect Gaines deliberately employed to symbolize the very real confusion about identity and place and action in the immediate post-Civil Rights South. In important particulars, Candy, the paternalistic white plantation owner who ultimately loses her power to speak for "her" blacks in Gaines's novel, is strikingly similar to Atticus and Scout finch, both of whom were also in the habit of speaking and acting for African Americans.

By contrasting *A Gathering* with *To Kill a Mockingbird*, therefore, students learn important insights about authorial voice, representation, and perspective. More than mere technical conventions in the art of narrative, these story-telling devices also convey a moral sensibility about race and hence can be productively exploited to raise vexing questions about whether the region's whites could ever "speak" for, or even genuinely know, its African Americans. *A Gathering* also beautifully shows that only by speaking for themselves--by acting in concert and autonomously--did southern blacks achieve self-determination, a form of equality, to return to the overarching theme of the conversation between region and nation, not so commonly articulated in idealizations of "America."

My students learn, too, that race is inseparable from gender in the making of the region. Gaines's novel, for example, is very much about masculinity, really the gendered meanings of racial existence in the South: through their actions, the "old men" of the title become, fully and for the first time, "men," *black* men. Another assigned text is Melton McLaurin's *Celia: A Slave* (1991), an extraordinary history of an enslaved African American female who, in 1850, was purchased by her owner for reasons of sex and who later killed him for repeatedly raping her. Using the killing and Celia's subsequent trial as interpretive vehicles to explore the practice and contradictions of slavery, McLaurin concludes that the white jurors deciding Celia's fate could not have defined her action as "protecting her honor," and thereby absolve her for the killing, because to do so would have created an intolerable inversion in the region's racialized sexual hierarchy: it would have given enslaved African American women a right white males withheld from their own legally free wives, the right to rebuff, with violence if necessary, unwanted sexual advance from their "masters" (or husbands).

Gender also is central to the section of the course that I find the most emotionally exhausting to teach, that about lynching. This is a sorry story indeed, but one that must be told to convey just how discrepant the region was from the rest of America. If students do not squarely confront both the motivating/exculpatory (and hideously inaccurate) constructions of race and gender, they cannot understand why white southerners for fifty years or more after Reconstruction resorted so willing to lynching. The white justification for lynching rested on the self-serving mythology that white women were (or were to be) pure, asexual, and defenseless. As "southern ladies" of this sort, they were thus thought dependent on the protection of white men from African American males, who, in the sick collective psychology permeating much of the white South at the time, were thought to be continually lusting after white women.

Harper Lee very deliberately unmasks this pathology in *To Kill a Mockingbird*. During Mayella Ewell's testimony against Tom Robinson, she declares that she had been "violated" by Tom and then added that "if you fine fancy gentlemen don't wanna do nothin' about it then you're all yellow stinkin' cowards, the lot of you. Your fancy airs don't come to nothin'...." (p. 188). The allegation of black-on-white rape elicited such outrage from southern whites because the act did not simply "defile" what were thought to be defenseless white "ladies": it also contaminated the purity of the white blood line--the "white race" could be preserved only by white women--and hence was the ultimate taboo in the Jim Crow South. The only winners in all of this, of course, were white men, who, by manipulating the gender constructions underpinning racial lynching, were able to turn privilege into "necessity" and thereby perpetuate their dominance over African Americans of both sexes and white females.[13]

Most students are uncomfortable (as am I) with the lynching statistics and accounts they read or see (of the lynching of Emmett Till, for example) in the *Eyes on the Prize* documentary series. I sense also that some white men in the class have not agreed entirely with the inference about how the entire process worked to perpetuate the privilege of their racial and gender identities. I would not have done so either at their age; indeed, I did not even have the bald facts from which such

---

[13] Some of the class readings on this and similar points include J. William Harris, "Etiquette, Lynching, and Racial Boundaries in Southern History: A Mississippi Example," American Historical Review 100 (April 1995): 387-410; Stephen Whitfield, A Death in the Delta: The Story of Emmett Till (Baltimore: Johns Hopkins University Press , 1988); and Sara Evans, "Myth Against History: The Case of Southern Womanhood," Pp. 149-154 in Patrick Gersten and Nicholas Cords (eds.), Myth and Southern History, vol. 2. 2nd ed. (Urbana, Ill. : University of Illinois Press, 1989).

inferences are drawn. This, too, is humbling and leaves me little room for self-righteousness or even excessive impatience.

Like gender and race, class is everywhere in the making of the modern South. My students see its racially decisive (and usually toxic) operation in Woodward's *Strange Career*, in Moody's *Coming of Age in Mississippi*, in Gaines's *A Gathering of Old Men,* and in Lee's *Mockingbird*, where Atticus Finch, surely a member of the white South's "better element," defends Tom Robinson against the depredations of Bob Ewell and other (typically) lower-strata "rednecks." Perhaps the single most provocative reading in the entire course, in fact, is an unorthodox class analysis of the region's rednecks by Will Campbell, a native white Mississippian, civil rights activist, and Southern Baptist preacher Campbell depicts southern rednecks as both victimizers and victims, scapegoated by a self-satisfied, "enlightened" America for the racial privileges accorded more advantaged, liberal, whites.[14] "What must be understood," Campbell says:

> "is that *all* whites...are racist because racism is the condition in and structure under which we live and move and have our being....[Racism] has nothing to do with how liberal or radical or enlightened or educated or good I am. Nor does it have to do with how reactionary, conservative, ignorant or bad I am. It just has to do with *being white within these structures*" (p. 93, emphasis in original).

Yes, "rednecks" have, Campbell readily admits, too often acted on their bigotry, suspicion, and frustration. They have done so though--at least in his analysis (one surely unusual for a man of the cloth)--because they too deeply drank the intoxicating brew known as evangelical Protestantism, a mind-numbing elixir the South's white elite used to entice those on the bottom rail from union with even more oppressed blacks and one therefore ultimately addicting poor whites to a self-defeating, burning religion of hate.

By depicting, often with first-hand accounts, gender, class, and racial differences in what Richard Wright once called "living Jim Crow," all of these texts help insure that students leave the course knowing that there is no totalizing "southern heritage," no essentializing "southern experience," no single "southern identity."[15] Students learn also that race has indelibly shaped the region's economy, polity, its cultural appetites in religion, food, music, and leisure, and even its religious beliefs and practices, and, finally, that "our" culture is not a

---

[14] Campbell, "Used and Abused: The Redneck's Lot," pp. 90-104 in Dudley Clendinen (ed.), *The Prevailing South: Life and Politics in a Changing* Culture (Atlanta: Longstreet Press, 1988). Once the Chaplain at the University of Mississippi, Campbell migrated to Nashville in the mid-1950s. When I asked him why he left the state, he said, simply, "They would have killed me if I had stayed."

[15] Richard Wright, "The Ethics of Living Jim Crow." Pp. 9-22 in Wright, Uncle Tom's Children: Five Long Stories. (Cleveland: World Publishing, 1938).

white culture at all, but a *southern* culture, the syncretic accomplishment of two races, never really equal in principle, never fully separate in practice, each always looking to the other for place and definition. Students now realize that to study the South is to study race.

Part Four

"Relative satisfaction" with the course is not to suggest that it be beyond improvement. Despite the addition of material on the Southern Appalachians in recent offerings the reading list probably continues to concentrate too much on the "Deep South" and on black-white relations. Other geographic sub-regions and the ethno-racial complexity stamping the region today (e.g., in the late 1990s, there were an estimated 50,000 Hispanics in Nashville alone) get too little attention, as do the South's original inhabitants, Native Americans.[16] Issues of social class permeate the course, but most often when configured with race, making me unsure if my students, my *Vanderbilt* students, appreciate as fully as they should just how meaningful class is to the region's history and culture. Rick Bragg's *All Over But the Shoutin'* (1997), his memoir about growing up abjectly poor and white in the region, might work wonders here. Also too little represented in the course is the South's religious traditions and practices. The writer Flannery O'Connor once referred to the South as "Christ-haunted," a sentiment echoed in Will Campbell essay I assign. Nonetheless, there is need for more on the topic, perhaps Donald Matthews's *Religion in the Old South* (1977), with its incendiary final chapter on the awesomely redemptive power of what had once been the slavemaster's tool, now appropriated and transmuted by African Americans, evangelical Christianity. Gender, clearly, figures prominently in the very design of the course, but I occasionally think about using Lillian Smith's autobiography, *Killers of the Dream* (1949). Smith was a novelist (*Strange Fruit* is her most famous), an authentic white southern radical on matters of race and sex, and a feminist, lesbian and Christian, who beautifully metaphorized racial segregation to bodily "avoidance rites." Speaking of autobiographies, one by an African American male with roots in the South, Richard Wright's *Black Boy*, say, or Henry Louis Gates's *Colored People: A Memoir*, would prove an insightful gender (and for Gates, who

---

[16] Included here is the stunning documentary, *Stranger With a Camera*, made by Kentuckian Elizabeth Barret. The film tells the story of the 1967 murder of a Canadian film-maker who, having gone to eastern Kentucky to portray the poverty of southern mountain whites, was killed by a native of the area apparently incensed by the barrage of unflattering (if sympathetic) images of hungry children, pinched faces, and squalid living conditions. It does not rationalize thekilling, but Stranger does provoke wide-ranging questions about how and why "the downtrodden" are represented by "outsiders" and about the ownership of these images.

grew up in West Virginia, geographic) juxtaposition to Anne Moody's *Coming of Age in Mississippi*. Each of these works, and much more, deserve to be taught in the course. That I've no room for them–the syllabus is stuffed now (7 books, 25 essays)--does not mask the fact that I've a long way to go before the course is what it ought to be. Humbling.[17]

I will also confess that though I conclude with Peter Applebome's *Dixie Rising: How the South is Shaping American, Values, Politics, and Culture* (rev. ed., 1998)--an interpretation of the region's present-day tensions, identities, inequalities, and national import by an experienced *New York Times* reporter-- there is no doubt that the discussion of the South of today is too hurried. Still, history is essential to any serious study of the region. The region's past is a tragically rich repository of social institutions and cultural practices of perennial moral urgency--arrangements voicing death and desire, exploitation and exclusion, class and courage, and fanaticism and freedom, to name a few—and that past persists in, haunts, the South's present, more so than is seen in any other region of the country. Even to pose the question of continuing southern distinctiveness, or of the region's "otherness," necessarily pushes the class (and its instructor) to chart the extraordinary changes in the region's laws, racial practices, migration patterns, economic and political institutions, and ethnic composition that have occurred in just one generation.

Despite all of these changes, the "South" continues to this day to function as a prism, filtering how Americans, northern and as well as southern, evaluate the moral grounding of our communal life and so refracting, always, our vision of such essential matters as freedom, equality, justice, and guilt.[18] To teach about life in the South, past or present, then, is to teach about human horror and pain, human yearning and possibility. To teach the South, finally, is necessarily to make moral commitments to oneself and to ask for moral reasoning from others. And this, most assuredly, teaches the teacher--himself indelibly of the region--humility.

Discussion and Essay Questions

1. Is it appropriate to study the history of the south based on two separate histories, one black and one white?

2. If the history of the south is one, is it possible to study the history of the south from an African American perspective and still cover the history of the south?

---

[17] The fine movie, "Mississippi Marsala," which I should show more frequently, makes the point about racial and ethnic complexity with a rare sensitivity.
[18] In "Southern Distinctiveness, Yet Again, or, Why America Needs the South," I explore several of these themes in greater detail, including the "pastness" in the South's present and what "the South" might mean today.

3. Why does there seem to be a tipping point in classes that discuss race? Meaning, at what point do students begin to feel that there is an over emphasis on African Americans in a history class?

4. Is it painful to study slavery and segregation?

5. Is it appropriate to separate the study of slavery and segregation from the study of contemporary society?

Chapter 2

Too White To Teach Race? Student Perceptions of Racial Identity-Based Professor Credibility

Andrea Malkin Brenner

Classrooms do not exist in a societal vacuum. Both students and professors bring to the teaching environment conflictive criteria by which knowledge and identity are deemed relevant or irrelevant. At one time, the academic debate focused on who should be admitted to colleges and universities and what they should be taught (Woodward 1991, p. 41). Currently, the concern is about who should teach them. More specifically, the question is whether experience can be taught or if it must be had. Since the 1970's, minority constituencies on campuses have begun to scrutinize the relationship between professors' identities and their claims to professional authority.

Until recently, there were few grounds on which a college professor's authority could be impeached. Students might complain about a course's workload, a professor's teaching style or professionalism, but for the most part, charges of "pedagogical malpractice" (Mayberry, 1996) were unthinkable. Currently, the debate over identity-based credibility is arguably the most visible expression of identity politics in higher education (Mayberry 1996, p. 3). Who has the credibility to define what counts as knowledge? This is a difficult question, and it is the function of universities to grapple with it.

Over the past fifteen years, most efforts within curriculum reform movements have been to integrate race and ethnic studies into the mainstream curriculum and scholarship rather than to encourage the development of new specialized ethnic studies programs. This inclusivity has given rise to a series of observations and questions about the relationships between knowledge and group identity. Does one have to be of a group to credibly teach about it? Are intellectual perspectives expressions of particular social standpoints? Does understanding require firsthand experience? Is it possible to teach courses from a perspective different from one traditionally taken (Scott 1992)? These questions have led to an identity-based definition of credibility as an entirely new precondition of professional authority (Mayberry 1996, p. 3) and have introduced a series of problems involving student perceptions. If students, regardless of their own racial identities, assume that the minority teacher who is teaching about race and racism "teaches what he/she is"—from experience— then by nature, the White professor who is teaching about race and racism "teaches what he/she is not." Thus, based on the perceptions of the students, the classroom can become a potential site for discrimination.

Research in the area of "outsiders" to a field, such as men in women's studies, suggests that the outsider meets great resistance (Tieman and Rankin-Ullock 1985). Regardless of actual performance, the person may be forced into a deviant status where every behavior is judged as fitting a typical, and negative characteristic of that person's identity. Before this study, no research existed that questioned whether a White professor is considered an "outsider" to the field of race/ethnic studies by students.

Specifically, students of color may perceive a White professor who teaches a race-related class as an ally but not a member (Culley and Portuges 1985, p. 142). While students may welcome the professor's lecture as an academician, as a White person he/she remains marginal from the lack of lived experience. In this context, courses on race and ethnicity may unintentionally mirror and reinforce the students' daily experiences of White domination.

Gershick (1993) maintains that an instructor's personal characteristics such as race do matter, yet he questions why students' perceptions, needs, and concerns involving these issues are rarely taken into account when instructors plan their courses and develop their teaching styles. In addition, the reaction of a student of color (still a statistical minority in most college classrooms) to the professor of color teaching the class on race may vary according to the professor's race.

The student may feel empowered by the "sameness;" this empowerment may even take an aggressive stance toward the "dominant" majority (Shankar 1996, p. 198), or it may lead to a false universalism of groups based on racial identity. In another scenario, students of color who, either because of economic or other privileges, have not experienced (or at least not perceived) discrimination, may be disbelieving of what they assume to be the teacher's politically correct focus on race and, thus, this "sameness" becomes a burden. Other students of color may feel angered at being segregated from their peers by the professor's discussions regarding race.

The Authority of Experience

In the late 1970s, Joan Wallach Scott explained that academic freedom rests on the protection afforded individuals by their disciplines against "incompetent outside authorities." However, research beginning in the 1990s began to ask who really is on the inside and who really is on the outside. What happens in a classroom when a faculty member's perspective on the world, based on his/her experiences, conflicts with the ideas of the established academic community? What happens when it conflicts with the students' understanding of what and how they should be taught?

The problem of "speaking for others," or trying to describe their situation or some aspect of it, is that one may also be speaking in place of or for them. This teaching practice, discussed in detail by Alcoff (1991/1992) has come under increasing criticism, especially with reference to topics of gender and race. There is a strong vibe which holds that "speaking for others is arrogant, vain, unethical, and politically illegitimate" (p. 6).

According to Alcoff, the recognition that there is a problem in speaking for others has arisen from two sources. First, there is a growing recognition that a speaker's social location affects the meaning and truth of what one says, and thus has an epistemically significant impact on his/her authority. Departments and programs that specialize in race studies were founded on the belief that the study of and the advocacy for the oppressed must come to be done principally *by* the oppressed.

Thus, it is imperative that scholars acknowledge that the divergences between speakers and those spoken for will have a significant effect on the content of what is said. The second recognizes that certain privileged locations are obliquely dangerous. Specifically, "the practice of privileged persons speaking for or on behalf of less privileged persons has actually resulted (in many cases) in increasing or reinforcing the oppression of the group spoken for" (Alcoff 1991/1992, p. 7).

In spite of the obvious importance of student perceptions of professor credibility, we know very little about how perceptions of credibility differentially include the way people interpret and respond to other people, and, specifically, their personal characteristics.

Theoretical Framework

In the past two decades, one of the most important theorists who has combined the fields of education and sociology has been Michel Foucault, whose major theoretical contributions explain the interconnection of power and knowledge. Foucault explains that all scientific investigation and social discussion ("discourses") about human nature, cultural activity, and social history, emerged from societal agents engaged in processes of power. Power, he explained, brings "objective" scientific knowledge into being, and the social relations of power were masked by people who accepted, whether they knew it or not, the distribution of power in society.

Much of the existing research on student perceptions of professor credibility is set within the parameters of Foucault's theory about the relationship between power and knowledge. This image of the student as the disciplined subordinate presumes that the teacher is powerful and has high credibility with students. In addition, Foucauldian theory suggests that the teacher's power may dilute the students' ability to find their own identities.

However, Foucault's image of the power-knowledge relationship in the classroom fails to account for the increasing complexity of student perceptions of their professors' teaching credibility (Foucault 1980). In this study, I argue that students are judged and examined by their professors, but also that they judge and examine their professors back, closely and with a powerful self-identity. Students are exercising enormous power in controlling or attempting to control what is taught in the classroom and who is teaching it. They are paying clients of the university system; they are not simply audiences.

While Foucauldian theory prescribes a rational and coherent plan from which one's teaching choices flow, the theoretical framework for this research is better centered around a perspective that focuses on subjectivity. It is for this reason, amongst many others, that critical theory guides the methodological and theoretical design for this qualitative study. A number of educators, Pierre Bourdieu and Paulo Freire among them, have argued that education represents both a struggle for meaning and a struggle over power relations. "Education starts with a belief in people, that they come with substantial experience and can be creators in their own learning to shape their own lives" (Mohanty, p. 147).

I would argue that students' perceptions of their professors' racial identities play a more significant role in the success or failure of individual students than the syllabi and text selection. Students' beliefs about the importance of and the differences between the personal stories, experiences, and races of their college professors who teach about race/ethnic relations suggest that there is a connection between racial identity and students' perceptions of their professors' credibility.

Critical Theory

Critical theory's practicality analyzes what works within a particular context without the necessity of logical consistency. This is particularly important when studying students' perceptions in general and in studying something as subjective as racial identity in specific. Critical theorists assert that objectivity depends on the "knowers" place in the social world and argues that to use the methods and assumptions of the natural sciences in the study of society would hamper the pursuit of truth. Thus, theorists believe that only through embracing critical theory can the realities of the social world be authentically disclosed and understood. It is for this reason that critical theory is often linked to research on education and specifically to research on teaching.

Because critical theory is not simply explanatory, but instead is committed to enabling change towards better relationships and a more just and rational society, it enables teachers to place their own practice and experience at the center of their studies. "Although schools claim to be fair and neutral transmitters of 'culture', they in fact actively maintain inequality whilst claiming to provide equal opportunity" (Gibson 1986, p. 54). Theories of education and cultural reproduction claim to show how education (through its language, values, processes, knowledge and so on) ensures the reproduction of cultural, hence economic, inequality.

While the other paradigms assume that the educational system can successfully intervene and help minority students attain social, and political equality, critical theory assumes that the school is part of the problem and plays a key role in keeping certain groups oppressed. Thus, it is not possible for the school to help liberate oppressed groups because one of its central purposes is to educate students so that they will willingly accept their assigned status in society (Banks 1986, p. 19).

But what happens when the topic of class discussion is race and racial oppression? More specifically, do White professors who teach race-related classes perpetuate the belief that oppressors maintain their status by defining and reproducing the "knowledge" of inequality? I believe that the suggestion that professors should refrain from teaching what they are not insults the intelligence of our students and the ideals of learning and scholarship altogether. As critical theory attempts to do more than explain the origins of everyday practices and problems, it offers a framework in which to answer questions that ask what should be taught and who should teach it.

Methodological Framework

The research framework for this study is guided by critical theory. The ultimate goal in using this model is to capture students' perceptions of their professors' credibility in race-related classes. The long individual interview and focus group questions capture the intersection of students' racial identity with their perceived racial identities of their professors, and the area of study. This approach advocates a framework that explores the diverse opinions of students, the strength of students' racial identities, and how students conceptualize the link between credibility and lived experience. A qualitative approach examines how differently each student experiences the same college classroom. The qualitative software QSR (Qualitative Solutions and Research) NUD*IST 4 (Non-numerical Unstructured Data Indexing Searching and Theorizing) was used to organize and categorize the vast quantity of data.

The 63 subjects of this study are students at American University, a private, co-educational four-year institution in Washington, DC who were enrolled in race-related courses during the Spring, Summer and Fall 2000 semesters. For clarity, this study defined race-related courses as 3-credit courses in which the main or one of the main focuses of the course is race, ethnicity, multiculturalism, or racism. The diversity of the student body at American University is not atypical in comparison with that of other four-year higher education institutions in the United States. American University's enrollment distribution by racial/ethnic groups approximates: Caucasians (61%), Blacks (6%), Hispanics (5%), Asian/Pacific Islanders (3%), and American Indians (less than 1%). In this study, students were asked to self-identify their race.

Findings

Identity-based Definitions of Race and Professor Credibility

Racial definitions were important to respondents; not only were the students pleased to self-define their races, but most responded that their professors had self-identified their races as well. In general, students believed that it was *positive* for their professors to self-identify their race if they were to credibly teach about race/ethnicity. However, when the data was controlled for race, it became obvious that if the professor was White, students believed that it was not only positive but *necessary* for the professor to racially self-define if he/she was to credibly teach about race/ethnicity.

Although some students believed that credibility was reached only by a combination of academic credentials and personal lived experiences as people of color, almost every student interviewed believed that his/her professors' lived personal experience as a racial minority increased his/her credibility to teach about race/ethnicity. Students enrolled in White professors' classes explained that although their professors had the academic background to teach the class, they were unable to offer personal lived experience with racial oppression which, they believed, would lead to credibility to teach about race/ethnicity.

Students also presented their ideas about what they believed was appropriate information for race/ethnic professors to share in class. While they expressed the need to hear about their professors' personal experiences, respondents reported that they were more comfortable listening to stories about past racial oppression from professors of color than from White professors. In addition, respondents also discussed the fine line between sharing personal stories and bias-free teaching.

Students' reasons for enrolling in race-related classes spanned from the general to the personal. These respondents were quite different than many of the students who Paulo Freire believed subconsciously expected little else than "banking" in the classroom. Students in this study were anticipating (if not expecting) a classroom which not only provided an open arena to discuss potentially volatile topics about race and ethnicity, but also offered an environment in which they could pursue their own exploration into topics of race and identity. Respondents' discussions about the empowering connections (i.e. mentoring) between professors and students in race-related classes proved especially interesting when the data was controlled for race.

Only students of color in the study reported a personal connection with their professors of color in race-related classes; this empowering relationship was also witnessed by White students who observed a closeness between their minority peers and their professors of color. When students were asked if they felt more empowered if they had a common racial identity with their professors in race-related classes, the majority of students of color responded that they had, while *all* White students responded that they had not. Many students of color who were enrolled in White professors' race/ethnicity classes referred to previous classes they had taken with professors of color to emphasize the importance of the racial connection they had experienced with their professor at the time.

In addition, although students of all races doubted (if not disputed) the credibility of White professors teaching race-related courses, there was a distinct *dis*connection or distance between students of color and their White professors in race-related classes. Students of color were also noticeably more negative than White students about the *dis*connection they felt with their White professors in race/ethnic classes and the doubts they held about their professors' teaching credibility.

Another important race-specific finding was that many students believed that their White professors' credibility to teach the topic of race/ethnicity was enhanced considerably if they were in multiracial relationships or marriages. These conclusions were reached by students regardless of whether their professors were actually involved in multiracial relationships (and told the students about it as part of class or personal discussions), or fictitiously engaged in multiracial relationships (students *hypothesizing* that they would feel their White professor's credibility would be enhanced if they were engaged in a multiracial relationship). Students who did feel that their White professor's credibility would be enhanced if they were involved in a multiracial relationship expressed that the relationship would serve to "increase" the professor's lived experience.

In addition, most students believed that the use of other voices in the classroom enhanced the credibility of White professors teaching about race. Even the small minority of students who did not view this as a credibility issue agreed that guest speakers, films and literature positively enhanced any White professor's class on race. Students discussed how the use of other voices in the race/ethnicity classroom brought the (White) professor "one step closer to a primary voice."

This was similar to the students' responses about their White professors who were involved in multiracial relationships. Responses to early interview questions offer the first glimpse into the significance of students' dual definitions of identity; not only were students' perceptions of their *professors'* racial identities meaningful, but also *students'* self-defined racial identities were important, as well. Throughout their responses, students continually made connections between the credibility they perceived was necessary to teach about race and both their own and their professors' racial identities. While the writing thus far has opened a host of questions about the differences between credibly teaching racial inequality and truly understanding it, the following sections focus in depth on the factors which students believe define the authority of that experience. The next section will specifically address these questions by discussing students' perceptions of the varying levels of racial understanding, analyzing the complexities governing the responsibility to teach the topic, and exploring the assumptions and realities of White professors who are slotted to teach courses about race and ethnicity.

The Authority of Experience: Who Should Teach About Race?

Respondents first defined oppression, experience and understanding. While most students believed that lived experience with racial oppression was necessary in order to truly understand it, there were a few students who found a unifying quality to all the "-isms." Respondents' opinions about their professors' credibility to teach about and to understand racial oppression were described as categorical in nature and were linked to lived personal experience. Also discussed were students' definitions of the mutually exclusive levels of understanding of racial oppression, which ranged from the simplest form, based on academic knowledge, to the deepest level, based on lived personal experience.

Next, I addressed the importance of audience (the other students enrolled in the course) and discussed how students' racial identities and their personal experiences enhanced class discussions. The significance of the specific subject matter in the race-related class was also addressed in light of the professors' racial identities. I then described students' opinions about which professors should be slotted to teach race-related classes in the university setting. Responses about the complexities of stereotypic teaching assignments were controlled by students' race and analyzed; those who would be categorized as *extremely* opposed to White professors teaching race-related classes were students of color.

Typecasting, or what student respondents in this study refer to as "pigeonholing," is a form of stereotyping that must be observed from the students' perspective as well as from the professors' perspective, because it prevents students from seeing professors of color from being fully integrated into all areas of academia. This "reverse discrimination" further confines students' already limited access to professors of color to ethnic/racial areas and offers students assumptions as to where professors of color will be found in departments. As a result, the students hypothesized, professors of color are pigeon-holed into teaching about minority issues because of their racial identities and White professors are often seen as "the other" in discussions of race/ethnicity and racial/ethnic oppression.

Presented last are the characteristics which students believe are necessary in order for their White professors to credibly teach race-related classes. These include racial self-identification, travel or field work, open-mindedness, and "proving their worth." Also introduced is the opinion of a small but vocal group of students who suggest that their White professors' "racelessness" offers a bias-free approach to teaching about racial oppression that I believe should not be discounted solely on the basis of racial identity.

The study of racial inequality introduces students to assumptions and debates about human behavior. These arguments include theoretical, practical, and epistemological concerns about the processes, structure, and dynamics of social change. By integrating multiple perspectives in the collaborative classroom, students are able to recognize the power that each discipline brings to the investigation of racial inequality in American society.

Many student respondents described co-teaching scenarios as the ideal environment in which to teach race/ethnicity courses. Co-teaching offers students the opportunity to learn from two or more instructors who hold varied perspectives about the same topic; it affords them the chance to observe certain interaction that would not be available to them in a solo-taught class. For collaborative teaching to be successful, professors must respect the different teaching and learning styles of their colleagues as well as their distinct differences in philosophies; this respect must be obvious to their students.

This teaching method provides students an opportunity to observe how professors with strong disagreements can negotiate and work together. The literature indicates that students exit a co-taught class with a richer perspective of issues as well as the ability to see how varied opinions can be. This includes not only the obvious diversity (a collaborative team of racially or ethnically diverse professors), but also an opportunity to observe professors comparing and contrasting their own personal experiences and academic backgrounds.

The great majority of students in this study expressed a positive reaction to a co-taught course, and many described it as the ideal teaching model for a race-related class. In addition, when respondents were asked which characteristics they believed to be the most important if their professors were to credibly teach about race and ethnicity, students listed their professors' personal lived experiences, their willingness to offer contrasting views of an issue, their race, and their ability to discuss volatile topics. These are similar, if not identical, to the benefits of co-teaching previously described.

Clearly, this study reveals that although students believe their White professors have the academic background and often the ability and charisma to teach race-related classes, as a group, they are unable to offer the personal lived experience which students believe is necessary to increase their teaching credibility. I argue that combining these ideal professor characteristics with the benefits of a diversity of opinions 6would suggest co-teaching as an ideal model in which to teach race-related classes. In addition, this teaching method would not only encourage students' awareness of the subjectivity of information about race and identity, but also provide them their much-needed voice.

Why then, has collaborative teaching with two professors of diverse races not been explored as the obvious choice for a model in which to teach race-related classes? What particular variations of co-teaching meet the characteristics that students perceive as so important for their professors to possess? How can the challenges of time, planning, and workload that collaborative teaching present be faced?

Summary and Recommendations

This study has explored the significance of dual definitions of racial identity. It has illustrated, as have other studies, the importance of students' *self-defined* racial identities in the classroom. This work is unique in that it displays how meaningful students' perceptions of their *professors'* racial identities are, as well. Respondents made connections between the credibility they perceived was necessary to teach about race and both their own and their professors' racial identities.

Respondents believed that their professors' lived personal experiences as racial minorities increased their credibility to teach about race and ethnicity. Not surprisingly, students enrolled in White professors' classes explained that although their professors had the academic classes explained that although their professors had the academic background to teach the class, they conveyed a lack of experience or lack of credibility to some students, simply by the nature of their race. Thus, one of the most important findings of this research echoes the transitive property of algebra which states that if the relation holds between a first element and a second and between that second element and a third, then the relation also holds between the first and third elements.

This formula, defined as: if A ~B and B~C, then A ~C, relates to this study in the following manner: •if a professor of color (or a White professor) (A) is to be viewed by students as someone who has personal lived experience (or viewed by students as someone who does not have personal lived experience) (B), and •students believe that personal lived experience (or lack of personal lived experience) (B) leads to increased credibility in teaching (or lack of teaching credibility) (C), then •according to students, the professor of color (A) is credible to teach race/ethnic classes (C) and the White professor is not.

The perspectives of students and the importance of their identity-based definitions of professor credibility must be explored. In many race-related classes taught by White professors, there are concerned students for whom the professors' racial identity has an effect on their ability to identify and to learn. Their concerns raise important questions about the ability of White instructors to teach courses on inequality and oppression. While it would be easy to argue the political risks of selecting particular faculty for specific classes based on their racial identities, we must listen to our students and not overlook their connections between racial identity and credibility. Just as the link between race, class and gender cannot be separated, neither can that of racial identity, lived experience, and credibility.

One of the most important findings of this study was that the great majority of students expressed an extremely positive reaction to a co-taught course. Several described the collaborative teaching of a White professor and a professor of color to be the ideal teaching model for a race-related class. Many of these students had been adamantly opposed to White professors teaching race-related classes alone.

Clearly, this study reveals that although students believe their White professors have the academic background and often the ability and charisma to teach race-related classes, alone, they are unable to offer the personal lived experience which students believe is necessary to raise their teaching credibility. I argue that combining the ideal professor characteristics previously mentioned with the benefits of a diversity of opinions would suggest co-teaching as an ideal model in which to teach race-related classes. In addition, this teaching method would not only encourage students' awareness of the subjectivity of information about race and identity, but also provide them their much-needed voice.

Why, then, has collaborative teaching with two professors of diverse races not been explored as the obvious choice for a model in which to teach race-related classes? In addition to investigating co-teaching as an option for race-related classes, there is a need for teacher education programs to sufficiently address cultural diversity by adequately preparing teachers to work comfortably with diverse students.

Today, more than ever, there is a great need for teachers who can effectively serve diverse student populations. Moreover, regarding the development of a successful pedagogy, I would argue that another important component must be included in teacher education programs—teachers' reflection about their own cultural biases and assumptions. In order for pre-service teachers to constructively and effectively assist students from diverse ethnic, racial, and cultural backgrounds, they must be given opportunities during the course of their teacher education programs to thoroughly comprehend and explore their own cultural and personal values and identities (Obidah and Teel 2001, p. 102).

What are the implications of this study in relative to its theoretical framework? Pierre Bourdieu discusses how the higher education system is an object of continued political struggle. In addition, the racially-based professor credibility and authority presented in this study can be derived from Bourdieu's work on the "formal equality" system of education, which encourages people to believe that they succeed or fail by their own individual merit, but in fact, one's position is the result of more covert channels based on cultural knowledge. Similarly, connections can be made between this study and Freire's work on the necessity of teachers and students to be co-learners if the educational setting is to prepare students for their lives outside the classroom. In addition, Freire's emphasis that people come to the classroom setting with substantial personal experiences that shape their learning is presented in this study by the students' perceptions of the importance of their professors' racial identities in determining credibility.

Clearly, this study has shown that researchers need to explore the expanding literature on the debate between lived personal experience and academic experience, "teaching what you're not", in the context of race and education. More important, however, are the practical steps that need to be taken in the race-related classroom. Diversity brings a wealth of resources to the university setting in the form of opportunities for cross-cultural interactions among students. As teachers, we must promote mutual respect and trust among students while we help students counteract bias and enable them to distinguish myth from reality (Abdi 1997, p. 34). We cannot deny the statistics that as a group, university students are becoming multi-racial while professors are not keeping up with these changing demographics (De la Luz Reyes and Halcon 1991).

What ways do our students define themselves and others racially and culturally? What do these definitions mean to them as individuals? In teaching introductory and intermediate courses on race, ethnicity, and multiculturalism in the United States, it is particularly important to encourage each of our students, including White students, to see themselves and their experiences as part of the course issues that the class will explore.

Thus, another recommendation based on the data collected in this study, is for professors to make an effort to legitimate the "White experience" as a racial experience with stories to be told and categories of oppression to be studied rather than dismissed. This includes several important elements.

First, in the race-related classroom, similarities must be found between diverse racial/ethnic groups and those of Caucasians such as cultural heritage and migratory patterns. Second, professors must include the expanding literature on Whiteness studies in their race/ethnic syllabi and make an effort to select texts that do this, as well. Some of the problems that White professors confront in the debate over teaching race-related classes is in their approach to the subject.

Therefore, third, I suggest a shift of the knowledge base in the race-related classroom. If the aim of White professors is to *explain* the experiences and oppression of people of color, their cultural background puts them at a distinct disadvantage. But, if they change their aim and focus more on pondering the way their historical, cultural, and personal identities connect with those of people of color, White professors might better be able to connect their experiences to those of marginalized cultures.

The National Association of Scholars (1988) argues that entertaining the question of who can teach whom unnecessarily politicizes the academy. It argues that "academic freedom is based on disciplinary competence and entails a responsibility to exclude extraneous political matters from the classroom" (Short 1988, p. 7). Thus, according to the Association, one's gender, class, sexual orientation, and race do not have an effect on an instructor's ability to teach; only one's competency matters.

I argue that this not only disregards the connections that students make between their professors' racial identities and credibility, but also insults the ideals of learning and scholarship altogether. Clearly, the students in this study were anticipating, if not expecting, a classroom which not only provided an open arena to discuss potentially volatile topics about race and oppression, but also one that offered an environment in which they could pursue their own exploration into topics of racial identity. We owe our students and our discipline a broader and more inclusive view (Darling 2000, p. 6). The debate over credibility and identity is taking place at a time when the demographic forces that have transformed American higher education are themselves meeting powerful challenges. In short, "the American university system is on the defensive, and the current debate about identity politics is up for grabs as a weapon in the struggle" (Mayberry 1996, p. 5). The controversy over identity politics in higher education is at a crossroads because the discussion has turned its focus from scholarship to teaching. The relationship between a professor's racial identity and his/her credibility to teach is now in question. I argue that nowhere is the challenge by students against a professor's credibility more an issue than in the race-related classroom where the politics of racial identity cannot be denied.

Discussion and Essay Questions:

1. What does the author mean by "identity-based credibility?"

2. The author mentions that students are "paying clients." Is this important to remember when designing curriculum and deciding who teaches in the classroom?

3. Do you believe that the expectations students may have about a class are different based on the race of the student, the race of the professor and the subject being taught?

4. Are there some subjects or courses whereby the race or sex of the instructor plays little if any role on the credibility of the instructor to teach the class?

5. Do professors of color have to prove that they are competent when in the classroom more so than majority professor?

References

Abdi, S. Wali. "Multicultural Teaching Tips." *The Science Teacher* (February 1997): 34-37.

Alcoff, Linda. "The Problem of Speaking for Others." *Cultural Critique* 20 (Winter 1991-1992): 5-32.

Banks, James A. "Multicultural Education: Development, Paradigms and Goals." In *Multicultural Education in Western Societies*, ed. James A. Banks and James Lynch, 2-28. London: Holt, Rinehart and Winston, 1986.

Beatty, Michael J. and Ralph R. Behnke. "Teacher Credibility as a Function of Verbal Content and Paralinguistic Cues." *Communication Quarterly* 28, no. 1 (1980): 55-59.

Bérubé, Michael and Cary Nelson, eds. "Identity Politics and Campus Communities: An Exchange." In *Higher Education Under Fire: Politics, Economics, and the Crisis of the Humanities*. New York: Routledge, 1995.

Bourdieu, Pierre and Jean-Claude Passeron. *The Inheritors: French Students and Their Relation to Culture.* Translated by Richard Nice. Chicago: University of Chicago Press, 1979.

Bourdieu, Pierre, Jean-Claude Passeron, and Monique de Saint Martin. *Academic Discourse.* Translated by Richard Teese. Stanford: University Press, 1994.

Culley, Margo and Catherine Portuges, eds. *Gendered Subjects: The Dynamics of Feminist Teaching.* Boston: Routledge and Kegan Paul, 1985.

Darling, Rosalyn Benjamin. "Footnotes." *The American Sociological Association* (May/June 2000): 6.

Davis, Nancy J. "Teaching About Inequality: Student Resistance, Paralysis, and Rage." *Teaching Sociology* 20 (1992): 232-238.

De la Luz Reyes, Maria and John J. Halcon. "Practices of the Academy: Barriers to Access for Chicano Academics." In *The Racial Crisis in American Higher Education,* ed. Philip G. Altbach and Kofi Lomotey, 167-186. Albany, NY: State University of New York Press, 1991.

_____. "Racism in Academia: The Old Wolf Revisited." In *Harvard Educational Review,* Thomas Bidell (ed.), Cambridge, MA 58: N3, 299-314, 1988.

D'Souza, Dinesh. *Illiberal Education: The Politics of Race and Sex on Campus.* New York: The Free Press, 1991.

Foucault, Michel. *Power/Knowledge.* New York: Pantheon, 1980.

Freire, Paulo. *Pedagogy of the Oppressed.* New York: The Continuum Publishing Company, 1970.

Gershick, Thomas J. "Should and Can a White, Heterosexual, Middle-class Man Teach Students About Social Inequality and Oppression? One Person's Experience and Reflections." In *Multicultural Teaching in the University,* ed. David Schoem et al, 200-207. Westport, CT: Praeger Publishers, 1993.

Gibson, Rex. *Critical Theory and Education.* London: Hodder and Stoughton, 1986.

Gitlin, Todd. "The Rise of 'Identity Politics': An Examination and a Critique." In *Higher Education Under Fire: Politics, Economics, and the Crisis of the Humanities,* ed. Michael Bérubé and Nelson, 308-325. New York: Routledge, 1995.

Mayberry, Katherine J., "White Feminists Who Study Black Writers." *The Chronicle of Higher Education,* 12 October 1994, A48.

_____, ed. *Teaching What You're Not: Identity Politics in Higher Education* New York: New York University Press, 1996.

McCroskey, James C. and Lawrence R. Wheeless. *Introduction to Human Communication*. Boston: Allyn and Bacon, Inc., 1976.

McCroskey, James C., W. Holdridge, and J.K. Toomb. "An Instrument for Measuring the Source Credibility of Basic Speech Communication Instructors." *Speech Teacher* (1974): 26-33.

McIntosh, Peggy. *White Privilege and Male Privilege: A Personal Account of Coming to See Correspondences Through Work in Women's Studies*. Wellesley: Wellesley College Center for Research on Women, 1988.

_____. "Interactive Phases of Curricular and Personal Revision with Regard to Race." Working Paper 219. Wellesley College. Wellesley: Center for Research on Women.

McIntyre, Alice. *Making Meaning of Whiteness: Exploring Racial Identity With White Teachers*. Albany: State University of New York Press, 1997.

Mohanty, Chandra Talpade. "On Race and Voice: Challenges for Liberal Education in the 1990s." In *Between Borders: Pedagogy and the Politics of Cultural Studies*, Giroux, Henry A. and Peter McLaren, eds., 145-166. New York: Routledge, 1994.

National Association of Scholars, "Is the Curriculum Biased?" A Statement of the National Association of Scholars. Princeton, New Jersey: National Association of Scholars, 1988.

Obidah, Jennifer E. and Karen Manheim Teel. *Because of the Kids: Facing Racial and Cultural Differences in Schools*. New York, NY: Teachers College Press, 2001.

Renzetti, Claire M. and Daniel J. Curran. *Living Sociology*. Needham Heights: Allyn and Bacon, 1998.

Scott, Joan Wallach. "The Campaign Against Political Correctness: What's Really at Stake." *Radical History Review* 54 (1992): 59-79.

_____. "The Rhetoric of Crisis in Higher Education." In *Higher Education Under Fire: Politics, Economics, and the Crisis of the Humanities*, ed. Michael Bérubé and Cary Nelson, 293-303. New York: Routledge, 1995.

_____. "Untitled." *Academe* (July-August 1995): 46-48.

Scott, Michael and Jon Nussbaun. "Student Perceptions of Instructor

Communication Behaviors and Their Relationship to Student Evaluations." *Communication Education* 30 (1981): 44-53.

Seldin, P. *Successful Faculty Evaluation Programs*. New York: Coventry Press, 1980.

Shankar, Lavina Dhingra. "Pro.(Con)fessing Otherness: Trans(cending)-national Identities in the English Classroom." In *Teaching What You're Not: Identity Politics in Higher Education*, ed. Katherine J. Mayberry, 195-214. New York: New York University Press, 1996.

Sheffield, E.F. (Ed.). *Teaching in the University: No One Way*. Montreal: Mc Gill—Queen's University Press, 1974.

Short, Thomas. "'Diversity' and 'Breaking the Disciplines' Two New Assaults on the Curriculum." *Academic Questions* 1, no. 3 (1988): 6-29.

Tieman, C.R. and B. Rankin-Ullock. "Student Evaluations of Teachers." *Teaching Sociology* 12 (1985): 177-191..

West, Cornel. "Paulo Freire." In *Beyond Eurocentrism and Multiculturalism*. Vol. I. Maine: Common Courage Press, 1993.

_____. "Identity: A Matter of Life and Death." In *Beyond Eurocentrism and Multiculturalism*. Vol. II. Maine: Common Courage Press, 1993.

Woodward, C. Vann. *Equal But Separate*, a review of The Disuniting of America: Reflections on a Multicultural Society by Arthur M. Schlesinger Jr. *The New Republic* (July 15 and 22 1991): 41-43.

Woodward, T., ed. "The Teacher Trainer: A Practical Journal Mainly for the Modern Language Teacher Trainers." *The Teacher Trainer* (1990): 4, 13-15.

Chapter 3

Beyond the Veil: Black and White Perspectives on Teaching about Racial Inequality

Wanda Rushing and Zandria Robinson

Teaching a Sociology course in racial inequality poses many challenges. Both subjects — race and inequality — arouse discomfort in mixed racial settings in twenty-first century America. Cities like Memphis, sites of noted conflicts over racial inequality, may pose special challenges[1]; however, the problem of the color line, identified by W.E.B. Du Bois a century ago, pervades all of American society, including colleges and universities, and classroom settings (Du Bois 1903/1994; John 2003).

The problem of the color line, and White ambivalence about it, generates tensions and provokes powerful student emotions (Tatum 1992). Most published accounts of complex student responses to inequality courses focus on student reactions, predominantly those of White students, to courses taught by teachers and professors of color (Hendrix 1998; Hunter and Nettles 1999; Tatum 1992; John 2003). Few studies relate the experiences of White faculty, male or female (Killian 1994; Cannon 1990; Gardner et al. 1992; Rushing 2002), especially in classrooms where the majority of students are African American.

---

[1] Memphis was the site of the 1968 Sanitation Workers' Strike and the assassination of Dr. Martin Luther King, Jr.

This paper examines the racial inequality course at the University of Memphis, and student reactions to it, from the perspectives of a White Southern woman who teaches the course and a Black Southern woman, now completing her Master's degree in Sociology, who took the course as an undergraduate. The course offers students an opportunity to actively participate in a classroom dialogical community as a means of analyzing the complexities of race globally, locally, and personally (Rinehart 1999). It encourages them to develop and share "outsider within" ways of seeing racial inequality (Collins 1991).

Through an analysis of our experiences as teacher and student, as well as student journals, class discussions, and faculty evaluations, we demonstrate how use of the "outsider within" standpoint forms an epistemological and pedagogical basis for examining personal experience and "in-group" knowledge of the "other," as well as sociological knowledge. We explain how life histories and racial identities, as well as the structure of the course, affect perceptions of instructor competence and credibility, validate student experiences, and affect classroom climate and student learning processes (Moulder 1997; Tatum 1992; Davis 1992). Ultimately, this paper demonstrates that students and faculty in racial inequality courses can create and sustain serious dialogue, establish trust and mutual respect, renew hope, and build alliances to courageously cross the color line.

Student Characteristics and Expectations

Co-author Wanda Rushing has taught Sociology 4420—"Racial Inequality"— at the University of Memphis for seven years. Once an all-White campus, the University now enrolls a large number of minority students-- approximately forty percent of the student body.[2] Enrollment in this particular class ranges from 50% African American and 50% European American to 100% African American. Infrequently, class membership includes Native Americans, Asian Americans, Middle Eastern Americans, and foreign students, but generally the classroom demography follows the typical Black-White configuration. Most of these students originate from Memphis and the Mid-South region, and most of them are women. Typically, 20 to 30 students enroll in the class. The class usually includes a few sociology majors, as well as many students who earn course credit toward a major or minor in African and African American Studies.

Co-author Zandria Robinson, a 2003 graduate of the University of Memphis, double majored in English and African and African American Studies. In 2002, Zandria registered for Racial Inequality to fulfill the Social Sciences

---

[2] The University of Memphis is an urban university whose student population is becoming more representative of the City of Memphis where African Americans constitute a majority.

requirement of the interdisciplinary degree. She perceived it as one of the "Blackest" of the courses offered. After having taken African American History, African American Rhetoric, and African American Literature from Black professors, Zandria was bewildered when she discovered a photo of a White professor on the Department of Sociology's website. What a White woman was doing teaching the "Blackest" of classes she could not imagine. Zandria's reaction is a fairly common one expressed by minority students who take the class. For example, at the end of last semester another student said: "My reaction the first day of class was what is SHE going to teach US about racial inequality?"

For Zandria, and many students whose parents came of age during the era of the civil rights movement, Black professors and courses in African American studies play important roles – symbolically and instrumentally – in developing Black consciousness. These students, unlike their parents and grandparents, struggle to develop an intellectual consciousness of race, class and gender, and the complexities of power and institutional racism from WITHIN the system. They do not expect to find a White woman talking about white privilege, institutional racism and internalized oppression. Their expectations and reactions can be seen as part of a postmodern (e.g., in this case, post civil rights movement, and post affirmative action backlash) problematic. Today's students, unlike those a generation ago, do not expect White faculty, even Sociology faculty, to address issues of inequality from a "minority" perspective.

> [The 1960s] was a time when sociologists confidently thought they had something to contribute to our understanding of the changes swirling around us. Younger colleagues, in contrast, were introduced to the field during the height of the Reagan-Bush backlash, with its assault on affirmative action and its effort to roll back some of the achievements of the civil rights movement...at a time that postmodernism, cultural studies, and other currents of thought called into question disciplinary traditions and that earlier confidence (Kivisto 2003:530).

Pescosolido and Rubin (2000) contend that the postmodern era not only calls into question the "disciplinary confidence" of faculty, but also the limits of "modern" methods for the social scientific analysis of postmodern life.

> Postmodernism...illuminates the limits of using a "modern" metaphor to understand contemporary circumstances, and the limits of using methods developed under that metaphor to study contemporary circumstances. [It] has identified a real problem in the sociological analysis of social life and social science that we should not ignore. (Pescosolido and Rubin 2000:58)

But, for Black students who seek intellectual validation of the continuing struggle for social equality, the Racial Inequality classroom, and other classes about race, serves as intellectual initiation grounds for learning to critically assess inequality—personally, locally, and globally — in a postmodern context. White students who take Racial Inequality also experience a postmodern problematic. First, White students who find it unsettling to examine the contradictions between our nation's ideological commitment to equality and the persistence of inequality may elect not to take a course that probes two hotly contested subjects—race and inequality. Consequently, many students at the University of Memphis opt to take a lower division Sociology course, "Racial and Ethnic Minorities" which focuses on *difference* rather than *inequality*. But White students who take the inequality course may expect to hear that the civil rights era either solved the problem of the color line, or reversed racial inequality by creating so-called reverse discrimination. When the course fails to confirm their expectations, many White students drop the class because they are unwilling to question their own assumptions about racial identity and white privilege. Anecdotally, it appears that many of the White students who stay for the duration of the semester have some personal connection to racial difference, which they sometimes reveal in their journals or privately disclose. But in class, these students rarely disclose the details of inter-racial dating, bi-racial siblings, or their own "mixed race" children.

Structuring Collaboration

The objectives of Sociology 4420—"Racial Inequality"—are to develop a macro-theoretical perspective on racial inequality, to become aware of one's own racial identity in a theoretical context, to understand Whiteness as a form of racial and social identity, and to understand that race is given meaning through historical and social contexts and is not a natural or biological category. Through class discussions and written assignments we work to establish a balance between knowledge about racial inequality gained from theoretical sociological perspectives, and the knowledge that students bring with them from their own life experiences (Rinehart 1999, 217; Lengermann 1981).

Recognizing and validating the knowledge of lived experience in an academic setting encourages students to develop and share "outsider within" ways of seeing racial inequality (Collins 1991). The standpoint of the "outsider within" is described in diverse sociological literature beginning with Du Bois (1903) and Simmel (1921), and continuing with Collins (1991) and Smith (1992). Both Du Bois and Simmel emphasize the outsider within's role in creating new knowledge. Du Bois used the metaphor of "the veil" to convey the outsider within status of African Americans, whose "double consciousness" offers a different perspective on life "behind the veil." This perspective of life "behind the veil" emerges when Black students exhibit a willingness to discuss "insider" knowledge and experience within a mixed university setting, i.e., beyond the veil, to nuance class discussion and foster alliances.

Simmel described the "stranger" who is privy to "inside" information from his standpoint as an "outsider" as having a special ability to "see" social patterns. Significantly, even when the course demographics are predominantly African American, Black students still assume the socially defined role of "the stranger." As White students become privy to the "insider" information provided by Black students, they shift perspectives. The class provides White students with the unique opportunity to become the stranger, to experience their own double-consciousness—intimacy with this new "Black" world, both theoretically and practically, and knowledge of their own experiences within the White world of privilege—and exercise this special ability to "see" otherwise invisible social patterns made visible. Contemporary feminist and Black feminist thought emphasize the importance of self-valuation when knowledge of practical everyday activity is taken from the background (outside) and placed at the center of inquiry (inside). As students articulate the knowledge afforded by day-to-day existence in a society marred by inequality, their personal experiences are analyzed with as much care and scrutiny as theoretical principles and historical examples.

Our class uses the "outsider within" standpoint to form an epistemological basis to critique sociological readings and personal experience, and to examine both types of knowledge from "other" standpoints. From the outset we acknowledge that members of all racial groups, including Whites, have racial identities (Tatum 1992; Tatum 1994). We work at relating racial identities to gender and class identities, in light of historical and global processes. We want to debunk the hierarchy of quantified oppression (Collins 1993) and avoid dividing the class into victims and victimizers, or oppressed and oppressors (Rose 1996, 39; Davis 1992; Bohmer and Briggs 1991; Cannon 1990) as we seek to understand the complexities of the matrix of domination. We create a classroom situation where members of all groups can speak for themselves, define the terms of interaction, and create a classroom climate sensitive to difference (Hartsock 1990). Consequently, discussions of rigorous readings about the complexities of structured inequality constitute a strong basis for establishing trust and collaboration, not only to criticize dominant institutional arrangements, but also to raise hopes for creating more equitable alternatives (Hartsock 1990; Moulder 1997).

Classroom Dialogue

By reframing the dialogue about race to stress power dynamics and situating the "problem" of racism within mainstream institutions and ideologies, students learn to discuss structures of power and privilege, and relate them to the social construction of race (Collins 1991:38). We examine individual experiences to understand the institutional processes at work in everyday life, as well as to validate those experiences as constructs and consequences of racism. Students struggle to reconcile the contradictions between popular denials of racial inequality and scholarly analyses of its impact on all Americans, including Whites (Killian 1998). Because the course creatively interweaves "lived" experience and "learned" theory, students become less resistant to sociological findings and more open to the possibility of being changed by the student-to-student dialogue (Rau and Heyl 1990; Davis 1992; Rigney 2001:192). White students often comment: "I didn't realize how much I benefit from White privilege," or "I didn't think I was a racist until I read this." Black students often express surprise that White people don't "know" this information. Initially, many of the Black students who hope to validate their own experiences from living in a racially divided society express disbelief and frustration to learn the complicated ways that White students think about race and racism, or how they deny it (Suter and Schweickart 1998, 129). Gradually, men and women begin to see race and gender differently, and to understand that racism negatively affects members of all racial groups.

Many students remark that the course validates their own experience. Others, usually White students, express amazement and alarm at the correspondence between readings and class discussions. It is difficult for them to believe that racial discrimination is an artifact of the past after listening to classmates recount personal experiences with violence and racial profiling. Some students report feeling shocked to see Whiteness made visible and treated as problematic. They prefer to attribute the "advantages enjoyed by Whites to their family values...and foresight—rather than to the favoritism they enjoy through their possessive investment in Whiteness" (Lipsitz 2002:75). A number of White students talk about how uncomfortable it feels to be a minority in the class. Whereas in the vast majority of their classes, White students see themselves as members of the numerical and ideological majority, Racial Inequality, particularly with its pedagogical commitment to anti-racism (Law 2003:520) and its epistemological basis of the "outsider-within" standpoint, often renders them the minority in both of these respects. Students explore these feelings in their journals and class discussions and wonder how minority students feel in other classes.

Through candid exchanges, students learn to trust each other and to see the perspectives of others, not only making it possible for us to discuss sensitive issues in class, but also creating opportunities for discussion beyond the classroom. We are amazed at the courtesy and concern shown by class members for each other, efforts at conflict negotiation and resolution within the class, the composition of study groups that emerge, and long-term friendships that blossom. Only twenty percent of our students live on campus. Many students relate that they just do not get to know people in most classes. Yet they form bonds in a class addressing subject matter that many Americans feel uncomfortable talking about. We share different points of view, and life experiences, without "pretending" to agree, engaging in aggressive verbal attack, or lapsing into passive, compliant note taking and memorization (Cannon 1990; Rinehart 1999). Black and white students typically continue conversation after class ends, and often maintain these new friendships beyond the semester.

Student Journals

Students write weekly journal entries. Each week's assignment appears on the syllabus. Journal topics vary, and some weeks students choose their own topics. The syllabus assures students that journals are private communication between the student and teacher. As a result of keeping journals, students learn to apply sociological knowledge, become more involved in class discussion, and seem more comfortable talking about sensitive racial topics (Wagenaar 1984). The journal also provides a tool for each student to process information about his or her own racial identity.

Initially, a few students use their journals to comment on class discussions and to explain their personal reasons for remaining silent in class. Some use journals to vent frustrations with the class or air grievances with classmates. Occasionally, White students use journals to reveal "insider" information about racial discrimination that occurs on campus or at work. Black students discuss conversations with family and friends about their university experiences. Minority students often express disappointment with the under representation of White students in Racial Inequality class and other classes that deal with racial or ethnic topics. One student wrote:

> I want this class to be a place where people of various races can come and talk to one another.... Looking at the first week of classes, I do not believe my last expectation will be met. Everyone here is of the same ethnicity. It seems as though Caucasians and other minority groups are never as well represented in classes such as these, like African Americans are. I'm wondering if they are scared and think they are going to get jumped on for their beliefs. The funny thing is, minorities on a day-to-day basis, attend classes where we are the only minority in the class. – Black Female Student

That semester another student commented:

> I think the fact that there are no Whites enrolled in our racial inequality class at this time is quite revealing. It is of interest to me, a student minoring in African American Studies, that in my other classes with an African American emphasis there is at least one White student after drop date. I theorize that while Whites acknowledge that African Americans are here, they don't want to confront the

fact that individual, institutional, and symbolic racism exist and are thriving. – Black Male Student

Minority students welcome White students to the class, including those who express disagreeable points of view. They criticize White students who drop and wish for more White male participation:

> We need more people like the lady that was in our class, but dropped. I was very disappointed that she did not stay in the class ... We needed the kind of feedback that she gave. In a way she was a coward because she did not stay for the duration. Nothing in life is going to be easy and racism is the hardest to deal with. But if people don't join together to pull all resources together we will not go any further.... I would like for more White males to be in this class, because this world is primarily run by White males, but I guess this was not an important subject for them to deal with. – Black female student

A White female student admits finding it difficult to discuss race with White students and family members outside of class, particularly defensive White males:

> I hope to benefit from this class...so that I can learn how to discuss this issue with White males that I am close to and who I know have not had good experiences with discussing issues on race. I often feel uneasy trying to discuss race with White males because they are automatically, and to some extent rightfully, on the defensive when it is brought up. –White Female Student

During semesters when no White males take the class, students often "take the role of the other" to include the White male standpoint. They synthesize lived experience and learned theory to articulate what the "typical" White male would say in the context of various discussions. This symbolic inclusion of a generic White male response illustrates a high level of frustration with their absence. Not surprisingly, the Black students symbolically charge the White women in the class with taking the message beyond the classroom and sharing it with the White males in their lives.

Occasionally, students write about the under representation of Black men in the class:

> I found my first week in class to be quite disturbing as far as who takes the class and who doesn't. I found myself quite bewildered as to why I could count up to seventeen girls of African American descent and only two African American males. Where are my fellow African American brothers? Why is it I can see them in abundance in front of the UC [University Center] building or in large attendance for some fraternity event, but not in any of my Afro-centric classes?
> – Black Male student

Near the end of the semester, students tend to reflect on the class. Some note the important contributions of their classmates, i.e., the people who do not drop the class:

> I think that part of the success of this course also has to be attributed to the students. The honesty and forthrightness with which students express themselves is different from what I've witnessed in any other class I've attended at this university. In this age of political correctness it is refreshing to at times engage in dialogue in which people openly and honestly share their views. — Black male student

Co-author Zandria found the candor and openness of students to be unnerving at times. Satisfied that she kept her own in-group loyalties intact, she found herself revealing some of her experiences of life behind the veil in the interest of meaningful, political dialogue infused with an assumption of praxis.

Study Groups and Group Projects

Each semester students take three essay exams, including the final, and they complete one group project. These activities promote collaborative learning. One week prior to each exam we distribute a review list of possible essay questions and concepts for identification which encourages students to use all readings and notes and to study with their classmates prior to exam day. These questions are designed to help students review the material and identify major themes. The actual in-class exam contains two or three of the essays and five or six terms. The group projects usually focus on a particular racial controversy, and students participate in groups according to their interests. Occasionally, we reserve a few minutes of class time for students to talk to group members and plan project meetings outside of class.

These activities benefit students in several ways. First, students learn to probe more deeply and critically into course materials; consequently, they learn a great deal about the subject matter. The essay exams are more than bureaucratic necessities for assessment in that they creatively reinforce our gained sociological knowledge and render the opportunity to integrate lived experience and theory in course papers. Indeed, they validate discussions within and outside of the classroom. Second, because student collaboration promotes greater cognitive and emotional perspective taking, students learn a great deal about themselves and about each other. Not surprisingly, study group membership changes from one test to another. In racially diverse classes, study groups tend to be less racially segregated by the end of the semester. Also, students seem to be more comfortable speaking in class after working in groups. Frequently, as stated above, group discussions continue outside of class when there is no exam or project to prepare, and after the semester ends.

Student Assessment

All students carefully scrutinize the professor who teaches the class, expecting to find evidence of academic competence along with personal credibility. Studies show that credibility standards vary according to a combination of race and subject matter. In one study, students admitted they assigned more credibility to Blacks teaching courses having an "ethnic" content than to Blacks teaching non-ethnic courses. As for Whites teaching "ethnic" courses, students indicated that a White person could be viewed as credible if he or she met the criteria of believability, truth, and experience, but some students preferred a "minority" perspective (Hendrix 1998:749). Minority students initially express surprise, disappointment, or skepticism to a White, Southern woman from North Carolina, teaching the class. One ambivalent student wrote:

> Before entering this class, I had some reservations. One, sometimes I get very emotional when speaking about racial issues with another ethnic group. And, two, I really feel that White America will never know how I or any other Black feels, if they have never been oppressed. So, to take a class where I know that the "dominant race" (no offense to you) would be teaching it, was probably going to be very interesting. –Black Female Student

Co-author Zandria felt similar sentiments, but realized that oppression was more complex than Black and White. Before the first day of class, but after her internet search revealed that the Professor was White, Zandria marched over to the bookstore to inspect the texts selected for the course. She was appalled by all of the "White" in the titles: *White Privilege* (2002), *Impacts of Racism on White Americans* (1996), *White Man Falling* (1998), *The Wages of Whiteness* (1999). But scanning the texts restored credibility for Zandria. Then she began to fear that this White professor might be arrested for telling the truth.

Most students do not investigate the texts. They believe that only a person of color can express a "minority" perspective, but they express hope that gender will help. A Native American woman brought up the issues of "life experience" and gender:

> I am wondering if our teacher will be able to relate to the issues regarding race, as it is difficult to address these issues if one has not had to fight the daily battles that a person of color must fight. Maybe just being a woman will help. – Native American Female

An African American male expected to find a person of color teaching the class and expressed his disappointment:

> When I first saw the petite, White woman with a strong Southern accent enter the classroom on the first day of our Sociology 4420 class, I was somewhat disappointed. In anticipation of this class, I had taken for granted that we would have a 'minority' instructor, one that was not of European descent. I expected an instructor that experienced first hand the devastating effects of racial inequality....I decided that I would have to make the best out of what I thought at the time was a less than perfect situation. However, after the first week of class, I decided this was a very unique opportunity to expand our minds about racism in ways that we never thought possible. Not only was I totally wrong concerning my initial disappointment relating to the professor, but everything about this class meshed, everything seemed to come together. – Black Male Student

Interestingly, one White female student wrote about her decision to enroll in the class, partly because she learned a White instructor would be teaching it and presumably would be more "objective." She explains her decision two years earlier to drop a course with racial content. She criticizes the teacher, a member of an ethnic minority group, for lack of objectivity, a criticism reminiscent of that encountered by John (2003), and reveals her own defensive reaction to sensitive subject matter:

> Two years ago I registered for ... class.... Unfortunately, that teacher handled this topic in a way that put me on the defensive. She made no bones about thinking that the White middle-class, especially males, created all of the racial problems that exist in our society. She was not objective in her approach to the topics in the class and I was extremely offended. – White Female

Many students, Black and White, become more engaged when we discuss articles that recognize White privilege, such as Peggy McIntosh's "White Privilege and Male Privilege: A Personal Account of Coming to See Correspondence Through Work in Women's Studies" and Abby Ferber's "What White Supremacists Taught a Jewish Scholar About Identity." One student wrote:

> I never realized that some White people don't know they are privileged. I always thought they knew. I thought they knew because they could see the unfair treatment of non-Whites and realize they are privileged. – Black Female

Another student wrote:

> I am a White female who grew up in a White neighborhood, went to a White school, and attended a White church. My parents never taught me to hate people

on the basis of their skin color, but they did teach me to discriminate. I think for many students there is a fear of taking courses like this one because if they are White they will have to examine their own lives and beliefs. However, I think that students should be encouraged to take this course in order to understand truths about racism and how it affects not only non-White people, but also how dehumanizing it is for White Americans. – White Female

Occasionally, minority students openly challenge White authority without disputing course content or questioning competency. For example, each semester we watch Stephen Jay Gould's video "Evolution and Human Equality," which discredits scientific racism and usually sparks lively class discussion. One semester a young African American man who agreed with Gould's assessment of racial inequality, criticized his classmates for readily accepting the authority of a White, male, natural scientist at a prestigious university. He said: "Black people have *been* knowing this. I don't know why we find it more acceptable coming from the mouth of a White man at Harvard." The student's criticism of White authority continued when he added that his mother doesn't believe him when he tells her his "natural hair" (i.e., long and braided) is healthy. Looking directly at me, he said, "Maybe if you told her, she would believe you." We considered the remark a challenge to scientific knowledge, and took the opportunity to ask who produces "scientific" knowledge, who controls its production, and who benefits from it (Harding 1991). We stayed focused on the issue of scientific racism, power, and privilege and avoided a potentially damaging confrontation. For other Black students, however, Gould's contentions are not held as privileged knowledge, rather recognition of Black knowledge by White people in positions of power.

White students pose different challenges to authority on racial matters. Many of them grew up in a time when public officials denied the existence of inequality and celebrated the virtues of colorblindness (Davis 1992). These students struggle to reconcile contradictions between their idealistic view of the world and scholarly views of racial inequality. Some find fault with readings that dredge up the "past" and stir up negative feelings. A few disgruntled students drop the class, but those who stay usually express positive views of the decision to remain.

Anonymous course evaluations conducted by the University at the end of the semester reveal that Racial Inequality students think a lot about instructor credibility and competence. In response to open-ended evaluation questions asking students to identify "positive characteristics or strengths of instructor," students emphasize competence and credibility as well as courage in their anonymous remarks:

> She is an extremely competent professor and I commend her courage for teaching this course.

> This material is hard to discuss and she presents it with respect and patience.
>
> This is difficult to discuss in a mixed group.
>
> Dr. Rushing focused on many issues that other professors would have been afraid to approach, but I really admire her efforts to teach the truth.
>
> Dr. Rushing is to be highly commended for her courage, honesty, and expertise in this area of study. This course must certainly test her true character.

Also, evaluations indicate that students sometimes end the semester with a different view of the world:

> This is the best class I have ever taken – good not specifically for me to learn about one specific area of study – but for life in general.
>
> Very enjoyable class. I was made aware without guilt about racism.
>
> This course encouraged me to think/look past my present beliefs and change some negative ideas about racism.

Building Alliances Across the Colorline

Teaching an undergraduate racial inequality class at the University of Memphis challenges all of us to find ways to build alliances across the color line. In Memphis, racial matters tend to be dichotomized as Black-White, but the color line is changing due to new immigration from Asia, Africa, and Latin America. Nonetheless, many students initially find it difficult to accept being in a class led by a White, Southern female professor who rejects an "orientation to Whiteness" (Frankenberg 1993) as well as the notion that a color-blind society is desirable or attainable. From the outset, as students deal with their own taken-for-granted assumptions about race, class, gender and region, they begin to establish the groundwork for open discussion and class participation. Minority students who find validation for their experiences through class readings and class discussion become more willing to study and learn course materials, more willing to engage in discussions with White students, and more capable of developing a critical perspective. A few students become more interested in pursuing a graduate degree in sociology. Zandria, for example, who came into "Racial Inequality" relatively certain that she would pursue graduate work in Literature, is preparing to enroll in a PhD program in Sociology. White students, who actually begin to "see" Whiteness for the first time, learn to listen and value "other" perspectives, work harder to understand course materials, and find themselves thinking critically about race. Together, students of different races find the courage to discuss theoretical and historical issues about race in a classroom environment that they share responsibility for creating and maintaining.

Crossing the color line in a racial inequality course requires collaboration, reflection, and a willingness to try new strategies for reading and discussion. A successful class begins with the understanding that teaching and learning are "collaborative acts that occur within social relationships" (Rinehart 1999, 217). Positive relationships are more likely to occur when teachers recognize and affirm the knowledge and experience about race that all students bring with them into the classroom. This mutual respect allows students to examine their own racial identity and link personal experiences to sociological processes. Then, students become more apt to engage diversity, more receptive to "other" points of view, and more interested in analyzing reading materials that challenge and validate their personal knowledge and experience. Subsequently, each class is better prepared to practice critical reflection and conflict negotiation skills, and less likely to lapse into denial, resistance, paralysis, or rage (Davis 1992). Further, a pedagogical and epistemological commitment to anti-racism, deconstructing institutional racism and endeavoring to change various systems of privilege, serves as an overarching purpose linking all members of the class to a broader goal beyond the academy.

Du Bois recognized that "education...always has had, and always will have, an element of danger and revolution, of dissatisfaction and discontent" (Du Bois 1994:20). Indeed, on the steps outside of class each week, talk of revolution between Black and White students was lively, inspired by the sociological education we received in inequality. Feelings of dissatisfaction and discontent may increase when our comfortable and familiar ideas about the world, and about ourselves, no longer fit our knowledge and experience. These feelings do not necessarily lead to denial or rage. Instead, these feelings, along with a cognitive, emotional commitment to discourse and change, can motivate us to take steps to cross the color line and look for opportunities to change the status quo on campuses and in our communities.

Discussion and Essay Questions:

1. Can someone who is an "outsider" ever become an insider even in a safe environment such as a classroom?

2. Why may it be unsettling or a source of discomfort to discuss issues of race in situations where the participants are of different racial backgrounds?

3. Can the concept of race be replaced in classroom discussions with another concept such as class and still not lose the significance of the conversation?

4. Why might white students feel uncomfortable in a class about race? Are there some white students who feel more comfortable than others?

5. Are white females privy to vantage points about race that white males are not?

6. Does the presence of a white professor make it "easier" for a white student in a class to discuss issues related to race?

References

Bauman, Zygmunt. "A Sociological Theory of Postmodernity." In *Contemporary Sociological Theory*. Craig Calhoun et al, ed. Blackwell, 2002:429-440.

Bohmer, Suzanne and Joyce Briggs. 1991. "Teaching Privileged Students about Gender, Race, and class Oppression." *Teaching Sociology* 19:154-163.

Cannon, Lynn Weber. 1990. "Fostering Positive Race, Class, and Gender Dynamics in the Classroom." *Women's Studies Quarterly* 1 & 2:126-134.

Collins, Patricia Hill. 1990. *Black Feminist Thought: Knowledge, Consciousness, and the Politics of Empowerment*. New York: Unwin Hyman.

------. 1991. "Learning from the Outsider Within: The Sociological Significance of Black Feminist Thought." Pp. 35-59 in *Beyond Methodology*, Mary Margaret Fonow and Judith A. Cook, eds. Bloomington and Indianapolis: Indiana University Press.

------. 1993. "Toward a New Vision: Race, Class, and Gender as Categories of Analysis and Connection." *Race, Sex & Class* 1:25-45.

Davis, Nancy J. 1992. "Teaching About Inequality: Student Resistance, Paralysis, and Rage." *Teaching Sociology* 20: 232-238.

Du Bois, W.E.B. 1903/1994. *The Souls of Black Folk*. Toronto, Canada: Dover.

Frankenberg, Ruth. 1993. *The Social Construction of Whiteness: White Women, Race Matters*. Minneapolis, MN: University of Minnesota.

Gardner, Saundra, Cynthia Dean and Deao McKaig. 1992. "Responding to Differences in the Classroom: The Politics of Knowledge, Class, and Sexuality." Pp. 131-145 in Education and Gender Equality, edited by Julia Wrigley. London: Falmer Press.

Harding, Sandra. 1991. *Whose Science? Whose Knowledge?* Ithaca, NY: Cornell University Press.

Hartsock, Nancy. 1990. "Foucault on Power: A Theory for Women." Pp. 157-175 in Linda J. Nicholson, ed. *Feminism/Postmodernism*. Routledge.

Hendrix, Katherine Grace. 1998. "Student Perceptions of the Influence of Race on Professor Credibility." *Journal of Black Studies* 28:6:738-763.

Hunter, Margaret L. and Kimberly D. Nettles. 1999. "What about the White Women? Racial Politics in a Women's Studies Classroom." *Teaching Sociology* 27: 4: 385-397.

John, Beverly M. 2003. "The Politics of Pedagogy." *Teaching Sociology* 31:375-332.

Killian, Lewis. 1994. *Black and White: Reflections of a White Southern Sociologist*. Dix Hills, NY: General Hall.

Kivisto, Peter. 2003. "The View from America: Comments on Banton." *Ethnic and Racial Studies* 26:528-536.

Law, Ian. 2003. "University Teaching in Ethnicity and Racism Studies: Context, Content, and Commitment." *Ethnic and Racial Studies* 20:517-522.

Lengermann, Patricia M. and Ruth A. Wallace. 1981. "Making Theory Meaningful." *Teaching Sociology* 8:2:197-212.

Lipsitz, George. 2002. "The Possessive Investment in Whiteness." Pp. 61-84 in *White Privilege: Essential Readings on the Other Side of Racism*, edited by Paula S. Rothenberg. New York: Worth Publishers.

Moulder, Frances V. 1997. "Teaching about Race and Ethnicity: A Message of Despair or a Message of Hope?" *Teaching Sociology* 25:120-127.

Pescosolido, Bernice A. and Beth A. Rubin. 2000. "The Web of Group Affiliations Revisited: Social Life, Postmodernism, and Sociology." *American Sociological Review* 67:52-76.

Rau, William and Barbara Sherman Heyl. 1990. "Humanizing the College Classroom." *Teaching Sociology* 18:141-155.

Rigney, Daniel. 2001. *The Metaphorical Society*. Rowman and Littlefield.

Rinehart, Jane A. 1999. "Turning Theory into Theorizing: Collaborative Learning in a Sociological Theory Course. *Teaching Sociology* 27:216-232.

Rose, Lillian Roybal. 1996. "White Identity and Counseling White Allies About Racism." Pp. 24-47 in Benjamin P. Bowser and Raymon G. Hunt, eds. *Impacts of Racism on White Americans*. Second Edition. London, Sage.

Rushing, Wanda. 2002. " 'Did you Hear What that White Woman Said?' Speaking for Change and Chance in Memphis, Tennessee." Pp. 143-159 in Robert M. Moore III., ed. *The Quality and Quantity of Contact: African Americans and Whites on College Campuses*. University Press of America.

Simmel, Georg. 1921. "The Sociological Significance of the 'Stranger.'" Pp. 322-27 in *Introduction to the Science of Sociology*, edited by Robert E. Park and Ernest W. Burgess. Chicago: University of Chicago Press.

Smith, Dorothy. 1992. "Sociology from Women's Experience: A Reaffirmation." *Sociological Theory* 10:1:88-98.

Suter, Diane and David Schweickart. 1998. "The Biology and Philosophy of Race and Sex: A Course." *NWSA Journal* 10:2:117-136.

Tatum, Beverly Daniel. 1992. "Talking about Race, Learning about Racism: The Application of Racial Identity Development Theory in the Classroom." *Harvard Educational Review* 62:1:1-24

------. 1994. "Teaching White Students about Racism: The Search for White Allies and the Restoration of Hope." *Teachers College Record* 95:4:462-476.

Wagenaar, Theodore C. 1984. "Using Student Journals in Sociology Courses." *Teaching Sociology* 11:4:419-437.

II

Student Groups

Chapter 4

Black and Gay Identity Selection on College Campuses: Master and Subordinate Status Strain and Conflict

Tim Baylor

It would be naive, or perhaps hopeful at best, to believe that college campuses are "ivory towers" where society's ideals find fertile ground and flourish in terms of lived experience. While this is the ideal, it must be realized that student interaction on college campuses does not occur in a vacuum. The social patterns, structures, norms, values, and beliefs of the surrounding society are more often than not replicated within the boundaries of educational institutions. In addition, students themselves come to college with habits, beliefs, and prejudices already in place as a result of their previous social experience. This does not mean that there are not any observable differences between college campuses and the surrounding social milieu, or that there is not greater space for seeking alternative social relations than those weighing on one in the larger society. However the ability to shrug off, even if only for a few years, some of these acquired norms and constraints on social interaction varies greatly from campus to campus. Variables such as the degree of selectivity in student admissions, residential or commuter campuses, the social class make-up, coupled with the racial and ethnic mix of the student body each affect campus dynamics. From published stories and informal conversations with colleagues, it appears that even the most highly selective college with a high degree of social class homogeneity cannot avoid the fact that we live in a society were race is still relevant for understanding social dynamics. Even where class differences are absent, the color of one's skin still acts as one filter through which the world is seen and understood. I suggest the role of race is even greater at the average, less prestigious educational institution where most students receive their education. For instance, I recently read a student journal in which the student, who was white, related over-hearing a conversation between some black[1] students following the World Trade Center bombings. One of the black students said something to the effect that, "he didn't care what happened to the people in New York since his forefathers were brought here against their will." This thought reveals so much about how one's personal experience acts as a filter through which we see and understand things, including race and its effects in society. I'm sure that this was not a common reaction among black students. However, it does show how one black student from the Midwest could not perceive that there were numerous black people who were inside this symbol of power and economic influence in New York City who also lost their lives. In the same way, I have encountered many white students in my race and ethnicity classes whose view of race is somewhat limited to the concern of "reverse discrimination" that they see as significantly impacting their educational and employment outcomes. Whether accurate or not, the perception surely affects their attitudes and interaction with others. This essay is concerned with how the filter of race interacts with an equally pervasive and problematic filter – sexual orientation,[2] especially when the person is both black and gay.

College campuses are often the first place where young people begin to escape some of the constraints of family and arrive at their own system of values and norms. Certainly, this is true regarding sexual orientation. As someone who found greater freedom, space, and support on a college campus to come to terms with my own sexual identity, I have maintained an interest in the struggles students undergo in coming to terms with their own sexual orientation. This concern has led me to serve as a faculty advisor to gay, lesbian, bisexual student groups on two different college campuses. Interaction on a college campus between students having a shared identity (sexual orientation) but also different identities (black-white) provides an interesting space from which to think about black-white relations in the larger society, since these larger patterns are often replicated in smaller microcosms like the college campus. While my thoughts are based on my own experience as a college student and my role as faculty advisor to two different student groups, and is therefor limited, I still think my experience reflects a much wider and common pattern of student interaction, or more accurately, the lack thereof.[3]

Student's of color lack of involvement in gay student groups on campuses struck me as unusual as I began to consider this piece and reflected on my own experience over the years.[4] I could only remember two black students, one black male during my own days as a student and one black female in one of the groups for which I served as faculty advisor, who ever participated in the gay student groups I had experienced. Yet from my attendance at gay dance clubs and bars and online in computer chat rooms, it was clear that black-gay college students existed in greater numbers than their representation in the gay student groups I've encountered. As an academically trained professional sociologist, I began to ask myself "Why?" this was so. Part of the answer, I think, rest on the sociological distinction between what is called our "master" verses "subordinate" statuses.

Hughes (1945) observed that each of us has multiple social statuses, i.e., socially defined positions within a large group, or society in general. For instance I have the social status of "son" in relationship to my family, the social status of "professor" in relationship to my employment, and the social status of a "White male" in relationship to my society. Attached to each social status is also a set of socially constructed "roles" which define ways individuals are supposed to act. Hughes (1945) also observed that a process occurs whereby a society, subculture, or social group selects one or more of these different statuses as being more important, what he called one's "master status."[5] Compared to our "master status," our remaining statuses become subordinate in their consequences and social significance. This process of status sorting is often an area of contention between the individual and society as there is sometimes disagreement about which status should serve as one's master status and what roles are appropriate for each status. Much is at stake since it is our master status that determines how most people relate to and interact with us.

Many of our potential statuses are obvious in that we cannot escape other people being aware of them, such as our sex or race. While the attempt to avoid having one's sex or race determine one's master status, if one was female or non-White, led to the very interesting phenomenon of "passing" where one attempted to assume another status, notably male or white because these statuses enhanced one's social position, these were less frequent although theoretically important responses to status discrimination.[6] Some statuses, however, such as sexual orientation are not so obvious and present the bearer of such a status with a choice of whether to make the status known to others. In revealing an unobvious status, the potential revelation must be weighed in terms of whether it enhances or detracts from one's position in society at large or in other groups to which the individual belongs. Something akin to a cost-benefit analysis occurs. A person must ask oneself, "What do I gain, and what do I loose by revealing my unobvious status? I will argue that from the perspective of a gay black student, revealing one's sexual orientation in a public manner by becoming involved in a gay, lesbian, or bisexual student group is perceived as having more costs than benefits. Due to these greater costs, black-white gay, lesbian, and bisexual student interaction is decreased.

The costs of being an "out" gay black student on a college campus come from several sources. Many of these costs are tied to the prejudice and discrimination resulting from a general climate of racism, homophobia, and heterosexism existing at-large in society.[7] Other costs are tied to historical and cultural experiences or aspects about the black community itself that uniquely impact and interact with racism, homophobia, and heterosexism The interaction between these two sources of prejudice and discrimination, one external to and the other internal to the black community, creates some powerful forces that ultimately reduce the likelihood of social interaction and support between black and white gay, lesbian, and bisexual students. Examining the source of these costs demonstrates some of the complexities involved in intra-racial and interracial group relations.

No one would argue college campuses are devoid of racism. While some high profile incidents of racism sometimes occur and gain the attention of the national media, behind these high profile examples of racial tensions are more fundamental differences in attitudes and beliefs about groups that students bring with them from their prior socialization experiences. For example national surveys asking respondents "Are blacks treated less fairly than whites?" consistently reflect major differences between blacks and whites regarding discriminatory treatment in the workplace, while dinning out, shopping, or while driving, with blacks agreeing that discrimination takes place at a rate 2-3 times higher than white respondents.[8] Even if these responses only reflected "perceptions" and not the actual state of affairs, perceptions still matter as they make people apprehensive or cautious, or in some manner complicate social interaction that occurs or doesn't occur whether on campus between students or elsewhere.

Minority students I have interviewed report "divided campuses" with "boundaries" separating groups from each other, "They were here and we was over there." Crossing these boundaries took extra effort. One black student reported, "I learned that I have to initiate things. White kids will not come to me, I have to come to them. It's like I have to show them it's okay to talk to me, or something like that."[9] However, white students are not the only ones constructing boundaries. One multiracial student described how she was ostracized from a black student campus group after she joined an all-white sorority.[10]

On college campuses, minority students report being discriminated against or victimized at increasing rates the longer they have been on campus. For instance in one study, fourteen percent of incoming minority (black, asian, and hispanic) freshman reported being victimized, twenty-eight percent for those having completed between one and four semesters, while forty-one percent of minority students who attended at least five semesters reported being victimized.[11] Faced with such discrimination many minority students, including black students, especially on integrated campuses, often seek support in largely racially segregated student organizations such as Greek fraternities and sororities or Black Student Unions, etc. The observation that people subject to prejudice and discrimination often seek social support within their own community is nothing new in the study of racial and ethnic relations. It does though, for purposes of this essay, emphasize the role of the black student community as an important support mechanism for black students. Therefor, for a gay, lesbian, or bisexual (GLB)[12] black student, outing one's self by participating in a racially mixed gay, lesbian, or bisexual student support/educational organization jeopardizes an extremely important source of social support from the black student community itself. This assumes of course, that a GLB black student would loose much support from the black student community because of its own homophobia and heterosexism, a point considered latter in this essay.

The potential loss of support from the black student community, besides the additional prejudice of having one's status as a GLB person known, obviously represent substantial costs, especially if the loss of black community support is not compensated for by support from the GLB community. The degree of support and other benefits from participating in the GLB student community, however, is also dependent on the absence or at least negligible presence of racism in the GLB student community; a problematic assumption to make as a quick examination reveals.

That GLB individuals are subject to prejudice and discrimination in the U.S. is obvious. For instance, during 1999 a total of 7, 876 "bias-motivated" crimes were reported to the Federal Bureau of Investigation by various local law enforcement agencies. Of those crimes, seventeen percent (1, 317) were based on sexual orientation.[13] In addition, although general societal attitudes towards GLB people have improved, approximately fifty-nine percent of the U.S. population still respond that "sexual relations between two adults of the same sex" is "always or almost always wrong."[14] A 1993 report for the Massachusetts Governor's Commission on Gay and Lesbian Youth found that 97% of public school students reported regularly hearing various anti-gay remarks, while a 1997 study of Des Moines, Iowa high school students reported students hearing about 25 anti-gay epithets per day.[15] High profile hate crime murders like that of gay student, Matthew Shepard, at the University of Wyoming on October 6, 1998, only add to this general climate of prejudice and discrimination and therefor concern on the part of GLB people regarding being open about their sexual orientation. Given this general social climate towards GLB persons, the black GLB student would have to be fairly secure about the support available from the GLB community to risk the loss of support from the black community in the face of racism, homophobia, and heterosexism. Unfortunately, such secure compensating support from the GLB community is not the case as racism also affects black-white GLB relations.

Perhaps it is not surprising that white GLB persons have also been conditioned by the general racism present in society. Given that white GLB persons come from all social and economic levels, they too have been socialized with either overt or subtle aspects of racism present in the groups and families to which they belong. Just because they may understand what it is to be discriminated against due to their sexual orientation, does not mean that they have become what sociologist Robert Merton called the "all-weather liberal," i.e., someone who lacked any prejudicial attitudes and therefor did not engage in any form of discrimination.[16] Indeed, Mandy Carter, a black lesbian activist, has said, "I think –bottom line– even though we're queer, we can still be racist" when commenting on both black and white racism within the GLB community.[17] Within the GLB community, claims of racism from people of color are common. Decades ago the well-known writer James Baldwin, who was both black and gay, articulated his observation that "The gay world as such is no more prepared to accept black people than anywhere else in society. It's a very hermetically sealed world with very unattractive features, including racism."[18] The black GLB community's claims of racism by the white GLB community have been articulated, again and again, most recently by Keith Boykin.[19] Boykin documents either from his own experience or stories he has heard, numerous examples of racism within the white GLB community. Other sources confirm the existence of racism and the difficulty of black & white GLB people working cooperatively, even in the form of interracial relationships. In one computer message board, one person wrote:

> This is all beautiful and stuff . . . but come on! Love has no color, but the world does. Our society does. And everyday that race prejudice is made manifest. I am in an interracial relationship and it is the best one I have ever been in simply because we don't hee and haw about "Love knowing no color". We acknowledge that we are from different cultures and try to grow with and in each other by learning and understanding those differences. We also try to make sure we understand internalized racial oppression and inferiority and internalized racial superiority because that tears a relationship up worse than anything in my experience. Love sees no color, but we do.[20]

Racism in the white GLB community represents one more cost the black GLB person, including students, must weigh in terms of "coming out" by participating in something like a GLB college campus group. Given the potential loss of black community support discussed earlier and racism within the white GLB community, it is not surprising that few black GLB students choose to participate in GLB student organizations, further reducing black-white interaction on college campuses and preventing mutual systems of support from forming. For instance I remember having one online conversation with a black student whom identified himself as bisexual. He vehemently denied and got angry when I suggested some similarities existed between the black community and the GLB community when it came to our mutual experiences with prejudice and discrimination. He saw no common ground at all.

Perhaps, the greatest cost though affecting a black GLB student's choice of whether to interact with white students in a GLB student organization is the probable loss of support from the black community due to its own homophobia and heterosexism. The black community's homophobia and heterosexism, however, must not be seen in isolation from the homophobia and heterosexism in the larger, dominant white community. Indeed, I will argue that black-white issues exacerbate the prevalence and degree of homophobia within the black community, increasing the costs for black GLB students, especially male students.

Homophobia and heterosexism within the black community can be seen as similar to the homophobia and heterosexism within the white community, except it is more complicated due to a history of subordination, discrimination, and differential treatment by the white community. As an ethnic subculture within the dominant white culture, the social norms and values of the white community have influenced the black community   This includes attitudes towards GLB persons. Some of this influence is seen among the black intelligentsia and leadership of the black church.

A number of contemporary black intellectuals, such as Frances Cress Welsing, Molefi Asante, Amiri Baraka, and Robert Staples have argued that homosexuality was unknown in Black African cultures. They suggest contemporary occurrences reflect European decadence and corruption, or it is the result of white racism which has weakened the black family and emasculated black men.[21] For instance, Cress (1991) states:

> The black male does not arrive at the effeminate bisexual or homosexual stance from any deeply repressed sense of genetic weakness, inadequacy or disgust . . . instead, the black male arrives at this disposition . . . as the result of the imposed power and cruelty of the white male and the totality of white supremacy social and political apparatus that has forced 20 generations of Black males into submission.[22]

A young black male expressed the same idea more simply, "Even though there are a lot of black homosexuals, a lot of blacks do not want to accept that fact . . . . [To them the] homosexual thing is a white thing."[23] It is interesting to note that the idea of no indigenous expressions of homosexuality in the black community is also found among some African intellectuals and political leaders who also identify white colonialism as the culprit responsible for introducing homosexuality and emasculating black men.[24] While the assertion of no same-sex sexual behavior among black Africans is historically and anthropologically inaccurate, the connection between homosexuality and emasculation is a substantive idea that needs closer examination.[25]   As Harlon Dalton, an Associate Professor of Law at Yale Law School has observed, "My suspicion is that openly gay men and lesbians evoke hostility in part because they have come to symbolize the strong female and the weak male that slavery and Jim Crow produced . . . . Thus, in the black community homosexuality carries more baggage than in the larger society."[26]

For the black gay or bisexual male student the gender construction of black male masculinity presents yet another cost to both "coming out" and interacting in a racially-mixed GLB student organization. To "come out," especially if one then interacts in a racially mixed GLB student group, is to fail to live-up to culturally prescribed standards of masculinity and bring upon the black community shame by "airing" one's homosexuality or bisexuality which are seen as stigma bearing social statuses. As one multiracial heterosexual student related, "Maybe some of it is African-Americans are themselves trying to be so accepted in general in the whole society, that to say within that particular community, 'okay we accept this [homosexuality and bisexuality],' and since this isn't a worldwide norm, they are losing some of the ground that they are trying to gain . . . ."[27] At the same time, a black student who "outs" himself must confront some ostracism from the black community in addition to potential racism from the white community with fewer resources and support than he would have otherwise had available. Cools (1998) has described black gay men as being "doubly 'othered': by race and by sexual preference and gender assumptions." Cool continues:

> The black homosexual comes to embody a condition of aggravated psychic unease. His skin color exposes him to racism and his gender exacerbates the anxiety he causes the white community. Compounding this marginalization is the fact that these men are 'othered' because of their sexuality. Unlike black men who subscribe to the heterosexual definition of black masculinity the black male homosexual finds little solace from the pressures of racism in his community for there is little or no acceptance of him in this community. This is because he makes more precarious, a masculinity which the black community has always 'engaged in a never-ending battle' to possess in the wider American community . . . . Thus the seeming loss of his masculinity isolates the black gay male and he is left with virtually no community to which to turn.[28]

While it might be argued that gay white male students also face similar demands of masculinity because of stereotypical gender ideas about homosexual men, such standards of masculinity are not constructed and standing counterpoised to those of another ethnic group as in the case of black male masculinity. The white gay male student by "coming out" does not risk opening himself to racism whether from his own ethnic community or one outside his own community. In addition as one recent black man writing about these issues has pointed out,

> There have been several white movie stars, athletes, politicians, and business leaders who have come out and continue to do their job without the backlash. It's a helluva lot easier for white folks to accept homosexuality, because they have their 'out' Elton Johns and Ellens, their

Queer as Folk and *Will and Grace*.[29]

These white gay "role models" that range from the stereotypical to the nonstereotypical provide a wider range of options for the white gay male student who contemplates "coming out." The same range of masculinities does not exist for black men. Instead, ". . . you think of RuPaul or the '70s singer Sylvester or Blaine and Antoine, the very feminine critics in "Men on Film' from *In Living Color*. That's gay."[30] As Boykin (1996), who is a gay Black man, has observed, "For black lesbians and gays, unlike straight blacks, our sexual orientation does not insulate us from the oppression of homophobia, and unlike white lesbians and gays, our skin color does not insulate us from the oppression of racism"

The situation for black lesbian and bisexual female students does not seem to be as oppressive compared to black gay and bisexual male students. While black lesbian and bisexual women still face similar issues in respect to potential racism, and some loss of support from the black community, gendered expectations are not constructed in such a juxtaposed manner in relationship to "race." Less emphasis is placed on female "femininity" than male "masculinity," according to Cools.[31] However, black lesbian and bisexual women still face prejudice and community sanctions for not conforming to general gender expectations, even if these expectations don't compromise their ethnic identity. Boykin (1998) cites the comment of Tony Brown, who hosts the television show *Tony Brown's Journal*, that "No lesbian relationship can take the place of a positive love relationship between black women and black men," as representative of homophobia based on the belief that women-women relationships endangers the black family.[32] Still, from a sociological perspective, other factors contribute to less attention given lesbians than gay men. Besides the general sexism existing in both the black and white communities, studies of "marriage markets" might also provide another reason why black lesbianism and bisexuality is seen in a different light than black male homosexuality and bisexuality.

Numerous social researchers, including one of the foremost sociologist of the black family, Robert Staples (1985), have argued there are simply not enough black men for black women to marry, especially black men capable of providing economically for a family.[33] For instance, Jaynes and Williams (1989) have calculated that at age twenty-six, black women with less than a high school education are in a marriage pool that has 651 men per 1,000 women. For the twenty-six year old black woman with some college education the pool grows to 772 men per 1,000 women.[34] This means that there are many more black women who will have to remain single or find alternative social relationships. I am simply suggesting that the oversupply of black women as it were, could lessen the social sanctions attached to black lesbians and bisexuals, whereas the opposite is true for black gay and bisexual men in a situation where marriageable black men are already in short-supply. Such an assertion seems to have face validity. Dr. Alvin F. Poussaint, an Associate Professor at Harvard Medical School, commented in an article in the magazine *Ebony* that:

> Many Black women in America's major urban centers, including New York, Chicago, Washington, D.C., and Atlanta bemoan the fact that finding "a good Black man" for the purpose of marriage or a committed relationship has become increasingly difficult, if not impossible. Justifiably or not, they blame this situation on what they perceive as a rapidly increasing number of upwardly mobile-looking, educated Black males who can be seen in upscale neighborhoods living obviously gay lifestyles.[35]

Given the dynamics described in the preceding paragraphs, it is not surprising that black GLB students remain closeted, which prevents them interacting with white GLB students. Besides the constraints based on gender expectations, including those that are ethnically specific, homophobia and heterosexism is further reinforced through popular culture and organized religion. While these sources of homophobia are not unique to black students, they may have equal or greater importance because they originate from their own community.

Boykin (1996) has suggested that black figures in popular culture may be the "worst offender" among all the sources of homophobia and heterosexism in black institutions. Among black musicians and singers the list would include Buju Banton, Tone Loc, Snoop Doggy Dogg, Brand Nubian, Lench Mob, Chuck D, Ice-T, Ice Cube, Queen Latifah, Shabba Ranks, Donna Summers, etc. Comedians and film stars such as Arsenio Hall, Eddie Murphy and the Wayan brothers regularly contribute to stereotypical notions of GLB persons.[36] Some of the material of black entertainers can be interpreted as historically and culturally reactive. Outlaw (1995) argues that the lyrical content of some black entertainers should be seen as a reaction to centuries of struggle in which black male masculinity has been assaulted. ". . . the queer is the worst kind of freak. He is not a real man, he's more of a bitch than any 'ho" could ever be."[37] Given the role and importance of popular culture, especially for youth, popular culture must be seen as a significant force constraining the expression of sexual identity among black adolescents and young adults. Even when black homosexuality is pictured somewhat positively, as in the case of the character "Carter" on *Spin City*, he is still not fully "masculine." For instance, in one show he artificially tried to appear more athletic to impress a boyfriend. In addition, different ethnic viewing habits meat that this show was less likely to be viewed by a wide black audience.

Another significant agent of heterosexism and homophobia in the black community is the black church. In this respect, the black church is not any different from the non-black church where heterosexism and homophobia have also been a part of its message. While this is decreasingly true of some denominations[38] strong strands of homophobia and heterosexism are prominent in Catholic and Protestant Christianity. Boykin (1996) has argued that in relationship to the black church, church dogma is more homophobic than the church community.[39] One black student I interviewed, for instance, related how she knew of one black male couple who attended a black Baptist church together where people were aware of their relationship.[40] Yet they were "in church" and that mattered more than their sexual orientation, although one should not assume that black GLB persons receive warm messages of welcome from black church pulpits. Unlike many white Christian denominations which are more centralized and hierarchical in structure and have "official" church statements or positions on homosexuality, the largest black or mostly black denominations (National Baptist Convention, USA Inc., Church of God in Christ, and African Methodist Episcopal Church) have no such statements. However, most black churches tend to disprove of homosexuality and bisexuality even though many acknowledge the presence of GLB people. As one Church of God in Christ pastor put it, ". . . it is no secret that gays and lesbian are in the church from the highest levels on down."[41] Still, the overall attitude one is more likely to encounter was expressed by a National Baptist Convention pastor who said, "All the ministers in the churches that I know of believe that God can change anyone. First, you must admit that you are wrong, that what you are doing is sinful, and then ask for change."[42] Thus one has a difficult time characterizing the black church as a supportive institution for GLB persons, a point which certainly upsets many black GLB Christians. "I find it despicable and a desecration," according to Jewelle Gomez, a black lesbian writer, "that our spiritual beliefs are perverted and used against Black gay people. Anyone who understands what the spirit of Christianity is supposed to be, would never use it against gays."[43]

It is also possible to see the homophobia and heterosexism in the black church as a product of white racism. Bishop Carl Bean, a black gospel singer provides an interesting viewpoint.

> All oppressed people try hard in that whole idea of assimilation to prove to the oppressor that they're okay. . . . If you tear that [assimilation] away and just look at the community, you'll find that the other side of the coin is great acceptance. There is no one in the church who doesn't know who's gay and lesbian. Everyone knows. . . . There is not a community, black, that I've ever known of where homosexuals were not living. Real honest-to-God, broken-wristed, twisting sissies don't get thrown out of the black community. That white phenomenon does not happen in our community.[44]

For the GLB black student, to understand and comprehend these potential racial dynamics on her/his own is a lot to expect. All that he/she knows is that another institution, that one former black man on the DL(down low) describes as the "anchor of our lives," and which has historically provided support indicates that it is wrong to be a GLB person.[45] He/she learns it is better to keep one's sexual identity hid, preventing participation and interaction in a GLB student group. What options then do black GLB students have available?

Options for gay black students, and gay black persons in general, are those any gay person must choose from, although within a different qualitative and quantitative structure of benefits, constraints, and costs. It is clear that most black homosexuals, male and female, when contemplating their own master status from the various statuses they possess, identify with their ethnic background before their other statuses.[46] One study found 81.4% of GLB online users identified themselves as "gay" when asked, "Do you identify more strongly with your ethnicity or your sexual orientation?" Important for this essay, however, were the differences between ethnic groups. Among white respondents, eighty-five percent (85%) identified more strongly with their sexual orientation than ethnicity, whereas sixty-three percent (63%) of blacks and fifty-five percent (55%) of Korean Americans identified more strongly with their ethnic backgrounds rather than their sexual orientation.[47] While these results were of a select group of GLB people, for instance almost eighty-nine percent (89%) had attended college, I would predict that ethnic group identification over sexual orientation would be more skewed among less educated minority group individuals, including blacks since homophobia tends to decrease with more education.[48] Individuals having lower levels of education would have even fewer resources to weather racism and homophobia and therefor seek greater support from their ethnic communities. I would predict that this would be especially true of black gay students since it appears that actual or perceived incidents of racial discrimination increase the longer one has been in college which increases the need for community support.[49]

Selecting ethnicity as one's master status because it carries with it more benefits than costs, does not however mean that "sexual orientation" is absent from one's subordinate statuses. It is still there but gaining the benefit of support from the black community cost the subordinating of one's sexual orientation. As one black lawyer and educator put it, "In exchange for inclusion, [black] gay men and lesbians have agreed to remain under wraps, to downplay, if not hide, their sexual orientation, to provide their families and friends with 'deniability.' So long as they do not put the community to the test, they are welcome. It is all right if everybody knows as long as nobody tells."[50] This response or social adaptation has been neatly summed-up by one black lesbian writer in the phrase, "Play it, but don't say it," an idea striking familiar to the United States' military policy of "Don't ask, Don't Tell."[51]

Another status/identity choice that appears more prevalent among black males is "bisexuality" as several studies have shown.[52] One member and observer of the black community referred to bisexuality as "black America's best kept secret" and ". . . a larger closet than homosexuality."[53] It is easy to see why self-identifying as bisexual rather than homosexual happens so frequently, especially within the black male community. Given the emphasis on "masculinity" within the black community, partially conditioned by white racism as described earlier, in addition to the other sources of homophobia and heterosexism described earlier, bisexuality reduces some of the potential costs. One can still claim to fulfill masculine gender expectations because of one's relationships with women, and since one still keeps one's same-sex relations discrete, one can continue to rely on the black community for support. But again for the black male and female student these benefits are conditioned on remaining politically inactive and relatively "invisible" when it comes to sexual orientation, something which involvement in an ethnically mixed GLB student group precludes.

The greater likelihood of young black men self-identifying as bisexual rather than gay holds several important implications for black students and the black community as a whole. First, some of those self-identifying as bisexual reflect cases where individuals have not been able to come to terms with their homosexual orientation due to societal and community prejudice and fear of discrimination that creates a degree of internalized homophobia in these individuals. One respondent in a study related how his friends saw themselves as "bisexual" even though they were only sexually attracted to men, but since they talked to women in clubs and flirted a little, they maintained their bisexuality.[54] This inability to accept one's sexual orientation is often manifested by secondary social, physical, and psychological problems.[55] Whether it is alcohol or drug abuse, stress and anxiety disorders, or a greater likelihood to engage in unsafe sex, internalized homophobia coupled with lack of community acceptance increases the occurrence of dysfunctional consequences.

Black men who are actively bisexual, report a higher proportion of female sexual partners than their white male bisexual counterparts.[56] At the same time they are less likely to disclose their homosexual activity to their female partners, an outcome predicted by arguments advanced in this essay.[57] The Centers for Disease Control (CDC) has indicated that black women account for sixty-four percent (64%) of new HIV/AIDS cases among women even though blacks make-up only 12-13% of the U.S. population. Seventy-five percent (75%) of these new cases are attributed to black women having unprotected sex with men. Further, health researchers estimate that sixty percent (60%) of these men are bisexual or living an alternative "secret" sexual life called "down low."[58] Another study by Ross and Rosser (1996) found that HIV seropositive men were less likely to publicly identify as being gay and less likely to be comfortable with other gay men, including belonging to a gay or bisexual group. A more recent study of black college student and non-student men in North Carolina who had sex with men, confirmed that fewer male college students identified as gay or revealed their sexuality identity to others than most people[59]

If we extrapolate the above findings to black students on a college campus, there should be a great deal of concern. The picture painted by research puts black women at greater risk of contracting AIDS through unprotected sex with "down low" black men who identify and act bisexually, although often secretively, in an attempt to mediate societal and black community homophobia and heterosexism and live up to community standards of masculinity, all of which is made more complicated by white racism. Research by Waldner, et. al. (1999) has also found that black university students scored higher on a measure of homophobia than white and hispanic students. At the same time, they also had the lowest levels of AIDS knowledge among the three ethnic groups, including knowledge about means of transmission, etc.[60] Since AIDS education and prevention is usually one of the activities of GLB student organizations, black GLB students lack this important informational source. Getting involved with an AIDS Awareness student organization if they exist on campus appears even less likely given the stigma surrounding AIDS and "fear of AIDS" which is greater among black students than white students.[61]

Examination of black-white GLB student interaction demonstrates campus patterns of black-white relations which replicate those found in the surrounding society. It also reveals the struggles centered about "identity" and the potential conflict within oneself in deciding on one's "master and subordinate" statuses, in addition to the conflict between the individual and society over status recognition and determination. While this study has primarily thought about these issues within the context of a racially mixed campus, it would be interesting to consider some of these issues at historically black colleges. While a preliminary, informal examination of web pages at some of the better known historically black colleges in 2002 revealed only one campus which had a student group that was clearly represented and identified as a GLB organization, and that was at a historically black women's college, things are changing[62] It would be desirable to hear the voices of black GLB students at both racially-mixed and historically black colleges (HBC) to determine what identity dynamics are similar or dissimilar when it comes to status choices. Some of these voices are beginning to be heard, especially those of GLB students at HBCs.[63] Finally, we need to think about ways in which bridges can be built over the chasms that currently exist between black and white students, black and white gay, lesbian, and bisexual students, and between heterosexual and GLB students whatever one's ethnicity. Because as it is now, managing one's multiple identities, trying to find some balance or compromise between different statuses creates incredible role strain and conflict in many cases. As one multiracial student put it, and something which would be equally true for black GLB students, "It's almost like you have to divide yourself, and that's just too much work."[64]

Discussion and Essay Questions:

1. How might one's master status change based on one's race or sexual orientation?

2. Does the situational context, i.e., being a college student versus living on one's own after college, influence what is someone's master status?

3. If one's socialization and experiences prior to attending college affects how one interacts with others at college, and possibly even the choice of master status while at college, how do you think urban verses a more rural residence, or a more ethnically integrated versus less integrated environment affects the outcome?

4. How might masculinity and femininity for black students be different than masculinity and femininity for white students?

5. Are there similar ways that someone is oppressed based on their race or sexual orientation? What do you think are the differences?

6. What affect does the shortage of black men have on the behavior of black women? Might this affect black women's views toward black men, especially gay black men?

7. What do you think is the strongest factor keeping gay, lesbian, or transgender black students from "coming out" or participating in a student gay, lesbian and transgender campus organization?

Notes

1. I will use the terms "Black" and "White" or "Black community" and "White community" rather than African-American or European-American for two reasons. First, the latter terms are more cumbersome. Second, and more important, I do not think that the real issue which causes so much conflict is tied to nationality as much as it is "skin color" and all the social baggage that gets attached to that variable.

2. The concept "sexual orientation" is used to represent the idea of an "identity" that goes beyond simple same-sex behavior. For purposes of this essay it does not matter whether one thinks this identity is established through nurture during the process of socialization or through nature in some form of fixed genetic biological predisposition. In either case, the emphasis is placed on the lack of a conscious choice regarding what one feels inside in a cognitive-emotional sense although choice may still exist in terms of whether an individual acts on these feelings.

4. One study of gay men at a college campus found that fifty-four percent (54%) of gay men who responded to the survey indicated that they participated in the campus gay and lesbian student organization. This figure may be high, however, since the sample was not random but selectively recruited. See D'Augelli, Anthony R. 1999. "Gay Men in College: Identity Processes and Adaptations." *Journal of College Student Development* 32: 140-146, p. 143.

5. See Hughes, Everett. 1945. "Dilemmas and Contradictions of Status," *American Journal of Sociology*, 50 (March):353-359.

6. For a recent discussion of "passing," see Sanchez, Maria Carla and Linda Schlossberg, eds. 2001. *Passing: Identity and Interpretation in Sexuality, Race, and Religion*. New York: New York University Press.

7. In this essay, "homophobia" refers to an "irrational and distorted view of homosexuality and of homosexual individuals." "Heterosexism" refers "an institutionalized enforcement of heterosexual 'normality' that is assumed by our culture." See Owens, Robert E., Jr. 1998. *Queer Kids: The Challenges and Promise for Lesbian, gay, and Bisexual Youth*. New York: The Haworth Press, Inc., pp. 7-8.

8. Gallup poll results cited in Schaefer, Richard T. 2000. *Racial and Ethnic Groups*. Upper Saddle River, New Jersey: Prentice Hall. P. 59.

9. Personal interview of 22 year old African-American college senior. 2001. Interview by author. Tape recording. Saint Joseph, MO, October 31.

10. Personal interview of 22 year old multiracial college senior. 2001. Interview by author. Tape recording. Saint Joseph, MO, October 29.

11. Smith, T., R. Roberts, and C. Smith. 1997. "Expressions of Prejudice Among College Students Over Three Assessments." *College Student Journal* 29(2): 235-237.

12. For brevity's sake "gay, lesbian, and bisexual" will simply be abbreviated "GLB."

13. Statistics are from the FBI National Press Office. Http://www.fbi.gov.pressrel/pressrel01/hate021301.htm

14. NORC. General Social Surveys, 1972-1998: Cumulative Codebook. Chicago: National Opinion Research Center, 1999, P. 236.

15. Studies cited in "Families & Educators Partnering for Safe Schools," by Parents and Friends of Lesbians and Gays (PFLAG). Http://www.pflag.org.

16. Merton, Robert K. 1949. "Discrimination and the American Creed," in Robert M. MacIver, ed., *Discrimination and National Welfare*, Pp. 99-126. New York: Harper & Row.

17. Cited in Boykin, Keith. 1996. *One More River to Cross*. New York: Anchor Books, P. 224.

18. Boykin, *One More*, p. 228.

19. Boykin, *One More* and Boykin's various columns archived at http://www.gay.com under "Channels" subsection "News."

20. Gay.com Interracial Relationships message board, Whimsy75, (#6 of 35) Sept. 21, 2000.

21. See Welsing, Frances Cress. 1991. *The Isis Papers*. Chicago: Third World Press, Asante, Molefi, 1989, *The Afrocentric Idea*, Philadelphia: Temple University Press, Amiri Baraka, 1965, *American Sexual Preference: Black Male*, reprinted in Baraka, Imanm Amiri. 1998. *Home: Social Essays*. Hopewell, NJ: Eco Press, and Staples,

Robert. 1982. *Black Masculinity: The Black Male's Role in American Society.* San Francisco, CA: Black Scholar Press.

22. Cress. p. 86.

23. Sears, J. T. 1991. *Growing Up Gay in the South: Race, Gender, and Journeys of the Spirit.* NY: Harrington Press, P. 68.

24. For a discussion of these ideas within the context of Zimbabwe, see Epprecht, Marc. 1998. "The 'Unsaying' of Indigenous homosexualities in Zimbabwe: Mapping a Blindspot in an African Masculinity." *Journal of Southern African Studies* 24(4): 631-651.

25. For a brief discussion regarding same-sex behavior among the Azande, see Herdt, Gilbert. 1997. *Same Sex, Different Cultures: Exploring Gay and Lesbian Lives.* Boulder: Westview Press, Pp. 76-80.

26. P. 217 in Dalton, Harlon L. 1989. "AIDS in Blackface." *Daedalus* 118(3): 205-227

27. Personal interview with 22 year old multiracial college senior. 2001. Interview by author. Tape recording. Saint Joseph, MO, October 29.

28. Cools, Janice. 1998. "The (Re)Construction of African-American Masculinity." *African American Male Research.* 3(1). Retrieved November 22, 2001 (http://www.pressroom.com/ ~afrimale/cools.htm).

29. King, J.L. 2004. *On The Down Low: A Journey into the Lives of "Straight" Black Men Who Sleep with Men.* Broadway Book: New York, p. 22.

30. King, p. 22

31. Cools, Janice. p. 4.

32. Boykin, Keith. p. 164.

33. Staples, Robert. 1985. "Changes in Black Family Structure: The Conflict between Family Ideology and Structural Conditions." *Journal of Marriage and the Family* 47:1005-13. See also, Bennett, Neil G., David E. Bloom and Patricia H. Craig. 1989. "The Divergence of Black and White Marriage Patterns." *American Journal of Sociology* 3:692-722 and Kiecolt, K. Jill and Mark A. Fossett. 1995. "Mate Availability and Marriage among African Americans." Pp. 121-142 in *The Decline in Marriage among African Americans: Causes, Consequences, and Policy Implications*, edited by B. Tucker and C. Mitchell-Kernan. New York: Russell Sage Foundation.

34. Jaynes, Gerald D., and Robert M. Williams, Jr., eds. 1989. *A Common Destiny: Blacks and American Society.* Washington, D.C.: National Academy Press, p. 539.

35. P. 126 in Poussaint, Alvin F., M.D. 1990. "An Honest Look at Black Gays and Lesbians." *Ebony* 45(11):124, 126, 130-131.

36. Boykin, *One More* p. 181.

37. Outlaw, Paul. 1995. "If that's your boyfriend (he wasn't last night)." *African American Review* 29(2): 347-350.

38. For a recent report and summary of the position towards homosexuality and GLB persons, see Bennett, Lisa. 1998. "Mixed Blessings: Organized Religion and Gay and Lesbian Americans in 1998." Washington, D.C.: Human Rights Campaign Foundation. (http://www.hrc.org/ publications/index.asp)

39. Boykin, Keith. *One More* p. 126.

40. Personal interview of 22 year old African-American college senior. 2001. Interview by author. Tape recording. Saint Joseph, MO, October 31.

41. Bennett, p.18. Similar acknowledgments are found in Boykin, Pp. 126-128 and

Zulu, N. S. 1996. "Sex, Race and the Stained-glass Window." *Women and Therapy* 19: 27-35.

42. Bennett, p. 16.

43. P. 53 in Smith, Barbara. 1990. "Talking About It: Homophobia in the Black Community." *Feminist Reviews* 34: 47-55

44. Cited in Boykin, *One More* p. 132.

45. King, J.L., p. 78.

46. For example one black lesbian related how most of the black lesbians she knew identify as "black women first and lesbians second." In Poussaint, Op cit. p. 131.

47. Garber, Jeffrey S. 2001. "2001 Gay/Lesbian Consumer Online Census." A Syracuse University, OpusComm Group, GSociety Study. Retrieved 10/22/2001. (http://www.glcensus.org)

48. Kim, Bryan S.K. Michael J. D'Andrea, Poonam K. Sahu, and Kiaka J.S. Gaughen. 1998. "A Multicultural Study of University Students' Knowledge of and Attitudes Toward Homosexuality." 36(3): 171-182.

49. Smith, T., R. Roberts, and C. Smith..

50. Dalton, Harold L. , p. 215.

51. Black lesbian writer Ann Allen Shockley cited in Gomez, Smith, p .49.

52. See Doll, L., and Beeker, C. 1996. "Male Bisexual Behavior and HIV Risk in the United States: Synthesis of Research with Implications for Behavioral Interventions." *AIDS Education and Prevention* 8: 205-225, Stokes, J.P., Vanable, P.A., and McKiman, D.J. 1997. "Ethnic Differences in Sexual Behavior, Condom Use, and Psychosocial Variables among Black and White Men who have Sex with Men." *Journal of Sex Research* 33: 373-381.

53. Rhue, Sylvia and Rhue, "Reducing Homophobia in African-American Communities," pp. 117-130 in Sears, James T. and Walter Williams. 1997. *Overcoming Heterosexism and Homophobia: Strategies that Work.* New York: Columbia University Press.

54. Stokes, Joseph P. and Miller, Robin L. 1998. "Toward an Understanding of Behaviorally Bisexual Men: The Influence and Context of Culture." *Canadian Journal of Human Sexuality* 7(2): 101-113.

55. See Chapter 6 "Outcomes for Sexual-Minority Youths," Pp. 101-122 in Owens Jr., Robert E. 1998. *Queer Kids: The Challenges and Promises for Lesbian, Gay, and Bisexual Youth.* New York: Harrington Park Press and Szymanski, Dawn M., Y. Barry Chung, and Kimberly F. Balsam. 2001. "Psychosocial Correlates of Internalized Homophobia in Lesbians." *Measures and Evaluation in Counseling and Development* 34: 27-38.

56. McKirnan, David J. and Stokes, Joseph P. 1995. "Bisexually Active Men: Social Characteristics and Sexual Behavior." *Journal of Sex Research* 32(1): 65-76.

57. McKiman, p. 72 and Ballard, Scotty R. 2001. "Why AIDS is Rising Among Black Women." *Jet* July 23. Retrieved 10/27/2001.
(http://www.findarticles.com/cf_0/m1355/6_100/76800067/ print.jhtml)

58. Ballard, p.1.

59. Centers for Disease Control. 2004. "HIV Transmission Among Black College Student and Non-Student Men Who Have Sex with Men—North Carolina, 2003." *Morbidity and Mortality weekly Report*. 53(32):731-734.

60. Waldner, Lisa K., Anjoo Kikka, and Salman Baig. 1999. "Ethnicity and Sex Differences in University Student's Knowledge of AIDS, Fear of AIDS, and Homophobia." *Journal of Homosexuality* 37(3): 117-133. See also, Dilorio, C., Parson, M., Lehr, S., Adame, D., and Carlone, J. 1993. "Knowledge of AIDS and Safer Sex Practices among College Freshman." *Public Health Nursing* 10: 159-165.

61. Waldner, Kikka, and Baig, p. 124.

62. An informal review of nine historically black college web pages conducted by the author.

63. The Human Rights Campaign, a national gay, lesbian, and transgendered rights organization, held its second annual conference in February 2005 for GLBT students at historically black colleges and universities. For more information go to http://www.hrc.org. Also, an account of one black gay college student at his HBC school can be found at http://www.keithboykin. com/ arch/001265.html.

64. Personal interview of a twenty-two year old multiracial college senior. Interview by author. Tape recording. Saint Joseph, MO, October 29, 2001.

Chapter 5

Facilitating Student Involvement and Cross-Race Contact: The Impact of Membership in a Black Greek Organization

Stephanie M. McClure

Introduction

It is an ongoing conversation on predominantly white college campuses (PWI's) across the country, appearing in student paper editorials and letters to the editor on what seems to be a regular basis – if students of color want to be integrated, don't same-race organizations, in particular black Greek organizations (BGO's), promote continued self-segregation? The question of so-called "self-segregation" can and should provoke multiple responses on campus and particularly indicates a poverty of understanding about the historical and contemporary experience of minority students on predominantly white campuses (for a great discussion of some of these questions at an earlier age see Tatum 1997). These are important questions but not ones to be addressed here. Instead, I present findings from a qualitative research project on black Greek membership that indicate, consistent with previous findings by Murguia, Padilla, and Pavel (1991) related to student development and research on voluntary association membership more generally that, as a voluntary association, minority student Greek organizations can in fact facilitate *increased* cross-race interactions for their members. This finding is particular to minority student organizations on PWI's in large part because of the demographics of the campuses and the realities of the minority student experience (see Massey, Charles, Lundy, and Fischer 2003; Feagin, Vera, & Nikitah 1996; Feagin and Sikes 1995).

Before presenting the findings, I will review research on several relevant topics, including previous findings on the impact of Greek organization membership, BGO membership specifically, and minority student involvement in same-race student organizations more generally. Although it is not often addressed in much higher education research, it is also important to recognize that Greek organizations are a form of voluntary association. As such it is appropriate to consider what we know about voluntary association membership in general to better understand the role and function of membership in a BGO at a PWI. I will then present excerpts from interviews conducted in the spring and fall of 2001 which reveal the ways in which membership in a BGO facilitate increased cross-race interaction.

Background and Literature Review

Although the origins of the black fraternal movement can be traced back somewhat earlier, the most common starting place for those interested in the history of BGO's is with the founding of Alpha Phi Alpha at Cornell University in 1905-06 (Kimbrough 2003). There are now nine national Black Greek organizations under the National Pan-Hellenic Council (NPHC). Current membership in the NPHC is over 1.5 million. According to the history of the NPHC, racism had prevented blacks from joining already existing white fraternal organizations (Ross 2000). Black students on both historically black campuses and predominantly white campuses founded fraternal organizations to enhance their college experiences and to deal with political and social issues facing the black community (Rodriguez 1995). Black fraternities and sororities have historically been and continue to be sources of identity formulation and social and cultural contact. According to an editorial by Dr. William E. Cox, publisher of *Black Issues in Higher Education* and member of a national Black Greek organization, these groups "play a vital part in the socialization process of thousands of Black students throughout the United States" (Cox 1986).

Most of the research on the influence or impact of Greek membership on college students however focuses primarily on the experiences of white students, with mixed results. A large proportion of this research points to deleterious consequences of Greek membership for college student development. These include findings on higher levels of rigidity in the attitudes of Greek members, lower moral and cognitive development outcomes, less concern for social issues than their non-Greek counterparts, extremely high levels of alcohol use and abuse, and increased incidences of rape and sexual assault in fraternity houses

(Fox, Hodge, and Ward 1987; Sanday 1996; Wilder and McKeegan 1999). Negative cognitive and academic outcomes have led to the suggestion that freshman pledging be abolished and deferred until sophomore year (Wilder and McKeegan 1999).

Other research has identified potentially positive outcomes associated with Greek membership, outcomes that are connected with the overall literature on student involvement, as well as some positive post-college outcomes (Thorson 1997; Pike 2000). These include increased opportunities for leadership development, higher levels of student involvement, and higher levels of post-college charitable giving and community involvement (Pike 2000, Thorson 1997). Many of these outcomes can be connected with Greek organizations as a form of voluntary association, as will be discussed in the next section.

The existing literature makes very few distinctions between those Greek organizations that are predominantly white and have very few, if any, minority members, and those organizations that are historically black. This is described in Wilder and McKeegan's (1999) review of the literature on Greek organizations and is exemplified in the following two quotes pulled from an article by Pascerella et. al (1996) that reviewed the impact of Greek membership on cognitive outcomes for freshman: "joining a fraternity during the first year of college has a significant negative impact on all four cognitive outcomes for men" and then, a few pages later, "Joining a fraternity had a strong negative effect on all four cognitive outcomes for White men, but a modest positive influence on all four cognitive outcomes for men of color." Fox, Hodge, and Ward write that their findings "indicate that characteristics most often associated with white fraternity membership may not necessarily be applicable to Black fraternity membership" (1987, 533). Thorson (1997) emphasizes that the findings of their national survey of Greek membership should not be generalized to black Greek organizations and Wilder and McKeegan (1999) state that although more research needs to be done on black Greek organizations the existing literature shows that "black Greeks appear to differ substantially from white Greeks" (Wilder and McKeegan 1999). These differences have been established across studies and yet even research published as recently as 2002 fails to make a distinction between membership in the different types of organizations (see Hayek, Carini, O'Day, and Kuh 2002).

Early research does reveal that the history and structure of the black Greek system serves a very different purpose than that of the predominantly white Greek system. In her research on the values held by black and white Greek and non-Greek students, Fox et al. (1987) found that the attitudes and priorities of members of black fraternities were very different from those most commonly associated with white Greek membership, which therefore "creates a different Greek membership experience for Blacks and Whites" (Fox et al. 1987). Whipple, Baier, and Grady (1991) review some of the major differences between black and white Greek systems.

"On most predominantly white college campuses, black Greeks provide the major social structure for most blacks on campus, both members and nonmembers alike, whereas white Greeks generally only provide social activities for their own members, guests, and members of other white Greek organizations. Black Greeks are also more service-oriented than are white Greeks" (Whipple et al. 1991).

The major negative findings associated with Greek organizations include lack of cognitive gains, negative influence of freshman pledging and Greek housing, and a tendency towards conservative values and less value for diversity. These conditions are not present for Black Greek organizations based on their different structure. They do not have freshman pledging, they do not have negative cognitive outcomes, they do not have Greek housing, and they do not show consistently more conservative attitudes than their non-Greek counterparts (Thorson 1997; Wilder and McKeegan 1999). There is concern about the occurrence and severity of hazing in black Greek organizations, an issue that has also been of concern for administrators regarding white Greek organizations (Ruffins and Roach 1997).

The experiences of members of a black Greek organization may therefore be seen as having some similarities to their white counterparts but also having some important distinctions. However, the specific experience of black students on predominantly white campuses (e.g. Bowen and Bok's finding that controlling for all other differences, race still matters, 1999) points to a greater need among minority students for same-race support groups (Murguia et. al 1991), something white students find through their participation in mainstream organizations that are predominantly white by default. What Tillar wrote in 1974 remains true today, "black students tend to gravitate toward black social organizations where more intimate social contacts involve students of their own race. Nonblacks continue to participate in the traditional social opportunities available on predominantly nonblack campuses" (Tillar 1974, 212).

Voluntary Associations in the Minority Student Experience – Same-race support groups

Several studies found that participation in same-race organizations did not increase isolation for African-American and other minority students, as commonly believed, but actually made them feel more apart of the campus community (Taylor & Howard-Hamilton 1995, Moran et al. 1994, Murguia et al. 1991). Students use these enclaves to scale down a large campus in order to deal with it more effectively. It is in this function that the black Greek organization can most clearly be seen as unique from that of white Greek organizations. Based on the incongruence in the overall campus environment and the needs and experiences of African American students, same-race organizations create a unique niche for these students (Tinto 1993). Kimbrough (1995, 1998) found that participation in a black Greek organization increases student opportunities for leadership development and involvement in other collegiate activities. As it functions to integrate African American students into the college campus, the black Greek organization can be seen as decreasing the isolation of its members (Moran et. al 1994), connecting them to other students on campus, and providing them with important information about black history and culture (Smith and Moore 2000).

These same-race organizations are a type of voluntary association and as such share many of the characteristics of this type of organization. Voluntary associations, defined minimally as any "formally organized named group, most of whose members – whether persons or organizations – are not financially compensated for their participation," figure prominently in discussions of the development of social capital (Knoke 1986, 2). Social capital is defined by Putnam (1995) through "features of social organizations, such as networks, norms, and trust, that facilitate coordination and cooperation for mutual benefit" (Putnam 1995, 67). Fraternity membership functions as an intermediate association linking its members to the university, to the larger black community, and also to society in general, serving to connect them to a group and lower their perception of isolation. It is in the context of this formation of social capital that the findings of the current research project are best understood.

Methods

The research was conducted at a large, predominantly white, southeastern university. Twenty members of one historically black fraternity on the campus were interviewed. The chapter on this campus averages approximately 20 active, undergraduate members. The interview subjects ranged in age from 19-23, all were at the sophomore level or above; most, based on the occupations of their parents and their attendance at the university, were middle to upper-middle class. Participation was voluntary and the men received no compensation for their participation, although the chapter did request and receive a copy of the original paper. Access to respondents was gained initially through a personal contact with one member. This was followed by asking members who had completed an interview for other contacts, then through further contacts with members at fraternity-sponsored events, and ultimately, by attending a chapter meeting and passing around a sign-up sheet for volunteers.

The interviews were conducted using a semi-structured interview style. There was an evolving interview schedule but the subjects were allowed to deviate from it. I followed up on any new ideas with probes to expand on the newly introduced topics. The open-interview style provided a greater opportunity for the interview subjects to address issues that were relevant to them (Denzin 1989). The taped interviews lasted from 25 minutes to two hours with most averaging around sixty minutes, largely depending upon the communication style of the interview subject and how many new topics were introduced and followed up on. I then transcribed the tapes verbatim. These transcripts were analyzed for common themes in comparison with the others. A method of constant comparison was used to identify those topics that occurred repeatedly as well as those that were unique or unusual (Strauss and Corbin 1998).

The data collection process occurred in two stages, with nine interviews being completed in the spring semester of 2001, after which an analysis of the themes and ideas was conducted for an initial write-up of the project. These themes were then used to inform and expand the interview schedule in the fall semester of 2001, at which time the final eleven interviews were conducted. In this way an attempt was made to follow a dialectical model of allowing the data to guide the development of the research project.

The findings presented in this paper were uncovered by focusing on the issue of cross-race contact and through identification of those findings that were unique or unusual. As opposed to the grounded theory method of analysis, which was used previously to analyze the data, I here deductively analyzed the data with the concept of contact explicitly in mind. The possibility for a same-race minority student organization to facilitate increased cross-race interaction existed in the literature but is counter-intuitive to conventional wisdom on campus.

Findings

The interviews indicate that membership in a BGO increases contact and interaction between members and other students, including white students, largely by facilitating involvement in other student organizations. Like most voluntary associations, BGO membership increases the social networks and self-efficacy of members, makes them aware of other opportunities and provides them with the tools to be successful in the context of a same-race support group which serves as the sort of axis of a wheel from which the members branch out into other areas of campus life. This then creates opportunities to work closely with white students in ways that would not have been possible otherwise. That is, they would have been possible for non-Greek black students but the fraternity structures and facilitates this involvement in a self-conscious, explicit, and effective way, as is clear in the following excerpts from the interviews. This occurs because social capital inheres in social structures – in an organization with a history, previous members with knowledge that is explicitly shared and passed down, and an organizational culture which encourages this type of social capital generation (Coleman 1988).

The idea of the fraternity facilitating increased contact with white students first presented itself in an interview with Jake, a junior business major. Contrary to the conventional campus wisdom described above, Jake described how his experience in the fraternity changed the perceptions of white people he had when he started college, having come from an all-black high school. "When I got up here I only had, I never would say I was you know a bigot or racist or anything like that but you always kind of have a, a little less comfort being around, you know, another race. I don't have that anymore. It's great, I done met so many wonderful people, I just, you kind of almost, if you really immerse yourself at this institution and [the fraternity] will help you do that. You know and it' just something where you kind of break out of that whole shell that you once were, you're almost like a totally different person."

David, a junior pre-medicine major focused more explicitly on how the fraternity had provided him with the knowledge and information to get involved in other student organizations on campus. David and another interviewee (Thomas, a sophomore political science major) had recently been elected to high visibility positions on campus and they attributed much of their success to the advice they received through the fraternity alumni listserv – the same success had been achieved by previous members and David and Thomas used the strategy suggested by them. David said, "the [fraternity members] were mentors to me, they told me what to do, what to get involved with, how to be success, successful on campus"

David continued by describing how the fraternity can "just be a resource for everyone because they were well in touch with everybody on campus you know. It wasn't just for the African American community, it was for everyone. . . that's what's so special about it. It's where you have a unique opportunity to um, I guess, go outside my culture, at a predominantly white school and have a major connection to people here. And I think that's unique because if you're just staying within your community of course it's always good to build your community but it's also good to get connections from everyone else and there's so many resources on campus you know. And if you stay isolated and segregated there's going to be so much that you're leaving behind." (my prompt – *so the frat has sort of connections to the rest of campus?*) "Yes, Definitely that, definitely. I mean if you look on campus now you know we have people in this organization in student government, in housing, all over the place, and it's just remarkable how it's only 22, 23 members and you can go on campus and be touched by [the frat].

Ryan's description mirrors that of David regarding older members passing down information gained from their experiences on campus, and clearly reveals the way in which membership in a voluntary organization assists in increasing the knowledge members have and creating new opportunities for them. "Had I not been a [fraternity member], because so much has been opened up to me through them, through older brothers who have come in and let me know of different opportunities and different things I could get involved in, that I know I wouldn't have been exposed to as a regular student who was uninvolved in the fraternity. Most of my, most of my involvement has come from brothers telling me this is a good program to get involved in, or brothers encouraging me, hey this is something new, you might want to check it out."

This increased knowledge and access meant that Steven had an experience with a fellow white student that he would never have been exposed to otherwise. He said, (in response to my question about if being a frat member makes being at the university easier) "Definitely, definitely, makes it a lot easier... a couple weeks ago I was at this leadership activity called LeaderSHAPE and you go away for a week and it was like a, that was the first thing that I did on this campus and that really changed me. My life, and this is like a tangent, but it was the first time I stayed with a white guy like in a room alone. And he was like in a fraternity, traditional you know, dirty hat, you know the whole thing going on. And I mean we thought we were like so different, the first day we were just like bs-ing each other or whatever but like by the fourth day we were crying in the room or whatever about like different stuff that we've long gone through in our life and stuff like that and I didn't, I wouldn't have gotten the opportunity if one of my bruhs didn't say like, Steven, here's the application, turn it into such and such, talk to such and such, and be prepared for this, this, and this in the interview. And that's exactly how it was."

While the primary focus was on the way in which the fraternity facilitated involvement in other student organizations and through that increased interaction with other student, several members mentioned just the friendship networks they developed through the other members. Jaeses, a senior business major, and Darin, a senior finance majored, both focused more specifically on how their circle of friends expanded across race through other fraternity members. Jaeses said, "joining it [the frat] I've seen like a whole new network just open up, a lot of access to things out there. And then in the fraternity we have like 20 guys, like 20 different guys who all come from different walks of life. Many of them, we have a couple of guys who grew up with nothing but white people so this is a whole new thing for them, around black people. You can learn a lot from them too. Of course, they interact their friends and everybody so that's another good thing about [the fraternity]. Everybody also has their own friends they came in with so, just those connections and it's real strong."

Darin, who had experienced a family tragedy during college, emphasized how the fraternity helped him to connect with the campus community. He attributed much of his success to this community. "I think it has opened my eyes up to a lot more opportunities to meet more people that I know I would not have met if I was not in the fraternity... it helped me meet a lot more people that it was something that I actually I think that I needed because it was more of a family away from home. It helped me grow up a lot because before then I was going home just about every weekend."

Conclusion

This analysis presents only one of the themes that emerged from the interviews, relevant to the question of contact between white and black students on PWI's. The conclusions reached in this study are in no way generalizable to the entire population, even to the entire minority student population. The very nature of the study forces that limitation. However, in the tradition of other exploratory qualitative research these findings can be used to inform future research that encompasses a larger population.

Nonetheless, persistent questions about the role and function of the black Greek system on predominantly white campuses point to a need for continued dialogue and education among students on campus, with particular attention paid to the ways in which BGO's are similar to and different from the predominantly white Greek system. This research is particularly significant in light of the increasing scrutiny directed at Greek organizations more generally (Kuh and Pascerella 1996). A review of the value of Greek organizations should distinguish between those that are predominantly white and those that are historically black, if only because the very structure of the two systems differs so dramatically. Based on their research, Taylor and Howard-Hamilton (1995) argue that "institutions need to work more cooperatively with the African American Greek-letter organizations to . . . increase the likelihood that African American students will be involved in more campus activities" (Taylor and Howard-Hamilton 1995).

The findings presented here indicate that, at the very least, concerns about the continued self-segregation of BGO's seem to be inconsistent with the actual experience of membership, which increases student efficacy and involvement across the spectrum of student organizations, thereby also increasing cross-race interaction between black Greek members and their fellow students of all races. This is not to deny that social distance across races is insignificant or easily overcome. However, for campus administrators concerned with improving the quality and quantity of student contact across racial groups it is essential to not only uncover barriers and difficulties which prevent this type of interaction (including white student attitudes, previous student experiences, and those organizations and campus structures which perpetuate existing student divisions) but to also look for and investigate those existing organizations and structures which may facilitate increased opportunities for interaction. This will also require educational and programming efforts to facilitate students moving past a naïve and impoverished understanding of minority student organizations, including BGO's, as agents responsible for perpetuating minority student segregation.

Discussion and essay questions:

1. What are the origins of black Greek organizations?

2. Should Greek organizations be racially integrated or do predominantly black Greek organizations still serve a purpose today? What might those purposes be?

3. In what ways do black Greek organizations actually increase contact between African Americans and white students?

4. Are the social lives of black Greek organizations generally different from Greek organizations that are predominantly white?

References

Coleman, James S. 1988. Social Capital in the Creation of Human Capital. *American Journal of Sociology* 94 S95-S120.

Cox, W.E. 1986. Black Fraternities and Sororities: Processing Growth, Learning, and Leadership." *Black Issues in Higher Education*, 3, 20.

Denzin, N. K. (1989). *Interpretive Interactionism*. Newbury Park, CA: Sage Publications, Inc. Feagin, Joe R. and Melvin P. Sikes. 1995. How Black Students Cope with Racism on White Campuses. *Journal of Blacks in Higher Education*, 8, 91-97.

Feagin, Joe R., Vera, Hernan, and Imani, Nikitah. 1996. *The agony of education: Black students at White colleges and universities*. New York: Routledge.

Fox, Elaine, Charles Hodge and Walter Ward. 1987. A Comparison of Attitudes Held by Black and White Fraternity Members." *Journal of Negro Education*, 4: 521-534.

Hayek, John C., Robert M. Carini, Patrick T. O'Day and George D. Kuh. 2002. Triumph or Tragedy: Comparing Student Engagement Levels of Members of Greek-Letter Organizations and Other Students. *Journal of College Student Development*, 43(5), 643-663).

Jones, R.L. 1999. The Hegemonic Struggle and Domination in Black Greek-Letter Fraternities. *Challenge* 10(1): 1-33.

Kimbrough, Walter M. 1995. Self-Assessment, Participation, and Value of Leadership Skills, Activities, and Experiences for Black Students Relative to Their Membership in Historically Black Fraternities and Sororities. *Journal of Negro*

Education, 64(1), 63-74.

Kimbrough, Walter M. and Philo A. Hutcheson. 1998. The impact of membership in Black Greek-letter organizations on black students' involvement in collegiate activities and their development of leadership skills. *The Journal of Negro Education,* 67(2), 96-105.

Kimbrough, Walter M. 2003. *Black Greek 101: The Culture, Customs, and Challenges of Black Fraternities and Sororities.* Cranbury, NJ: Fairleigh Dickinson University Press.

Knoke, David. 1986. Associations and Interest Groups. *Annual Review of Sociology,* 12, 1-21.

Kuh, George D. and Pascerella, Ernest T. 1996. The questionable value of fraternities. *Chronicle of Higher Education,* 42(32).

Massey, Douglas S., Camille Z. Charles, Garvey F. Lundy, and Mary J. Fischer. 2003. *The Source of the River: The Social Origins of Freshmen at America's Selective Colleges and Universities.* Princeton: Princeton University Press.

Moran, Joseph J., Yengo, Lisa, Algier, Anne-Marie. 1994. Participation in Minority Oriented Cocurricular Organizations. *Journal of College Student Development,* 35, 143.

Murguia, Edward, Padilla, Raymond V., Pavel, Michael. 1991. Ethnicity and the
Concept of Social Integration in Tinto's Model of Institutional Departure. *Journal of College Student Development,* 32, 433-439.

Pascarella, Ernest, Marcia Edison, Elizabeth Whitt, Amaury Nora, Linda S. Hagedorn, Patrick Terenzini. 1996. Cognitive Effects of Greek Affiliation During the First Year of College. *NASPA Journal,* 33(4).

Pike, Gary R. 2000. The Influence of Fraternity or Sorority Membership on Students' College Experiences and Cognitive Development. *Research in Higher Education,* 41(1), 117-139.

Putnam, Robert. 1995. Bowling Alone. *Journal of Democracy* 6, 65-78.

Rodriguez, Roberto. 1995. Pledging Relevance: From the Million Man March to Education Budget Cuts, Black and Latino Fraternities and Sororities Lock Step with Their Communities. *Black Issues in Higher Education,* November 30, 32-34.

Ross, Jr., Lawrence C. 2000. *The Divine Nine: The history of African American Fraternities and Sororities.* New York: Kensington Publishing.

Ruffins, Paul. 1997. A Brief History of the National Pan-Hellenic Council. *Black Issues in Higher Education,* June 12.

Ruffins, Paul and Ronald Roach. 1997. Frat-ricide: Are African American Fraternities Beating Themselves to Death? *Black Issues in Higher Education*, 14(8), 18-25.

Sanday, Peggy Reeves. 1996. Rape-Prone versus Rape-Free Campus Cultures. *Violence Against Women*, 2(2), 191-209.

Strauss, A. and J. Corbin. 1998. *Basics of qualitative research: techniques and procedures for developing grounded theory.* Thousand Oaks: Sage Publications.

Tatum, Beverly Daniel. 1997. *"Why are all the Black kids sitting together in the cafeteria?": and other conversations about race.* New York: Basic Books.

Taylor, Collete M. and Howard-Hamilton, Mary F. 1995. Student Involvement and Racial Identity Attitudes mong African American Males. *Journal of College Student Development*, 36(4).

Thorson, Esther. 1997. *Greek and non-Greek college and university alumni: Giving, community articipation, and retrospective college satisfaction.* Columbia: University of Missouri-Columbia Center for Advanced Social Research.

Tillar, Thomas C. Jr. 1974. A Study of Racial Integration in Southeastern Social Fraternities. *Journal of College Student Personnel*, May.

Tinto, Vincent. 1993. *Leaving College: Rethining the causes and cures of college student attrition.* Chicago: University of Chicago Press.

Whipple, Edward G., Baier, John L., Grady, David L. 1991. A Comparison of Black and White Greeks at a Predominantly White University. *NASPA Journal*, 28(2).

Wilder, David H. and Hugh F. McKeegan. 1999. Greek-letter Social Organizations in Higher Education: A Review of Research. In John C. Smart (ed.) *Higher Education: Handbook of Theory and Research*, 15, 317-366.

Chapter 6

History of a BSU at a Professional Health Science University

Joseph W. Ruane

Initiating a Black Student Union at a white professional college proved challenging even after the Civil Rights movement. The changes over time in the eventual development of the Black Student Union at a university chartered for health sciences are worth mentioning. Coming out of the civil rights era of the 1960's, the college, which at that time predominantly prepared pharmacists, had no association on campus for African Americans. In 1971 a group of 12 African American men and women approached a new white sociology professor on campus and asked him to be an advisor to a Black Student League. The professor checked with the Student Government, which funded all of the student organizations, and he checked with the Faculty Council, which granted permission to student groups to organize under the banner of Student Affairs and Student Government. Faculty Council, he was told, would not likely grant permission for a "Black Student League" and its presumed radical agenda to exist on campus in 1971.

This was a college which had experienced no civil rights protests, nor anti-Vietnam War protests, and was supported and led by a conservative Board of Trustees and a three- person administrative staff who were also officers of the corporation. Liberal faculty would joke that the college did not know there was a war going on, let alone protest actions in Vietnam. The only black faculty member on campus was a Jamaican chemistry professor who did not identify as

African-American, and declined to be the advisor to any such group. There were no more than fifteen black students on campus at that time.

The black students were, for the most part, working class street smart students who wanted a voice in how they might be treated in an all white school. The purpose was "to form a helpful and informing union for the black people (students) at the Philadelphia College of Pharmacy and Science."[1] Together with the professor they decided that if academics were what was important to the faculty, then academics would get them recognized. The black students called their organization the Black Academic Achievement Society (BAAS), and formally petitioned the Faculty Council to recognize them as a student organization.

The faculty, of course, favored academic achievement, and any group that would work toward that end should be recognized in a college setting. The group proposed a constitution which fostered a tutoring system to assist black students in remaining students at the college; encouraged BAAS officers to locate and obtain scholarships for black students to attend the college; informed incoming students what to expect academically upon entering the college; fostered a closer relationship among the black students on campus; provided a means for the expression of black opinions on issues on campus; and to achieve academic excellence above all. Membership in the organization was not to be interpreted as separation from the rest of the college.

Faculty Council approved BAAS after a bit of discussion. Who could object to "mom and apple pie?" The black students had their organization, and they interacted with the Black Student Leagues of other schools. In the early stages of the organization most of the activities were social. The group sponsored a men's basketball team in the intramural league and all the non-players turned out to cheer for them. In years when the number of men interested was insufficient, a couple of the women joined their team. As the population of the school shifted from 70% male to 60% female, the interest in having a team in the league waned. Most of the social activities were parties; they never waned.

The organization was most active during Black History Month, and always presented the work of prestigious African Americans in a prominent setting, the center hall of the main college building.

During the 1980's they tried to change the name to Black Student Union, but an African American advisor insisted they keep the name BAAS. She liked the academic connotation. However, in 1993, the organization voted to change its name in order to be uniform with similar associations in other colleges.

The students wished the organization to be known as BSU/BAAS, the Black Student Union/Black Academic Achievement Society, giving them both current acceptance, and bowing to their historical beginnings, as well as allowing that academic excellence was still part of their goals. Coincidentally, during the twenty years since their beginning, the organization was usually two organizations in one. All of the students were members of the Student National

Pharmaceutical Association, the African American pharmacy student component of the National Pharmaceutical Association, once called the Negro Pharmaceutical Association. Further, since the college student government rules declared all student organizations open to all and any students who desired membership, on occasion a few white students, often of Latino background joined the group. In 1997 there were enough Latinos on campus that a Latino Student Association was organized, but the original Latino students maintained their membership in both groups until they graduated. Now the two organizations occasionally hold joint projects.

The ease with which the 1993 change of name was approved by the administration demonstrates the change that had come over the college by that time. The support staff had become integrated through the work of a president who came from industry, and through his newly appointed Human Resource manager who was an African American woman. Jobs which once came only to whites by word of mouth, now were openly advertised, and today in the twenty-first century, all jobs are advertised and both black and white networks of family and friends, invite people to apply for open positions. This change in personnel helped shift the mentality of staff and students to accept the competency of peoples of color. While students may have little or no interaction with some of the staff generally, the whiteness on campus had changed noticeably for African American students with the addition of black secretaries and administrators.

The African American Human Resource manager contributed immensely in another way to the BSU. She met with the group on several occasions to make them aware of their black consciousness. Too often the students saw the world from the perspectives of the white majority, and did not look deep enough to their African roots to understand their present position as an African American minority which was beginning to stand tall to gain their proper role as equals in a white dominated society. Some African American students were even advised by their parents not to get involved in the BSU for fear they may get involved in black vs. white politics, and consequently get themselves in trouble in school. Fortunately, fewer students, if any, give this as a reason for not joining today.

With the presence of more African American staff on campus the students attempted to enlighten more of the campus about black involvement in American culture by bringing in professional stage productions such as a history of popular music put on by Freedom Theater. Sadly, while the production was great, the attendance was poor. Only the members of the Student association, a few of their parents, and some staff were present. Similar experiences followed with dancers from Philadanco. Here were two world-renowned Philadelphia groups receiving no attention on this white campus. The only consolation the students had was knowing that at that time during the late 1980's even had the groups been white, the apathetic attention would have been no different. Such was the narrow focus of the students and, for the most part, the science-minded faculty.

Things did begin to change in the 1990's, however. A Black History presentation on Black Ancestry and Black Inventions co-sponsored by BAAS and Student Government succeeded immensely. Also, one of the most popular multicultural dinners annually attended by all students is that provided by the BSU. Ribs, cornbread and yams seem liked by all.

A bigger change in BSU is the background of the students. Today's generation since the millennium comes from city and suburbs, and depending on parents' background, the difference in attitude may be profound. The founders of BAAS were mostly from the inner-city and had street smarts, and the street demeanor, complete with defensive attitudes. Today it is different. Most black students studying for a professional degree in a health science field today are at least a step up from the poorest neighborhoods, if not more. Some of their parents were professionals, teachers, or physicians, but many are still the first generation in their families to go to college. The life of the African American students in a professional health science university calls for dedication to one's career. Students of any color who graduated from the university know that they had earned their degree. No one, black or white, was given a free pass to get by.

After teaching at the university for a year, a colleague wrote:

> So far, my experiences with students have been my main point of reference. I tend to be student-centered to begin with, and I have spent a lot of time with students, since the visiting professor role has meant four courses each semester. I have not yet made as systematic or detailed a view of USP as an institution as I'd like, so please interpret my initial impressions in that light. From my perspective so far, USP seems to function as a school for good students, many of whom are from working-class or immigrant families who actively aspire toward upward mobility, even as they struggle with its meaning and implications. Paying for their education and balancing its costs with other claims on family resources seem to be major issues for a considerable number of students. Many students seem to have neighborhood-based urban, rural, or small-town rather than suburban or more cosmopolitan urban backgrounds. In relation to our geographic location, I think we have very few African American or Latino students. A good number of students seem to be first or second generation immigrants, especially from India or other parts of Asia. Even though our students embody racial/ethnic diversity, in its dominant ethos, USP seems oriented toward the kinds of values typically associated with white upwardly mobile males. The natural sciences function as carriers for values of logic, rationality, supposed neutrality, emotional inexpressiveness, assertiveness within the bounds of deference to authority, professional identity, and hard work (meaning putting in long hours and meeting externally imposed demands). Given this context, these are some reflections on its implications for two groups of students.

African Americans

Other than the efforts of individual faculty, I don't see much recognition of the problem of institutional racism or the difficulties faced by African American students throughout their careers as students. (I had been impressed that USP sponsored the DuBois conference each year, but I see that the financial commitment will be reduced.) White and Asian students sometimes assume that African Americans benefit from Affirmative Action, as if other groups rely more on individual achievements perceived without reference to social support of various kinds. A number of white and Asian students have difficulty acknowledging the extent to which racism colors every facet of life now, especially in its institutional and deep cultural forms and especially as directed toward African Americans.

Asian Americans

The stereotypical Asian student would seem at first glance to be a good match for the dominant ethos of USP: good at science, hard-working, focused, reserved. However, a number of Asian students struggle with oral and written expression, for reasons rooted in language barriers and in cultural values. While USP makes some resources available to students, the requirements of their major subjects, the values of the dominant ethos of the school, and the stigma attached to seeking help of any kind seem to discourage students from taking full advantage of resources such as the writing or tutoring centers.

In general, I think all students at USP, and especially minorities, are affected by trends in higher education. Traditionally, higher education has been more content than student-oriented, as if students were passive receptacles of knowledge rather than creative agents with much to share from their diverse cultures and the potential to help transform institutions and disciplines. More recently, higher education is experiencing pressure to identify more directly with corporate business interests. This identification can have some positive implications, such as the call for competencies beyond the technical, which could include an appreciation of cultural diversity. There are also negative implications such as the reinforcement of tendencies to reify all students in relation to monetary and status objectives of faculty, administration, donors, and others. For minority students especially, this focus can mean a negation of their experiences, perspectives, values, and senses of connection to their families and communities."[2]

The university has held diversity workshops for staff and faculty, and the student government has held successful multicultural nights and weeks, all of which have positive effects. However, while students enjoy the new food experiences and listening to the music and poetry of distinct cultures, such activities are layered over the existing structures without truly changing or integrating the dominant ethos of the university. Individual attitudes may be challenged by such events, and for now, that must be seen as growth as prejudices are questioned. Summer programs which exist to recruit minority and disadvantaged students through preparatory courses do assist in forming friendships among those working together in such programs.

University records indicate that 51% of the faculty is male, and 81% of faculty are white. Fifteen percent of faculty is Asian and 1% African American. Two of the faculty claim American Indian ancestry in their mixed backgrounds. There are three Latino faculty. The university at the undergraduate level has a more than 42% minority student body, however, only 6% are African American. Thirty-three percent are Asian. The families of the majority of the minority students come from India or Korea. There are also several Chinese and Vietnamese students in that minority. Fifty-two students identify as Latino, barely 2%. The identity of 46% as white in 2004 represents a change from a white population of 69% in 1996. There are 64% women in the undergraduate population. Each of the groups appear to segregate themselves from the other as well as from the whites, although many individual minority students integrate organizations and social groups comprised predominantly of whites. From the African American perspective many of the Asians students seem to see themselves as "almost white," thereby denying their own personhood as a people of color. These 2004 figures are interesting when one reflects on the population of the city of Philadelphia where the university is located. The city is 43% African American, 45% white, 4% Asian and 8% Latino. A large number of the students of Indian parentage live in New Jersey. About 95% of the students in the university come from the Mid-Atlantic states.

Student experiences and reactions to the white campus vary according to their own background, and the actual incidents occurring in their own history on campus.[3] One African American student from Connecticut found his time here exciting and stimulating. He made good friends and got a good education and a profession. He will go home with good memories of campus life, and even an appreciation of stressful classes. He, however, never joined the Black Student Union since when he was a first year student, he found them intellectually shallow and only concerned with intramural sports or partying. His distance from them remained even after a major turnover left intramurals behind and the BSU students became more service oriented. He lived in neighboring housing with a Peruvian, two Koreans, and a student from India and spent much of his time off campus working when not in class.

Another student of black and white parentage, and a native of the local area, had a sour taste in his mouth as a result of what he saw as an unfair treatment. He can't forget the poor resolution of a discipline problem in which he was unfairly targeted in a complaint, and the lack of understanding of his family financial problems when his parents lost work. He carried a good GPA but received no tuition aid to help him out. He was happy to shake the dust of the school off his feet at graduation. He, however, had no difficulty making friends on campus, and found having grown up locally gave him the option of enjoying campus or his own neighborhood.

Experiences of African American athletes give another perspective of campus life. One shy All-American graduate basketball star notes that he felt comfortable at the university since his own home suburban community was only 15 minutes away. While the university is in a mixed inner-city area surrounded on one side by relatively affluent predominantly middle class and upper middle class university faculty and staff intermixed with working class families, the other side of the campus borders a poorer section of the city. The neighborhood presence of African Americans gave him the ambiance of an African American community even though he knew none of those neighbors. However, being one of a small minority of black students on a white campus, he always knew that he could simply go home to his community to feel more comfortable.

This same athlete said that his high school had a large African American population, but also was predominantly white, so coming to a school 70% white (seven years ago) did not bother him. He had a white roommate in his campus apartment, and met a white student who became his best friend over the course of his career at the school. He now as a pharmacist spends much time with his white friend and the friend's girl friend in his social life outside of work. His own girl friend is an African American athlete still at the university.

One observation the male athlete said about the curriculum is echoed time and again by other students, black and white. Namely, they note that the science curriculum is so difficult that classmates begin to work together across racial lines in the struggle to get through their courses. No one hesitates to give another student help in learning a subject. This male athlete credits this joint struggle as an important element in overcoming any racial biases. The fact that students see that one another has succeeded for a year or two in the curriculum signals that the classmate is serious about graduating, so each is willing to help the other.

Another black male athlete had a similar experience with classmates. However, he understood his success at school in slightly different terms. He had gone to a high school in which he was the only African American except his brother who was the year ahead of him. When he arrived at this university, there were about fifty African Americans on campus, so it was that much less of a problem, and it was aided by the fact that his brother was also here a year ahead of him.

Comparing the two brothers is interesting, however. The younger brother found it difficult to date the females on campus. Dating is a persistent problem when there is a small number of African Americans on campus. Once a person dates a student on campus and then breaks up with the student, there is awkwardness in meeting each other in class or in the cafeteria when most are likely to see each other daily. Workers who date someone at the job find similar awkwardness. The younger brother preferred to date off campus in the community. He commuted from home for the first couple of years then moved into a house of athletes with his brother. His older brother, on the other hand, rarely dated African American women, but often dated the Asian and white women on campus, and eventually lived with an Asian woman after graduation.

A memorable student who came to the university on a basketball scholarship but then contracted cancer in his second year also dated a white woman. He overcame the illness and returned to school to graduate. Throughout his ordeal students and faculty befriended this personable young man. He could be found hanging out with the basketball team even though he no longer played on the team, or he could be found with black or white groups in conversational circles on campus. His ease in either black or white company might be explained by his interracial background. Sadly, he died after seven years of marriage to the same woman who stuck with him through his college illness. His cancer had returned. At his funeral just eight years after graduation his many friends, black and white filled an overflow Greek Orthodox Church, the church of his mother and him, in a ceremony jointly officiated with his father's Baptist pastor and the Greek Orthodox priest.

The history of another African American athlete was very different, however. Unlike the previous student, he came to the Philadelphia school from New York City. Far from his Bronx setting of black neighbors he found himself in a strange city on a mostly white campus expecting to play basketball. The struggle to be a good student and to give time to playing on the men's basketball team worked against him, so he gave up basketball to be a student in the pharmacy program. While he had a few black friends on campus, a certain insecurity about the friendships stayed with him. They still were students and played on the varsity basketball team. The isolation of being an obvious minority student, and possibly being seen as a basketball player who didn't make the team left him in a predicament that lasted until he graduated. He did have a few classmates who were friendly with him, but it would be difficult to say who really were friends. He readily accepted the friendly encounters with other students and faculty, black or white, but those who knew him well still considered him somewhat of a loner since he was often seen by himself. Of course, the perception could have been wrong. He saw himself as independent of any of the cliques on campus, but longed for the comfort of a black community like the neighborhood at home.

A student from Africa found that all of the students were politely friendly as far as aiding one another in class work, and also in extending invitations to fraternity and social parties. Nevertheless he said that even at the parties there was a certain distancing that inhibited getting to know someone. He found this among both the white and African American students. Consequently, many of the African students seemed to group together in social circles on campus.

The response from a Bermudan student showed similar distancing from African American students. Her interview noted:

Although I am a black student, I am not an American. My background has more of a British influence as my country is a British colony and for this reason I find myself placed in a rather unique position.

During my early years at USP, I often felt that I could not connect with the African American students on campus because my background/ my experiences were different. I could not understand their jargon, i.e. the Ebonics. I could not relate to their struggles as a black person living in America, because back home, blacks and whites lived, worked and played side by side. It was okay for black children to play with the white children. Interracial dating is not so much frowned upon in my country. My brother has dated white women for years, not because there is a lack of quality black women to date, but because my brother grew up working in a white dominated profession. My brother is an equestrian instructor/show jumper. Our country depends on tourism and international business for its survival, so we are much more tolerant and accepting of other races. However, yes there is racism in my country, but it takes on a different form. There is corporate racism, for example. The whites have the better paying jobs; however, I will say that educational opportunities for minorities are excellent. However, we have to fight a bit harder to get to the top.

So when I came to the United States, I did not have the attitude or express the bitterness that I've seen expressed among the African American community. I did not really understand their struggle because I come from such an affluent society. Please don't get me wrong, I don't want to sound arrogant, but I am just saying that when I came to the United States, I did not understand what all the bitterness was about. Yes there was slavery in my country; however, I believe that my country has learned to put the past in the past and move on whereas here in the United States, African Americans still choose to hang on to the past.

It has only been this past year that I have done a lot of thinking. I felt that I needed to connect more with my African American sisters in order to find out what all the hype was about. Boy have I learned a lot. In addition, I have experienced acts of racism toward me while here in the United States. This has prompted me to really get in touch with who I am as a person because I realize that my identity is so fragile and could easily be taken away if I did not stand firm and believe in where I came from and where I was going. That is so important.

One of the sad things I have experienced is a lack of acceptance from the African American students. As a person of a British background, I tend to have a formal nature about the way I speak and the way I carry myself. To me I have a very proper personality and I think that for people, who have not taken the time to get to know me, this may turn some people away. Other black people would stare at me or have this attitude and I could not understand it. I have been told that many of them have the perception that I think that I am better than them and that is not the case at all. So this year I have taken an extra effort to connect with my African American sisters and so far, things have gotten better. I am particularly committed to finding out more about their struggles in America and in doing so, it has reaffirmed my identity as a black person. I realize that it takes a lot more to be able to find one's place here in this society and so I think it is important for me to stand firm for who I am. Back home I could relax a bit, but here it's different. I don't mind it though because it will definitely make me a stronger black woman.

How do I feel among so many white students? It's not intimidating at all. I just wish that the black students on campus would come together more as a unit. We are so divided and that, I think, is where the major problem is. It is clearly evident that the black students from Africa have something against the black students from America. I could understand that to some degree, but when you really put things in perspective, we all share a common bond, regardless of our background, regardless of our history. My background was a bit different, and I too felt isolated for a while but like I said, I have matured enough to know that I must bridge the gap by finding out more about their background and that is something I have made a commitment to do. I believe that if we as a black people want to get ahead in this world and make things better for future generations, we've got to stop feeling like victims. We must start forgiving one another and realize that we have the power and the potential to make great things happen for ourselves. We as a black people like to complain when things are not going our way, but what are we doing to change it? That is a question I'd like for every black person to think about. If we continue to sit back on our "toosh" then nothing will get done. Yes, we'll have to fight and fight hard. But haven't we fought all our lives, so what is the big deal? So once again, I don't feel intimidated by a large white presence on campus, but I feel isolated because the black students are not united.

Yes, I can be myself but it has not been easy. Being myself meant being a black person with a British influence and that came across strange to students here. Just my friendly manner was foreign so I stopped being so friendly just to fit in a bit. I would smile and say "Hi" and people would look at me like I was stupid! But for the most part I am myself. I believe that being as independent as I am has made it easier for me to be myself.

Do I have white friends? No not really. I speak to them and we may exchange a few words but that is as far as it goes. There is quite a difference between American whites, Canadian whites and British whites. The white students here on campus can be a bit snobbish but I've gotten used to that. They treat me with respect, and I try to do the same. Sometimes, other black students treat them better than they treat me. This is particularly evident with the black cafeteria staff. But I refuse to stoop to their low level.

Do I mind interracial dating? Not at all. Who knows, I may have a white sister-in-law in the near future, It doesn't bother me, but I know that interracial dating is a big taboo among the African American community! When I listen to the reasons for it, sometimes I have to smile. Other times, I try and put myself in their shoes and that's when I understand their viewpoint. Don't get me wrong, interracial dating is frowned upon by some cultures in my country, in particular the Portuguese, but on the whole, interracial dating is much more accepted in Bermuda.

Did I come here with an attitude? Yeah I did. I was told before coming here that Americans are not as friendly as Bermudans. I was told that I had to watch my back and not be so trusting of others. I was told that Americans are more direct in their approach and that I had to be careful what I said and how I said it.

Did USP give me an attitude? No, not really. In fact, being here has opened my eyes a lot. WOW! I have learned a lot.

Are African Americans treated any differently from other minority students on campus? Most definitely. I can't really tell who is Chinese or who is Korean or who is Indian. I call them all Asians. They do treat us differently. Some of them act like they are scared of us. There is definitely an academic disparity. They are clearly more gifted in the natural sciences, computer sciences and mathematics. And what makes a lot of other students angry is that they, majority of the time, will get the better grades because they have access to the back tests. But definitely, we are treated differently.

Another female wrote

Well, ever since you've mentioned this I thought a lot about it, so I think that what I have to say will be of some value. This situation isn't anything new to me. I'm from Williamsport PA, and the black population there isn't really significant. The black population has grown enormously from the time I was in elementary school till the time I graduated but still, the blacks were definitely the minority. I guess it's because of this that I don't really have a hard time here at all. I'm used to being the only black girl in a classroom a lot of times, and honestly, on most days it doesn't bother me that much. Both my roommates are white, and one of them, I consider my best friend here. No matter what the situation, I'm still true to who I am. I don't put on masks anywhere that I go. I still do find that, on those rare opportunities where I'm not the minority anymore, for example BSU meetings, the cheerleading squad, which is predominantly black now, it feels really nice. Just to be able to talk and not to be asked to repeat myself, or to come in with hair extensions, and not be asked "how did my hair get so long?" or to be around other black girls who have the same body type as me and be proud of it and not think that they're fat. But, in the real world I know I will rarely be in situations like those so I've learned to answer the stupid questions and not get irritated, and in a way, I've taken the questions and stares as compliments. Every time I walk into a room where there is no one else like me, I become the center of attention and I've learned to love it. But for those of us who just want to "fit in" I could see where everyday life on a white campus might be too much for someone to handle.

Her comment about the cheerleading squad is significant. The cheerleaders were always white women, with an occasional black woman joining them, and the men's basketball team was always the same. A historic change came in the 1994-95 season when the college first started five black players. It came so naturally that the white coach was not aware of it until afterwards. It is not often that the team has had enough black players that they could put an all black team on the floor. All of the players were active in the BSU, as well as the Association of Student Pharmacists, the new name of SAPHA. Two of the players today manage pharmacies in major hospital medical centers. During that same era another Bermudan black woman, four white women, and four African American women formed the first student dance team to perform at the basketball games. The interracial group was almost as popular as the basketball team as some fans came to see the dancers rather than the game itself. The group has continued to be interracial, with members of the BSU now to be found either on the dance team, the cheerleaders, or as leaders in student government.

The institutional racism occurs infrequently, usually as the result of an administrator taking the complaint of biased students at face value rather than investigating the prejudice first. However, today thirty-four years later, no longer a ready scapegoat, the BSU leadership is strong enough to defend its position as an outstanding organization on campus, and is itself a source of leadership training for tomorrow's leaders in several health fields. Sometimes being black the BSU is the center of attention, but as the student above put it, "they have learned to love it." Stereotypes continue to degrade minorities on campus as when a white student dressed as a Woodlands Indian in war paint and loin cloth feigned kidnapping a white female, carrying her on his shoulder and then and raping her in a fraternity skit. When one minority is maligned, all are maligned. Racism comes in many colors.

Discussion and Essay Questions:

1. What functions or purposes does a Black Student Union play on a college or university campus?

2. Are there issues of class and geographic background that cut across an African American student body on a college or university campus?

3. Why might administrators, faculty and staff be initially apprehensive about the creation of a Black Student Union?

4. Why might administrators, faculty and staff be supportive of a Black Student Union?

Notes
 1. Black Student Union Constitution. The Philadelphia College of Pharmacy and Science changed its name to the University of the Sciences (USP) in 1996, and is chartered as a health science university.
 2. Barbara Hogan, Ph.D., Assistant Professor of Sociology, e-mail note, 5 July 2000.
 3. Students were promised anonymity in interviews or e-mail communications that follow.

III

Social Distance

Chapter 7

Racial Divides on a Diverse Campus: An Exploration of Social Distance at a State Liberal Arts University

Erica Chito Childs and Eunice Matthews-Armstead

Introduction

There are many stories about race on college campuses– debates over affirmative action, race in the classroom, as well as diversity issues on campuses among the faculty and student body.[i] In media reports, particularly, the university campus is most often heralded as a place that promotes cross-racial interaction, primarily because it has an ethos of tolerance, the assumption that education decreases negative racial attitudes, and the belief that the younger generations are more open about race. Yet there are also reports–some media and more academic– on the persistent (self) segregation of college students.[ii] In particular, while universities may have racially diverse student populations, this does not mean that there is an integrated, diverse social environment.[iii]

The racial climate of a college campus and the frequency of cross-racial interaction differ based on the college, the student body, and other factors such as geographical location, and affiliations. Still most colleges place an emphasis on diversity and promoting (at least in theory) cross-racial interaction. While the term diversity is incorporated in the mission statements of universities, corporations, and professional and social organizations, it represents a variety of meanings depending on the context in which it is used. Based on the tools colleges and university use to monitor diversity and how they rate their level of success in this area, it appears as though their concerns are centered more on what we refer to as "spatial diversity," the demographic make-up of the campus than on "interactional diversity," the levels and frequencies of interracial and interethnic interaction.

Today college campuses are more racially and ethnically diverse than they have ever been (Humphreys, 2002), which could provide the students the opportunity to engage in meaningful interactions with students from different backgrounds and worldviews. It is the meaningful interactions across racial and ethnic boundaries that bring about long lasting positive effects on students' learning and democracy outcomes extending beyond graduation (Antonio, 1999; Chang, 1997; Gurin, 1999; Smith, 2002). Colleges and universities need to redefine their understanding of diversity to incorporate interactional diversity and move beyond monitoring the numbers to include an examination of the depth and intensity of interracial interactions. For example, is the creation of a racially and ethnically diverse environment enough to bring about meaningful social interactions across racial and ethnic boundaries? Is opportunity the only barrier to meaningful cross-racial interaction? Do colleges and universities need to do more to ensure students experience the benefits of learning in a racially and ethnically diverse academic community?

In this paper we will share the findings of a case study conducted to explore both the quantity and quality of social interactions across racial and ethnic boundaries among students at a moderately sized public university where students of color make up approximately 18 percent of the student body. This study examines whether social interactions occur between White and Black students as well as the students' perceptions of factors that support and/or hinder such interactions. The intent of this study is to further the discussion on the issue of racial diversity and cross-racial interaction on college campuses and to provide insight that could be used to guide university policies in the development of more interactionally diverse college communities.

Method

For this study, two focus groups were conducted with two separate non-random samples of white students and Black students. These focus groups were mixed in regards to age, gender, and student status. The white focus group, lead by a white female researcher, consisted of five male and five female students who were all juniors and seniors. The Black focus group, lead by a Black female researcher consisted of five male and five female students who were all juniors or seniors. The focus groups were conducted after social distance questionnaires were completed with a larger non-random sample of 433 students and a preliminary analysis of the quantitative data had been conducted.

The social distance questionnaires were based on the Morrissey (1992) Social Distance Scale, a variation of the classic Bogardus Social Distance Scale, and were administered to 433 college students on the campus where the focus groups were conducted. The respondents were asked to respond to a four part Likert scale (never, once, a few times, frequently) to the following items in reference to their experience with a particular racial group for the following seven items designed to identify increasing levels of intimacy in social interaction: (1) converse with; (2) attend the same parties; (3) dine at the family home;(4) have as a roommate; (5) date; (6) engage in sexual relationship; (7) establish long term relationship (including marriage). The non-random sample was drawn from the body of students attending the university at some point between the Fall semester of 2001 and the Fall semester of 2002. Among the respondents 84% (363) were White, 12% (50) were Black, 5% (20) were Latino. The racial demographics of the study participants closely parallel that of the university. The racial demographics of the student body at the time of the study was 72% White, 8% Black, and 5% Latino. The ages of the respondents ranged from 17 to 52, with a mean age of 21. There was adequate representation among all four academic status groups, 32% (138) were freshmen, 18% (76) were sophomores, 30% (130) were juniors, and 20% (89) were seniors. Women comprised 68% (293) of the sample.

Table 1. Racial Makeup in Percentages

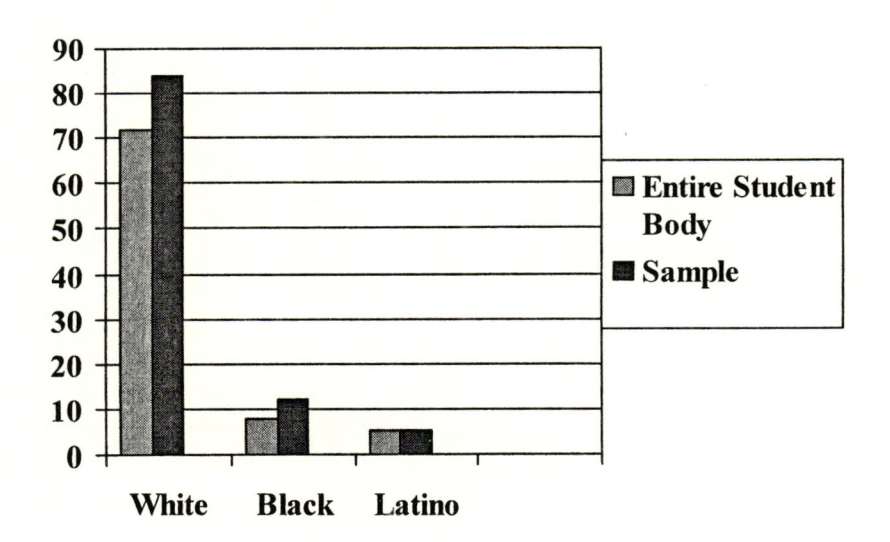

The focus group participants were presented with a summary of the results of the questionnaire, since the purpose of the focus groups was to gain insight regarding how the students explained the results of the questionnaire. In the focus groups, the students were asked open-ended questions about the results as well as their views on the frequency and extent of cross racial interactions and their motivation (or lack of) to engage in such activities. The focus group participants were informed of the purpose of the study prior to their participation and the sessions were video taped and reviewed by the researchers. The results of these surveys will be referenced in regards to the in-depth results of the focus groups to help understand the quality and quantity of cross-racial interaction among the white and black students.

Findings

According to the social distance surveys, 88 percent of the white students reported having frequent conversations with Black students while only 52 percent said that they frequently attended parties with Black students. As the level of intimacy increased the frequencies decreased even more significantly. For example only 12.4 percent of the students reported frequently having a Black student to their family home for dinner. Among the Black students, 80 percent reported having frequent conversations with White students, yet only 30 percent stated that they frequently attend parties with White students. In terms of interracial dating and sexual relations, 33.2 percent of the white students reported having dated a Black student, and 26.7 percent indicated that they had had sex with a Black student. Black students reported slightly higher levels of interracial intimacy with 54 percent stating that they had dated a White student and 44 percent reporting they had sex with a White student. Based on these reports from the preliminary surveys, we conducted focus groups to find out how white and black students explained these findings and their cross-racial experiences.

Table 2. Frequency of Cross-Racial Interaction in Percentages

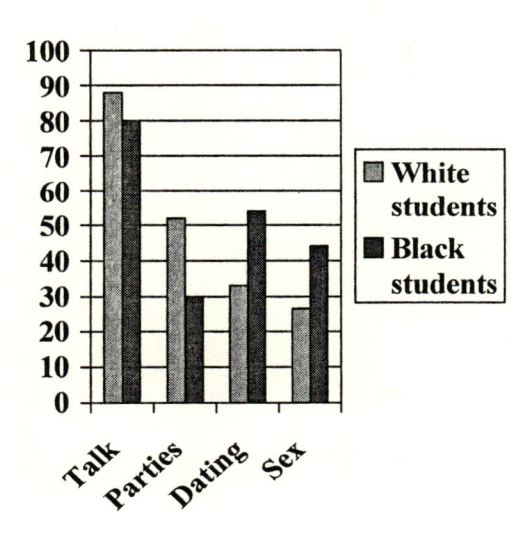

The White Students

During the focus group discussion, the white students were initially hesitant to discuss race, even in the all-white group. After being presented with the survey results, the white students stated they were not surprised at the relatively low levels of interaction, acknowledging that they also have limited contact with Black students also. One male student stated, "I mean, on a personal level I converse with them but I don't go parties and stuff with them." Other students gave similar responses, describing how they did interact with Black students in class or in casual conversations but they did not engage in lengthier interactions. The white students described themselves as different from the Black students in a number of ways such as using "we" vs. "them."

The students offered a variety of explanations as to why social interactions across racial boundaries were so limited yet the general view was that it is not intentional or deliberate. Furthermore, the White students also stated that the reasons for not interacting were not racial but based on preferences and comfort levels, which they described as beyond their control or responsibility. As one student stated, "It's not like you're racist but it's just not comfortable.... If you're not [use to being] around other races, it does feel awkward." According to the White students it is about "comfortability," which is not viewed as racial even though they acknowledge they are not comfortable with an entire racial group. The students' lack of comfort interacting with individuals who do not look like them illustrates their perceptions that "those" people are different from them. They attribute their lack of comfort to a lack of experience interacting with people from different races, referring to the racially segregated neighborhoods that they grew up in as part of the reason. The White students appear to view the racial segregation as something that is "natural" not intentional or exclusionary. They stated that the choice was about what they considered to be the "natural tendency to gravitate to people with whom you are more comfortable."

When the students were asked more specifically about social events, such as hanging out, parties and dating, the discussion continued to focus on perceived differences and lack of commonalities. The students stated that they did not attend parties with Black students because they "listened to different kinds of music and partied differently than them." In particular, the white students talked about not really listening to rap music and not wanting to dance. As the discussion continued, the students acknowledged their reluctance and unwillingness to be the only White person at the party. One student stated, "....being diverse would be going to that party and being the only white person and sure it shouldn't be a problem but unfortunately in the past they made those boundaries and now it just happens." As this student's comment implies, the white students characterize the Black students as the ones who self-segregate and do not want whites at "their parties." The white students described parties that were sponsored by a student organization that had primarily Black members to be a "Black party" and that they would not be welcomed. The students expressed the belief that they did not reject the Black students but rather the Black students segregated themselves. Racial and ethnic organizations were cited as evidence of the minority students' desire to self-segregate. As one White student stated, "I think those groups are full of crap, I don't like them I don't have anything against Blacks and Latinos, some of the coolest people I've met on campus are people of a different race, but I think when you make groups like that you are kind of segregating yourself and then they talk about segregation, people being racist but I think making a group like that you are doing it yourself." Another student added, "I think it is positive, but it's positive for them....it discourages us." In general the white students explained the lack of interaction by citing how white students grow up in predominantly white areas and how Black students segregate themselves. Not hanging out with Black students was viewed as based on commonalities and not seen as racial segregation, at least not on their part. The limited social interactions that occurred appeared to merely reinforce their existing stereotypes yet regardless of where the responsibility lies for its development or maintenance, they did not view the racial divide as a problem.

When asked about the survey results on interracial dating, the white students described interracial dating as uncommon. As one student stated, "I know a lot of black people and white people who just because of their culture they have a hard time even feeling attracted physically to people of the opposite race and I think that it is based a lot on the fact that it wasn't part of their growing up process, and it even was not directly but indirectly frowned upon so you get the idea and this goes to both races." From the perspective of the white students, not dating interracially was based on the lack of commonalities as well as limited acceptance from the larger society. Only one white female student disagreed with the group's responses and acknowledged that she dated interracially. She discussed how she routinely attended parties that were predominantly Black, yet she attributed this to having mostly all Black friends and a Black boyfriend. She described feeling "uncomfortable" at the "white" parties because of her friends and interests, and acknowledged she didn't hang out with many white students. After her discussion, one student responded, "I never have a problem on campus with Blacks and Latinos... I don't see any problems, I just have never thought about it, I mean I just don't see a problem." Another student added, "People need to interact on their own, you can't try to facilitate, or force it on people." For all but one of the white students, sharing the campus with students of a different race and engaging in superficial social interactions was as much diversity as they desired. Even the white student who does have close interracial friendships and relationships still does not describe a diverse social environment. Rather she is content to be the only white person in an all-black social network by simply crossing the color-line and not hanging out with whites. The racial divide that existed between white students and Black students is a reality that these white students are willing to accept.

The Black student focus group

When presented with the survey data, the Black students stated they knew the campus was segregated by race, describing a separation and limited cross-racial interaction between themselves and white students. As one student stated, "Diversity is just some political term that really doesn't mean much. You go to functions and hear the speeches about how we are a diverse campus I think it is a joke. Yea, we're diverse alright, this campus is a whole bunch of different people occupying the same space." The Black students described their interactions with the white students as primarily being limited to superficial conversations in class or about coursework.

Unlike the white students, the Black students acknowledged their role in the existing racial divide. They described the decision to form close Black social networks as something that exists "by design and out of perceived necessity." For example, some students mentioned the need for potential allies among other Black students. They spoke of seeking out other Black students as one of the first things they did when they came to campus. They described their racial clustering as a preference rather than a rejection of White students. Like the white students, the Black students stated that they did not have anything in common with white students. Yet even more importantly they emphasized the commonality and understanding that existed between them and other Black students, which helped them to feel more comfortable on a predominantly white college campus. As one student stated, "I would sit in the class on the first day and when I see another Black student walk in there is like a sigh of relief that I won't be the only one."

Beyond the necessity of grouping together, the Black students also discussed the pressure from other Black students to maintain close Black networks. As one student stated, "It's like if you see a Black girl and she is hanging around all White girls you know the Black students are going to talk about her." A few of the students came from racially mixed communities and had white friends in high school who came to the college with them, but once they got on campus, the cross-racial friendships did not last. Another student described it this way, "When I came here I had a white roommate and she was like cool and everything, I mean we were like best friends when we were inside the room but outside of the room if I saw her on campus we would barely speak. We didn't go to parties together and she didn't come to my house. But we were still cool." According to these students, the racial divide is a difficult thing to challenge.

When talking about their interactions with white students, the Black students described how they felt the need to adapt their behavior to conform to the expectations of the dominant white society. As one student states, "It is like that writer says its like we have to wear two masks, one for them and the one that is real." Another student added, "You have to be careful in class because you don't want to labeled as the angry Black Man so I watch what I say." The Black students' responses illustrated that they consistently monitored how they dressed and talked around whites on campus. Dressing a certain way, such as what they referred to as "thug wear," would result in whites on campus treating them negatively. They referenced having been told by family and other Black students the need to learn to deal with whites, especially in the "real world" after college, but there was little or no desire to hang out with white students. Like the white students, the Black students also spoke of "comfortablity" but it was mostly in terms of their perceptions of whites not being comfortable with them and having to make whites more comfortable rather than addressing their own comfortability.

When asked about why they did not engage in cross racial interactions such as attending parties with white students or dating interracially more frequently, they gave a number of different reasons. The white students' parties were described as "boring and unappealing." Also, the Black students discussed how white students did not join student organizations or attend campus events that were associated with Black students or racial organizations. Some of the Black students were members of the race-based organizations that the white students in the focus group disagreed with, yet they stated that they did not exclude members of other racial groups from joining their organizations. One student discussed that there have been occasions where they have attempted to actively recruit members from different races to join but white students for the most part chose not to. Another student stated, "Well it is like this for me if they join that's fine and if they don't that's fine too." The students also reported that many of their organizations were perceived as being race-based but were actually founded to be interracial organizations. As one student explained, if the founders of an organization or majority of the members are Black, then "white students assume that the organization is Black," and no matter how much they try to dispel that perception it does not seem to work.

Interracial dating was also described as uncommon, yet differed based on gender. The Black male students expressed more of a willingness to date interracially, yet did discuss having a problem with Black women dating white men. Some of the Black male students discussed how when they saw a Black woman with a white man they felt that "she could do better." The Black women also described being bothered by interracial dating, and not likely to date interracially themselves. Most of the Black women stated that they have never had the experience of having a White man approach them, yet the Black men did recount incidents where white women were pursued them. While all of the Black students expressed opposition to interracial dating for the opposite gender, the Black men did acknowledge more of a willingness to date interracially than the Black women.

Overall, the Black students described the racial segregation that existed slightly different than the white students. Like the white students, the Black students cited comfortability and lack of commonalities as reasons for the racial divide but they also clearly identified the role race plays and acknowledged the benefits of having a Black support network. Neither the white or Black students are interested or motivated to change the lack of diversity on campus. As one Black student stated, "I'm not sure I see the value in all this talk about diversity really. I mean I am going to have to interact with White people all my life if I want to get ahead because they seem to own and control most things and that's okay I'll play the game...but I'm not going to give up who I really am." These black students described experiencing rejection and differential treatment from whites that affected their decisions to interact with whites. The racial divide was something they saw as necessary to separate them from white students who were unable or unwilling to understand, and as a way to encourage a strong black social network amongst themselves for support and success.

Discussion

The racial dynamics that emerged from the focus groups on the college campus mirror those of the larger society. Supported by both the quantitative and qualitative data, there exists a reasonable amount of talking across racial boundaries. However, as the level of intimacy increased the amount of cross racial interactions significantly decreased. For example, the white students reported higher levels of talking and attending parties with Black students, when it came to close friendships (inviting someone over for dinner) or dating, the numbers dropped considerably. While white students may feel it is okay, even necessary to state that they would have a conversation with Black students, it is acceptable to state that they do not prefer to have close Black friends or partners. Both white and Black students admitted to preferring members of their own race and keeping separate. The white students explained their self segregation in terms of a preference for being with their "own kind" rather than a dislike for the other groups. For the white students it was a matter of "comfortability" not prejudice. This sort of attitude is consistent with the prevalence of color-blind ideologies, which deny the role of race, while simultaneously maintaining racial boundaries (Bonilla-Silva 2002; Bonilla-Silva and Forman 2000). The Black students described their self-segregation as a coping mechanism for being able to function on a White dominated campus. The students expressed a feeling that the campus community was merely a microcosm of what occurs in the larger society regarding race relations. Based on the Black students' discussion, the campus environment is subtly hostile, yet also a practice ground to prepare them for life in the larger society, which they viewed as helpful and necessary. Merely talking cross racially, which occurred frequently among the majority of the students in this study, was not enough to challenge the racial divide that existed. The white and Black students all used skin color as a marker of difference, with racial identity being one of the most significant determinants of social interactions on this campus.

While many of the students agreed the campus could be more integrated, and race relations could be better, none expressed the desire to work towards these goals. The students did not report having or wanting more interracial friendships, or challenging their existing perceptions of difference. None of the students in the focus groups defined the existing racial divide as a problem thus were not particularly motivated to do anything about it. They seemed to view it as a natural and acceptable reality. The Black students appeared to view their interactions with white students more as a necessity connected to their ability to achieve economic and social success than as a preference or desire to want to be around them. For the Black students it was about survival, expressing feelings of being forced to interact with White students because of the existing racial hierarchy, which appeared to foster some resentment. On this college campus, merely occupying a similar geographical area is not enough to create the meaningful cross-racial interactions associated with the benefits of having a diverse college community. A diverse student body, or in other words, spatial diversity, was not enough to alter the interaction patterns of any of the students. According to the students, the opportunity to engage in cross-racial interactions is not the only barrier.

The racial dynamics demonstrated here among the students of this study indicate questionable progress in regards to the existence and development of a more racially and ethnically integrated campus. Based on the results of this study, spatial diversity alone is not enough to sufficiently support interactional diversity among students on a majority college campus. This case study reveals that if colleges and universities truly want their students to experience the benefits of learning in a racially and ethnically diverse campus community they will need to be far more proactive. Colleges and universities have an opportunity to create a microcosm of an alternative type of community that works to redefine the dynamics of race relations in this country rather than reinforce them. Because colleges and universities can impose more control over their communities than what is found in the larger society they are better able to create an environment where cross racial and ethnic interactions are the norm and not the exception. One of the key barriers to cross-racial interactions indicated in this case study was the carryover from the larger society of the centrality of skin color in the determination of social groupings. As the students categorized themselves according to skin color the distorted reality of in-group similarities and out-group differences were employed, which appeared to limit cross group interactions.

The students of this study appear less motivated to challenge the existing dynamics of racial segregation, and most striking was the underlying apathy and tolerance for the racial divide. If we are to ever reach the ideal of a truly integrated society we must challenge the assumptions of racial difference and lack of commonalities that underlie students' decisions to remain separate. Moreover, if white students maintain that they are not comfortable and do not have anything in common with Black students, what implications will this have in the "real world" when making decisions about who they want to work with, live near, buy from etc? Therefore we must continue to struggle for change. Colleges and Universities have the potential of playing a critical role in the transformation of existing race and ethnic relations so that racial divides could become a description of our past.

Discussion and essay questions:

1. When is a situation diverse? How should we define diversity-spatial, interactional, or both/neither?

2. Does frequent contact between African Americans and whites mean that diversity has been achieved?

3. Does overall inequality of African Americans and whites have an effect on students' preferences to interact with members of the same racial group?

4. Does the sex and race of someone make a difference in the likelihood of greater or less interactional diversity occurring?

5. Should colleges and universities be concerned about doing more to promote more interactional diversity?

6. Is some degree of social segregation based on race desirable on college or university campuses?

7. What would it mean to have a completely integrated college or university campus?

References

Antonio A. L. (1999). Racial diversity and friendship groups in college: What the research tells us. Diversity Digest. Retrieved 4/20/2002, http://www.diversityweb.org/Digest/Sm99/research.html.

Bonilla-Silva, E. (2003) Racism Without Racists: Color-blind Racism and the Persistence of Racial Inequality in the United States. Lanham, MD: Rowman and Littlefield.

Bonilla-Silva, E. and T. A. Forman (2000)"'I Am Not a Racist But...': Mapping White College Students' Racial Ideology in the U.S.A.," *Discourse and Society* 11: 50-85.

Buttny, R.(1999). Discursive constructions of racial boundaries and self-segregation on campus. Journal of Language and Social Psychology, 18(3) 247.

Covers, D.J. (1995) The effects of social contact on prejudice. Journal of Social Psychology 135 (3) p403

Chang, M.J. (1997) Who benefits from racial diversity in higher education? Diversity Digest. Retrieved 4/20/2002, http://www.diversityweb.org/Digest/W97/research.html.

Gallagher, C. A. (1995) "White Construction in the University," *Socialist Review* 24: 165-187.

Gurin, P. (1999) New Research on the benefits of diversity in college and beyond: An empirical analysis. Diversity Digest. Retrieved 4/7/2002, http://www.diversityweb.org/Digest/sp99/benefits.html.

Humphreys D. (2002). Campus diversity and student self-segregation: Separating myths from facts. Leaders guide Retrieved 4/7/2002, http://www.diversityweb.org/Leadersguide/SED/studeseg.html.

Morrissey, M. (1992) Exploring social distance in race and ethnic relations courses. Teaching Sociology 20 p.121-124.

Smith, D.G. (2002). Diversity works: The emerging picture of how students benefit, Executive Summary. Research, Evaluation and Impact. Retrieved 4/7/2002, http://www.diversityweb.org/Leadersguide/DREI/dsmith.html.

Tatum, B.D. (1997). Why are all the Black Kids Sitting Together in The Cafeteria? and Other Conversations About Race. New York: Basic Books.

---

[i] Today college campuses are more diverse than they have ever been. D. Humphreys, "Campus Diversity and Student Self-segregation: Separating Myths from Facts," *Leadersguide*, http://www.diversityweb.org/Leadersguide/SED/studeseg.html (accessed April 7, 2002).Yet, the definition of diversity varies and what constitutes diversity among the students is not widely agreed upon. Some have even argued, "the rhetoric of diversity (and all the time we spend on it) is avoidance behavior, that it hides the realities of inequities in education and helps us evade the hard work necessary to overcome those inequities."

[ii] Eduardo Bonilla-Silva and Tyrone A. Forman, "'I Am Not a Racist But...': Mapping White College Students' Racial Ideology in the U.S.A.," *Discourse and Society* 11 (2000): 50-85. Charles A. Gallagher, "White Construction in the University," *Socialist Review* 24 (1995) : 165-187.

[iii] There is little agreement in regards to the extent to which colleges and university have been able to achieve such levels of social diversity. The debate continues regarding the reality of self-segregation on campus. While some emphasize the success of diversity with racially diverse student bodies, others point to "reports of increasingly tense racial climates and racial self-segregation among students"

Chapter 8

Self-Segregation and Friendship Formation Among Undergraduate Students

Bette J. Dickerson and Kianda Bell[1]

Introduction

In an increasingly global society, there is general consensus that individuals must develop cross-cultural understanding and tolerance. Such understanding and tolerance is most easily cultivated through natural friendships and associations, rather than through other means. A popular perspective, contact hypothesis, assumes that people of diverse race/ethnic backgrounds living in close residential proximity will "get to know, understand, and like one another, leading to long-standing cross-cultural understanding" (Bochner, Hutnik, and Furnham, 1984, p. 690). The college experience has achieved a significant role in exposing individuals to cross-cultural experiences in an attempt to create mutual tolerance and understanding. However, despite decades of legislated school integration in the United States and even in settings with high levels of

---

[1] Portions of this chapter were first presented in "Do Undergraduate Students Self-Segregate?" in The Quality and Quantity of Contact edited by Robert M. Moore III (University Press of America, 2002) and we thank Kathryn Lasso and Tiffany Waits for their contributions to that publication.

ethnic diversity, Buttny (1999 p. 247) reports "a climate of separateness, or a 'new segregation' on college campuses".

There are clear benefits to the support that comes from associations based on common culture, beliefs, and identity, but do the benefits of these associations tend to direct students towards forming friendships overwhelmingly within their own racial/ethnic in-group? Is this segregation self-imposed by students who, of their own free will, separate themselves by race or ethnicity? Are the effects of mandated and institutionalized integration of college campuses felt on an individual level? Does recruitment of diverse student bodies translate into a college experience characterized by diverse interactions and friendship circles? These questions have long been important in the United States and are best illustrated in the 1954 Brown vs. Board of Education case when the Supreme Court declared that separate is not equal, ushering in an age of conscious efforts to desegregate schools. Contemporarily, debates have moved beyond the quality of the formal classroom education into an examination of college as a microcosm of an increasingly pluralistic society and to the exposures obtained not only formally in the classroom but also informally through friendships.

In an attempt to answer these questions we turned to prior research on self-segregation at college campuses was reviewed and collected observational and survey data on patterns of friendship formation at a college campus (see Dickerson, Bell, Lasso, and Waits, 2002). There are clear benefits to the support that comes from associations based on common culture, beliefs, and identity, but do the benefits of these associations tend to direct students towards forming friendships overwhelmingly within their own racial/ethnic in-group?

Important information was gained for those seeking to create and maintain race and ethnic diversity on campus. Because data was collected from one of the most diverse campuses in the United States, it provided insight about the realities of race and ethnic relations and friendship formation in an environment that publicly embraces cross-cultural understanding. It also resulted in recommendations to begin and guide the process of change. Furthermore, the study results shed light on areas in need of future related research and action and that, hopefully, will inspire you, the reader, to further examine and engage with this important issue.

Our Review of the Literature

College is often the first time that most young people have been away from their families and familiar surroundings for an extended period of time. Friendships become an important way for students to "anchor" themselves in their new environment, serving as an affirmation of identity as well as providing a framework in which students can "'make sense' of their own behavior and the behavior of others" (Ting-Toomey 1981). During this important new stage of maturation, friendships also help young adults work through issues such as the need for independence, developing social skills, and conflict resolution (Marcus 1996). Naturally, college students seek to form friendships with others based upon perceived similarities which facilitate the development of a sense of intimacy. Among all characteristics differentiating individuals, ethnicity, the "cultural characteristic of the self" may be the most important contributor, at least to initial friendship pairings (Ting-Toomey 1981) because friendship is based "in part on perceived similarity of personality, values, attitudes, beliefs, needs, or, social skills between partners" (Blieszner and Adams 1992 p. 65). In fact, "[p]ersons belonging to similar ethnic backgrounds because of congruent cultural beliefs and values, possess a stronger degree of intimacy for each other than friends belonging to different ethnic groups" (Ting-Toomey 1981 p. 391).

Identity consists of a hierarchy giving order to various components of self in relationship to group. For example, gender or language (related to ethnicity) may be the salient factors that prescribe where we fit into some group situations, while race (equated with ethnicity) may be more important in other situations (Jackson 1998). Furthermore, Doane (1997 p. 375) found that the "ethnic identity of dominant groups ... assume[s] ... a position of dominance shape[ing] the nature of group ethnicity" within a social system composed of several ethnic subgroups. He defines a dominant group "as the ethnic group in a society that exercises power to create and maintain a pattern of economic, political and institutional advantage, which, in turn, results in the unequal (disproportionately beneficial to the dominant group) distribution of resources" (Doane 1997 p. 376).

Adler (1996) distinguishes between two complementary elements in the hierarchy of identity, which she calls *status*, prescribing popularity or relative dominance over others, and *relationship,* characterized by trust and freedom from loneliness. She states "Together, these two elements combine to stratify groups and their members along the identity hierarchy" (Adler 1996 p. 137). This hierarchical layering emerges through a process of "competing discourses" between individual self perception, perceptions of one's core subgroup, and perception of the larger social system outside of one's own subgroup, prescribing both status and relationship between and within groups and between individuals (Buttny 1999). Cohesion within the social system, then reflects both inter- and intra-group stratification, as social rules, especially as developed by more dominant individuals or subgroups, reflect acceptable attitudes towards individuals and subgroups belonging to the social system. Alternatively, less dominant individuals or subgroups, may resist the role prescribed to them by more dominant members and form "countergroups" (Yeh and Huang 1996).

Intergroup relations theory suggests that, across groups, "the greater the perceived dissimilarity, the greater the subjective intergroup distance....Perceived difference may result in increased levels of uncertainty and anxiety, which leads individuals to avoid contact with out-group members."

Communication between groups becomes vital for inter-group understanding and for decreasing uncertainty and anxiety (Buttny 1999).

With regard to friendship formation between individuals, several studies confirm that, as with inter-group relations, the most salient factors in strengthening friendships relate to frequency and quality of communication (Buttny 1999). Bliesszner and Adams (1992 p. 64) state that "As people get to know each other better, they discover and respond to each other's unique personality characteristics; stereotypes become less influential in the relationship." The more we communicate with our friends, the more we understand and trust them, and the greater intimacy we feel with them. As frequency and quality of communication between persons increase, the level of trust between those persons increases, and the feelings of uncertainty decrease while similarities between persons emerge (Ting-Toomey 1981). In an environment of low levels of inter-group familiarity and understanding and low levels of friendship pairings across ethnic divides, one would expect higher levels of stratification by ethnicity, with high risks associated with and more rigid barriers to crossing those divides.

In this context, self-segregation is defined as arising from the intent of the individual to preserve race/ethnic separateness in the process of forming friendships. Buttny (1999 pp.249-250) contrasts two different views about segregation versus integration. The *social support model* suggests that students segregate themselves in search of "the support of their own cultural groups and organizations to succeed in higher education". Intergroup integration can cause a loss of social identity, which can be more important for minority groups than dominant groups. On the other hand, the *integrational model* posits that if children of different backgrounds could get to know each other, they wouldn't develop racial/ethnic prejudices and stereotypes. His research also distinguishes between three distinct attitudes that can lead to self-segregation: *nonassertive segregation*, *assertive segregation*, and *aggressive segregation.*

Nonassertive segregation occurs when students are interested in having more interracial contact but don't know how to achieve it. Chavous' (2000) research suggests that pre-college backgrounds may contribute to a student's ability to manage his/her surroundings on campus, especially when coming from an ethnically homogenous neighborhood. This type of segregation could be related to uncertainty and inexperience with inter-racial groups. In addition, it is important to note that in an environment where one subgroup (such as Whites) is numerically dominant, that subgroup can more easily avoid contact with minority subgroups, while minority subgroups must make conscious decisions to avoid contact with the dominant group.

Assertive segregation occurs when students consciously seek out others with whom they have common ethnic traits. Assertive segregation is related to feelings of pride of one's own heritage as well as an expression of individuality.

This may be especially important for minorities surrounded by cultural expressions reflecting the social identity of a dominant group.

Aggressive segregation is related to conscious racial separation, based upon a rejection of "other." Principal reasons for rejection stem from feelings of threats. Chavous (2000) found "In entering mainstream college settings, ethnic minority students often face unique challenges regarding the meaning or value of their ethnic identity, which may represent threats to their identities." These feelings of threats may come from inter-group tension, where one group feels threatened by another, or intra-group pressure, where the culture of one's own group expresses rejection of other groups. "This construct taps into individuals' beliefs that they cannot express their cultural values in school settings, that their ethnic culture was incompatible with their college environment, causing them to engage in self-protective strategies in order to enhance self-esteem" (Chavous 2000 p. 80). While we often think of ethnic minorities engaging in aggressive self-segregation, Buttny (1999 pp.249-250) notes that "Whites often tell racial narratives structured around a complication that is not resolved by the end of the story, suggesting continuing problems with minorities. ... These can be characterized as an ideological dilemma, with Whites being critical of minorities on one hand, but not wanting to appear prejudiced on the other." Chavous (2000 p. 83) argues that "ethnic-related organization[s] may serve as a protective or supportive factor," while "students who identif[y] less strongly [with their ethnic backgrounds are] more likely to experience feelings of threat and have lower levels of collective self-esteem."

Ethnic segregation may occur for several reasons, including uncertainty about how to cross racial divides, accompanied by inexperience. It may result from a strong sense of "acceptance" and celebration of one's own ethnicity; or from a sense of perceived threat from others, and a need for self-protection. What becomes important, then, is to discover not only the relationship between individuals, but to understand the dynamics of group relations within the social system in which those individual relationships occur. Related to this is the *contact hypothesis* mentioned in our Introduction that Bochner, Hutnik, and Furnham (1984) tested by looking at the friendship patterns of overseas and host students in an Oxford, England, student international house. Their findings indicated that while these students had a great deal of contact with one another because they shared a dorm, most of the English students' friends were also English, and most of the foreign students' friends were other foreign students, although not necessarily from their same home country. It seems that the factor of being a "foreigner" in another country served as a commonality that brought foreign students together, perhaps because of the shared experience of being the "other."

The amount of racial homogeneity and heterogeneity also affects the salience of ethnic roles. Though interested in examining the factors that contributed to a heightened awareness of another person's ethnicity, Bochner and Ohsako (1977) examined three societies (Japan, Australia, and Hawaii) and found that in segregated societies, "the perception of another's racial role will have a direct and exaggerated effect on interpersonal behavior; whereas, in integrated societies, the effect will be more indirect and muted" (Bochner and Ohsako 1977 p. 490). This finding is applicable to other situations, including a university campus.

Ting-Toomey (1981 p. 385) further suggests forming friendships within ethnic groups is easier "because of congruent cultural beliefs and values, [creating] a stronger degree of intimacy for each other than friends belonging to different ethnic groups." When people first meet, they naturally differentiate others based on physical traits, which can lead to stereotyping – and possibly to self-segregation in friendship formation (Blieszner and Adams 1992).

Our Conclusions

We were curious about the extent that self-segregation exists, how it manifests itself and why it may occur and decided to gather information from undergraduate students and key faculty and staff informants at a major university (see detailed accounting in Dickerson, Bell, Lasso and Waits 2002).. Information was collected with regard to differentiation by ethnicity/race, gender, language, and age through three methods of qualitative data collection (observation, interviewing key informants, and administration of a survey questionnaire). We hypothesized that undergraduate students would tend to segregate by racial/ethnic similarities when forming friendships. Hypothesized reasons for self-segregation included: resisting opportunities to form friendships across ethnic divides because of a need to maintain a level of comfort; self-segregation as means to maintain peer support networks; resisting forming friendships across ethnic lines because of negative perceptions of racial out-groups. We also considered the possibility that self-segregation could be indirectly and unintentionally encouraged by university institutions.

The data we gathered both contradicted and confirmed elements of the previous research that self-segregation occurs among undergraduate students was confirmed. This could be attributed to several things, including conscious or unconscious segregation by the university regarding dormitory assignments, students feeling more "comfortable" with students of their own race/ethnic background, common language (especially in the case of international students), reinforcement of race/ethnic identity, and replication of the larger society, which segregates itself by race/ethnicity. Using Buttny's (1999) framework the data suggest that this segregation can be classified primarily as *nonassertive segregation*, where students are uncertain about how to form cross-cultural relationships and/or *assertive segregation*, where race/ethnic minority groups, due to their relatively small numbers, form groups in order to preserve their own sense of identity. Although the information gathered does suggest that some level of *aggressive segregation* may exist on the campus studied, this influence appears to be minimal. Indeed, during the course of our work, we found both an institutional commitment to cross-cultural understanding as well as an openness on the part of the students to learn about and benefit from the richness of alternative perspectives afforded by divergent cultural expressions.

However, as opposed to assumptions made in much of the literature, we found self-segregation occurred overwhelmingly on the part of Whites. The proportion of Whites in integrated settings was significantly lower than the proportion of non-Whites. Similarly, Whites self-reported having fewer friends from ethnic backgrounds different from their own. Insights from the key informant interviews support the importance of this dynamic. As a numerical majority, Whites are constantly self-segregating in everyday situations. This, however, is seldom perceived as separatist or cliquish behavior. As a sociological majority, Whites are powerbrokers in society who have higher degrees of social mobility. With the greater ability to move within and about the social arrangements in society comes a responsibility to challenge oneself to cross race/ethnic boundaries that can cause negative forms of self-segregation.

Another important conclusion is that not all forms of self-segregation are negative. Self-segregation based on *similarity attraction*, likeness of kind based on cultural and identity, is natural and can provide the necessary support system one needs to "make it". This is particularly true for disenfranchised groups who have had their "histories obliterated." This moves us to a discussion of why self-segregation occurs, and what positive and negative effects can ensue.

Self-segregation can occur as a means of support for marginalized groups or groups in culturally unfamiliar circumstances. This type of cohesiveness can be essential to a successful college experience. Likewise, "comfort level" can be an important factor in coping with pressures and feelings of detachment often felt by new college students. The latter mentioned type of support applies to all different race/ethnic groups, minority and majority. In no circumstances was self-segregation observed or self-reported to be practiced as a result of negative racial/ethnic outgroup sentiment.

Students overwhelmingly reported believing that cross-cultural understanding is important; however, this belief does not seem to be widely practiced by students. We found that friendships with persons of one's same race and ethnic background serve a purpose, namely "comfort." Yet, students acknowledged that friendships with students of other race and ethnic backgrounds were of importance. Perhaps what we see is a separation between what students are being taught versus the reality of living in a society where racism continues to exist, despite the talk of encompassing diversity and multiculturalism. It could also be that students are providing the socially acceptable answers to a sensitive topic. It is difficult to determine from the data at hand whether or not students are suffering from a subsequent lack of cross-cultural understanding and respect for difference.

Our Recommendations

Based on our conclusions, we offer several recommendations. First, self-segregation should not be treated solely as a phenomenon occurring primarily among non-White groups. Nor should the practice be perceived as entirely negative. Secondly, support groups and cultural groups that celebrate different race/ethnic identities should be encouraged since "a social system with a heightened awareness of ethnic differences may be a necessary condition for racial integration..." (Bochner and Oshako, 1977, p. 480). A cultural celebration that is inclusive of many different racial/ethnic elements could facilitate cross-cultural experiences and foster greater understanding and respect for difference. Third, include mandatory curricula, for all students, which address diversity issues and encourage cross-race/ethnic interactions, particularly those universities with relatively low numbers of race/ethnic minority students. To construct a genuinely diverse environment, a strong effort must be made to recruit racially/ethnically diverse students, faculty, and staff. However, professors may also tend to slip into their own race/ethnic "comfort zones." At the same time, they hold a visible position of authority and influence and their curriculum design must therefore reflect the institutional commitment to race/ethnic diversity. Therefore, the university should look at ways to provide in-service training to its professors to ensure that they are consciously representing it's commitment to cross-cultural understanding to students, and to help professors design their class curricula in ways that provide increased opportunities for course-related cross- cultural interaction.

The final recommendation involves increasing the amount of interaction among students on an individual level. Evidence suggests that rigidity between ethnic groups does still exist, yielding levels of nonassertive segregation, where students are unsure about how to successfully integrate and therefore retreat into "ethnic comfort zones," where they have a higher probability of experiencing success in social situations. This rigidity can then easily create social stratification on campus -- and dominance of one group over another -- by race/ethnicity, especially when one subgroup is numerically dominant. For example, we saw hints of dominance of the white undergraduates over multiethnic undergraduates manifested in the hierarchy of the student government, which may serve to heighten minority students' sense of alienation, resentment and powerlessness (Dickerson, Bell, Lasso, and Waits, 2002).

More ways must be found to coax – and push – undergraduates into situations where they will be exposed to students who are different from them, making the unknown more familiar and more comfortable to be around. Data suggest that the willingness to integrate and learn is there (Dickerson, Bell, Lasso, and Waits,

2002). At the same time, ways must be found to "guarantee success," so that this exposure leads to acceptance and not rejection, so that when self-segregation does occur, rather than reflecting a rejection of other (aggressive self-segregation), it is assertive, reflecting an acceptance, an embracing, a celebration of self.

In closing, it is important to acknowledge that almost everyone asked felt that cross-cultural understanding and respect for difference is important and that the university plays an important role. If self-segregation characterizes much of the actual interactions among students then this diverse interaction may not be occurring. If a university fails to prepare students to interact in a society that is increasingly multi-racial/ethnic, society on the whole will feel the negative effects. If the university is, indeed, a microcosm of the larger society, lack of cross-cultural understanding among its students will in turn translate into the same for this nation's future educators, leaders, and general public. While all of the causes and effects of self-segregation are not negative, it is important that the directive of fostering a diverse environment not be lost.

Discussion and Essay Questions:

1. When, how and why do whites segregate themselves?
2. Should all professors feel an obligation to promote de-segregation?

3. Can some university or college policies or lack of policies actually facilitate segregation rather than decrease it?

4. What is the opposite of segregation?

5. How do people benefit from living in de-segregated activity? Are the benefits different depending on the race and gender of the individual?

References

Adler, P. 1996. "Preadolescent clique stratification and the hierarchy of identity." *Sociological Inquiry* 66 (2): 111-142.

Adler, P. and P. Adler. 1994. "Social reproduction and the corporate other: the institutionalization of afterschool activities." *The Sociological Quarterly* 35 (2): 309-328.

Asante, M. K. and Al-Deen. 1984. "Social integration of Black and White college students: A research report." *Journal of Black Studies* 14: 507-516.

Babbie, E. (2000). *The practice of social research* (6th ed). Belmont, CA: Wadsworth.

Blieszner, R. and R. G. Adams (1992). *Adult friendships*. Newbury Park, CA: Sage Publications.

Bochner, S., N. Hutnik, and A. Furnham. 1984. "The friendship patterns of overseas and host students in an Oxford student residence." *The Journal of Social Psychology* 125 (6): 689-694.

Bochner, S. and T. Ohsako. 1977. "Ethnic role salience in racially homogenous and heterogeneous societies." *Journal of Cross-Cultural Psychology* 8 (4): 477-491.

Buttny, R. 1999. "Discursive construction of racial boundaries and self- segregation on campus." *Journal of Language and Social Psychology* 18 (3): 247-268.

Chavous, T. M. 2000. "The relationship among racial identity, perceived ethnic fit, and organizational involvement for African-American students at a predominantly white university." *Journal of Black Psychology* 26 (1) February: 79-100.

Crain, R. with R. Mahard and R. Narot (1982). *Making desegregation work how schools create social climates*. Cambridge: Ballinger Publishing.

Dickerson, Bette J., Kianda Bell, Kathryn Lasso and Tiffany Waits (2002). "Do Undergraduate College Students Self-Segregate?" In *The Quality and Quantity of Contact*. Ed. Robert M. Moore, III. Lanham, MD: University Press of America.

Doane, A. 1997. "Dominant group ethnic identity in the United States: the role of "hidden" ethnicity in intergroup relations." *The Sociological Quarterly* 38 (3): 375-397.

Duncan, Otis and Beverly Duncan. 1955. "A methodological analysis of segregation indexes." *American Sociological Review* March 20: 210-217.

Gay, Gary. 1985. "Implications of the selected models of ethnic identity development for educators." *Journal of Negro Education* 54: 43-55.

Grant, Carl. 1990. "Desegregation, racial attitudes, and intergroup contact: A discussion of change." *Phi Delta Kappan*. Special Section on School Desegregation September.

Greene, Jay P. and Nicole Mellow. 1998. *Integration where it counts: a study of racial integration in public and private school lunchrooms*. University of Texas September.

Greenberg, M.T., Siegel, J. and Leitch, C. 1983. "The nature and importance of attachment relationships to parents and peers during adolescence." *Journal of Youth and Adolescence* 12 (5): 373-386.

Jackson, L. 1998. "The influence of both race and gender on the experiences of African American college women." *The Review of Higher Education* 21 (4): 359-375.

Klaczynski, P. 1990. "Cultural-developmental tasks and adolescent development: theoretical and methodological considerations." *Adolescence* XXV (100) Winter: 811-823.

Kurtines, W. and R. Hogan. 1972. "Sources of conformity in unsocialized college students." *Journal of Abnormal Psychology* 80: 49-51.

Marcus, Robert. 1996. "The friendships of delinquents." *Adolescence* 31 (121) Spring 145-158.

Martinez, A. A. 2000. "Race talks: undergraduate women of color and female friendships." *The Review of Higher Education* 23 (2): 133-152.

Steitz, J. and Owens, T. 1992. *Adolescence.* 27 (105) Spring: 37-50.

Taylor, D and Rickel, A. 1981. "An analysis of factors affecting school social integration." *Journal of Negro Education* Spring 50 (2): 122-133.

Ting-Toomey, Stella. 1981. "Ethnic identity and close friendship in Chinese- American college students." *International Journal of Intercultural Relations* 5: 383-406.

Yeh, C. and Huang, K. 1996. "The collectivitistic nature of ethnic identity development among Asian-American college students." *Adolescence* 31 (123) Fall: 645-661.

Zack, N. (1995). *American mixed race: the culture of microdiversity.* ed. Lanham, MD: Rowman and Littlefield.

Chapter 9

"Let's Talk About *The Simpsons* or Something": Interracial Interaction at a Predominantly White University

Todd Schoepflin[1]

Black college students are most likely to attend institutions that have white students as their majority population base. If race did not matter, then there would be nothing to explore. However, since race continues to be a force in everyday college life--it can disrupt the flow of social interaction, impact friendship and dating patterns, and influence where a person sits in a dining hall--it is critical to explore its effects.

Although the opportunity for positive relationships between black and white students exists, the college campus often reflects the racial tensions in American society. I am in agreement with Altbach (1991: 3), who asserts "race is one of the most volatile, and divisive, issues in American higher education." At colleges and universities throughout America, racial issues have sparked curriculum debates, affected relations in dormitories, and influenced admissions decisions. Altbach makes an important point: if institutions of higher learning (which constitute the best-educated community in the United States) have racial problems, then there is cause for concern about the rest of society.

---

[1] "The author thanks Kenneth Feldman, Norman Goodman, Peter Kaufman, and Oyeronke Oyewumi for providing valuable insights."

In this article I discuss the quality of interaction between black and white students at a predominantly white university that I refer to as "Upstate University." Upstate University is a private, coed, liberal arts institution located in a suburban setting in the Northeast. Of the approximately 2,700 undergraduates enrolled at this university, there are about 120 black students in attendance. I analyze cases of social interaction in which communication between black and white students began to break down; as I will show, racial tension was at the center of these breakdowns. Although black and white students misunderstood each other in the course of social interaction, I will explain how communication was in some instances sustained. This article also includes an analysis of how power relations affect interracial interaction at Upstate University.

This study employs qualitative methodology; it describes the routine and problematic moments and meanings in individuals' lives (Denzin and Lincoln 1994: 2). As part of a larger project, data were collected through interviews with thirty-five black students and thirty-five white students. My approach was to elicit the students' perspectives of their experiences through detailed interviewing. The duration of interviews was between one and two hours. I recorded each interview onto audiotape and personally transcribed all interviews. I began interviews in September 2001 and completed interviews in May 2003. I use pseudonyms to conceal the identities of participants.

Terminology

One must be careful in using racial terminology. Issues of courtesy, accuracy, and identity are found in the use of group names (Simpson and Yinger 1972). In considering the proper terminology to use when referring to racial groups, it is instructive to note the terms used by reputable scholars who study race. West (1994) mostly uses the label "black." Patterson (1998: xxii), who uses the term "Afro-American," declares: "I refuse to call any Euro-American or Caucasian person 'white,' and I view with the deepest suspicion any Euro-American who insists on calling Afro-Americans 'black.'" Both Wilson (1996) and Gates (2004) alternate between "black" and "African-American." As we can see, there is not unanimous agreement for the use of one, single label. Nor is there a consensus with respect to whether a hyphen should be used between "African" and "American." Simpson and Yinger (1972) make an excellent point: since there are persons within any group who prefer different group titles, any choice will cause some discomfort. Furthermore, how long a particular term will remain acceptable is impossible to predict because the potential always exists for a newly preferred term to emerge.

Throughout this article, I use the term "black" rather than "African-American." I do not use the term "African-American" because only a few of the black participants in my study used that term. When referring to themselves or to friends from the same racial background, most subjects consistently used the label "black." In addition, I hesitate to use the term "African-American" because some of the black respondents with ties to the Caribbean region referred to themselves as "black." In using the same term that most students did, I believe I am being respectful and accurate. I use the term "white" because it provides balance with the term "black" and is the predominant label that white interviewees used when referring to their racial group.

Interaction Maintenance

There will always be snags with interaction; there are ebbs and flows to our interactions and, in some cases, people "rub us the wrong way." It is interesting when we consider that in some interactions, an individual takes it upon himself or herself to "fix" an interaction. We might say that he or she "cleans up" an otherwise messy interaction that makes it possible for future interactions to occur. I coined the phrase *interaction maintenance* after learning of instances in which black students repaired interactions that were breaking down. As we shall see, racial tension was at the center of these breakdowns.

When I interviewed Randy, a black student, he was very familiar with the Upstate University campus. Randy had spent four years on the campus as an undergraduate at Upstate and after earning his Bachelor's degree, he returned to pursue a Master's degree. I asked him to recall his freshman year:

> Big change--the party atmosphere, socializing in dorm rooms, the clubs didn't particularly pertain to my lifestyle, kind of music I like, or even the way the kids dressed, or the way they talked. Even as simple a thing as going to the dining hall was tough sometimes. Everywhere you went there were white people everywhere. I mean I don't mind, I don't have this thing with color; I don't even care, but it just took me off guard.

His last phrase, "it took me off guard," is compelling. This phrase suggests he did not expect a mass of white students to be present; nor was he used to the music, fashion, and vernacular that he associates with white students. Randy proceeded to describe awkward interactions with white students during that first semester. Interactions were often uncomfortable, he stated, because of preconceptions that others held. As an example he recalls a sentiment he heard after getting to know white students: "Oh, I didn't know you were like that," some would say, "I thought you were some thug." His roommate once asked him if he'd ever used a gun, to which Randy replied: "Don't say stuff like that to me, that's dumb." He had another roommate who made insensitive jokes when he would exit their room, leaving his wallet behind. Once, upon departing, he said to Randy "hopefully my wallet's there when I get back." Randy says he would "joke back" to hide his anger; although he was very bothered by his roommate's jokes, Randy would remind himself "don't start out bad." This is an example of what I call *interaction maintenance*: though angry, Randy would stay calm and complete the interaction in a peaceful way. The exchange would suit both parties so that interaction could occur again. Had Randy shown his anger and replied in a heated fashion, we can speculate that the next interaction might be even more uncomfortable, if it occurred at all. He learned through interaction that some white students have certain images of blacks: thugs, gun users, wallet stealers. "They play it off as a joke," he said, "but deep inside I have a feeling that's how they really think." Randy seemed vexed that race did factor into so many interactions:

> When you do it on this consistent basis, and your friendship is all these race issues, I'm like 'Just let it go, let's talk about *The Simpsons* or something.' Like 'Oh, you love that Tupac video, every time I come in here you're watching that.' What is that supposed to mean?

Yes, Randy told me, he likes the music of Tupac Shakur, the hip-hop artist who was murdered in 1996, but he also likes *The Simpsons*, the long-running animated television program. White students may have typecast him as a Shakur fanatic, but sometimes he'd prefer to discuss a funny, and race-neutral, television show. In describing his view of campus race relations, he noted the tension that was often present. People know that tension exists, he said, but they don't talk about it:

> Between students on the surface, race relations are pretty good; but when everybody separates and goes back to their rooms is when the whispering starts and the little snide comments begin. That you hear about weeks even months after, and you're like 'Oh, that's what they thought?' You think they're your friends but then one makes a comment about you: 'He tried to talk to some white girl at the club.' I guess the relations aren't as good as I thought they would be. It's like they smile in your face and behind your back. It's fake.

Listening to Randy made it clear that he had a reservoir of resentment because of certain interactions and it is probable that those specific interactions hampered the development of close-knit friendships with the white students who participated in them.

In an interview with another black student, I learned that a solid friendship had formed between a black student and a white student, and that an awkward interaction did not hurt that friendship. Tonya, a junior, recalled the time when her best friend at Upstate, who is white, made a verbal blunder:

> My best friend--it wasn't her fault, because of where she's from--a really small town. She's my best friend and I love her to death. One day we were walking back from the dining hall. She was talking about someone and said "She just doesn't sound like a colored girl." Me and my other friend, who is black, just stopped in our tracks and said "You don't use the term 'colored' anymore!" She said "Dude, I'm sorry, don't be mad." She didn't know. I said "We're not mad, you didn't know." Her family probably uses that term all the time. It was funny though.

Here Tonya exercised an impressive amount of understanding. It is easy to see how another student in the same situation would be offended by the use of such outdated language. Yet Tonya excused her white friend's comment for two reasons: she is from a small town and, perhaps, she learned the term from her family. She did not let the remark interfere with their relationship. Instead she repaired the interaction by letting the student know that she was not angry. She does not fault her friend's lack of awareness, and she even found humor in the incident.

It turns out that Jill, a black junior, also encountered the use of the term "colored":

> My friend and I were in class and the teacher kept using the term 'colored.' We kept looking at each other whenever she used the word. We wrote a letter to her asking why she used it. She said "that was the proper term to use when we were in school." She brought us in front of the class to discuss it.

Jill and her friend embarked on a sophisticated course of action by writing a letter to their professor and agreeing to discuss the issue in front of other students. It is stunning that a faculty member would use such an archaic term; at least, however, the professor turned the situation into a learning experience for other students. So, it is evident that black students practice interaction maintenance with white students, and they also repair interactions with white faculty.

Erica, a black senior, shared a story that indicated how differences between black and white students can cause an awkward interaction:

> I put extensions in my hair one time, and I went to get my hair re-braided; with extensions you have to burn the ends to keep the braids together, because it's synthetic hair. Someone in the dorm walked past the door as my friend lit the hair on fire, and the student walking by almost lost it: "Oh my God, are you burning your hair?" We just burst out laughing because we knew.

Erica and her friend knew that this white female student was unfamiliar with this re-braiding process. The practice seemed strange to the student, as expressed by the phrase "Oh my God." Her surprise regarding the possibility that someone might actually burn their own hair was met by laughter; therefore, a wall was placed between two black students who were "in the know" and one white student who was not. After laughing at the white student's expense, the two black students reacted to her gaffe by repairing the interaction:

> We were like "Just sit down." It's like "Ask me, I'll tell." I'd rather you ask me than say something ignorant that you don't know. "This is not my hair." I took out a braid and said "See, this is my hair, but this synthetic hair I bought." I explained that my friend was braiding within my hair.

The interaction was ultimately fruitful. A white student learned something new, and since the interaction ended on a less awkward note, there exists a chance for future interactions. These stories show how black students fixed interactions that otherwise may have broken down: Randy maintained a civil relationship with a roommate who teased him with a racial stereotype; Tonya maintained her close friendship with a student using offensive language; Jill corrected a professor using the same offensive language; and Erica explained a cultural practice to a resident.

Analysis

Interaction maintenance is related to Goffman's (1967) concept of *face-work*. According to Goffman, a person may want to save his or her own face because of pride or he or she may want to save the other participant's face because of a desire to avoid the hostility that may arise if the participant loses face. The first case is a defensive orientation toward saving one's own face; the second is a protective orientation toward saving the other's face. Goffman believed that the protective orientation occurs because during face-to-face encounters, participants are expected to sustain a "standard of considerateness," which means that participants are expected to go to certain lengths to save the feelings of others. In our society, as Goffman noted, this is sometimes called "tact," "diplomacy," or "social skill."

In a way, the episodes of interaction maintenance presented in this article serve as examples of face-work because black students saved the faces of white individuals. However, the concept of interaction maintenance is different from face-work in that it is not meant to designate general tact or social skill; rather, interaction maintenance involves a specific kind of diplomacy that I call *racial diplomacy*. In one example mentioned earlier, Randy was not just saving a white student's face--he was deflecting racial conflict and tension in the process of face-to-face interracial interaction. Randy was diplomatic despite the fact that the offending participant, a white student, insulted him during the course of interaction. Randy was not offensive, yet he engaged in interaction maintenance--he contributed to peaceful race relations despite being the object of the insult.

The reader may wonder why Randy engaged in interaction maintenance despite the fact that he was the person who was offended. One possible reason is that another individual--a white student--had more power in the situation. As Fine (1992) points out, relations of power affect the amount of control that actors have in situations. Power is a dimension of social structure that limits the choices of individuals. From this perspective, the reason that Randy did not "start out bad" with white students was because he had little choice. As a black student at a predominantly white institution, he did not have the luxury to alienate white students. As Snow (2001) asserts, social actors take structural factors into account as they develop their lines of action in the course of social interaction. Randy's approach to race relations takes into account the environment in which his interactions take place--situated at a predominantly white university, he did not think it was wise to trade insults with white students. In a different context, however, he might have responded to racial insults in a different manner.

To extend the analysis of Randy's encounters, we can apply Anderson and Snow's (2001) concept of *interactional affronts*. They ask us to consider the different ways in which systems of stratification manifest themselves at the micro level of social life. They are concerned with the consequences of affronts and insults that people face as they participate in everyday interaction. They view interactional affronts as manifestations of racial inequality. These interactional affronts are displays of antagonism between members of different races and hierarchical niches. Applying their perspective, Randy did not encounter insults--he encountered *racial insults*. These insults can be viewed as manifestations of racial inequality in the sense that white students, who are at the higher end of the social hierarchy at predominantly white Upstate University, used stereotypical insults to alienate Randy, a black student at the lower end of the social hierarchy.

Anderson and Snow (2001) might also say that Randy was resilient in the face of interactional affronts because Randy took measures to moderate the force of their impact. He would offset the affronts by using "jokes" of his own, a clever technique to maintain interactions. He would give himself mental reminders not to "start out bad" with white students. He would converse with other black students about, as he called it, the "race thing." As Anderson and Snow (2001: 401) point out, "humans are highly creative in interpreting, reinterpreting, and engaging the social world in ways that salvage a positive sense of self." Not only did Randy reject the stereotypical evaluations of white students but, as his testimony shows, he believes he became a stronger person for having faced interpersonal adversity: "It makes you so much stronger in every aspect of your life, socially, mentally, psychologically...because you know you can get over a hump like that." However, unlike for white students, a considerable cost emerged for Randy, in the form of psychological energy that he allocated to this process.

This examination of Randy's encounters demonstrates his experience with racial insults; now I will argue that some black students face race *and* gender insults. The analysis includes Nikki, a black senior who relayed the following incident:

> I experienced something else that turned me away. I was on my was to class and I walked by three white girls and they made a comment to me: "Keep that weave growing." That really affected me, because I felt as if they just assumed that since I'm a black female I'm not supposed to have long hair down to my back. My first intention was to say something, but I just walked by. I went back to my room, I was so upset. I was upset because to me, I don't see color. So when I see a person, I don't see them for white, Hispanic, black; that day I just felt weird.

The analysis also involves Erica, the student who was in the process of getting her hair re-braided. Recall that as her friend was burning the ends of synthetic hair, a white female walked past Erica's door and hollered "Oh my God, are you burning your hair?" Erica described the re-braiding process to the white student--an example, I argued, of interaction maintenance. However, an analysis centered on the hairstyles of Nikki and Erica will show that gender is a factor that affects interracial interaction.

The reader might ask: what is the social significance of hair? One answer comes from Wilson and Russell (1996: 92), who point out that America is a "hair-obsessed society," one in which women are bombarded with corporate advertisements that prey on their insecurities about hair. Williams (2000: 15-18) provides another insight, in asserting that hair texture plays a role in perceptions of beauty and privilege in America. For many years, as she points out, the media has projected images of white movie stars and models with "long flowing hair." The media that has portrayed white women as "delicate damsels of distress" is the same media that has portrayed black women as "nappy-haired heads of households." Banks (2000) offers a related point: what is deemed desirable in mainstream society is measured against white standards of beauty, which include long and straight hair (usually blonde). Therefore, black women's hair, in general, fits outside of what is considered desirable. When white women criticize black women's hair, they are in effect devaluing black physical characteristics and affirming physical standards associated with white females. Pejorative comments about hair may offend black women, who face a lack of understanding of their hairstyles; tensions surface and can inhibit the development of friendships. This point is apparent in Nikki's reflection that the experience "turned [her] away." The tension that surfaced involved both race and gender.

By blurting out the question "Oh my God, are you burning your hair?" to Erica, the white student expressed, simultaneously, fascination and discomfort. Within interracial environments, black women's hairstyles become representations of "mysterious" cultural practices that require explanations (Banks 2000: 17, 80). The white student invaded Erica's personal space, and in doing so, offered an overt message: race matters, and gender matters, and hair was the medium through which the message was expressed.

To return to Anderson and Snow's (2001) perspective, we can consider a question: what is the consequence of insults that Upstate students face as they participate in everyday interaction? It seems possible that some black students who face interactional affronts would be hesitant to join white peer groups and be reluctant to attend social events in which many white students are present. It is likely intimidating when white students, who represent a privileged majority group, use derisive comments toward black students. Racial insults, or racial *and* gender insults, serve as reminders that black students are situated on the margins of mainstream campus culture at predominantly white universities. I believe that negative interracial encounters facilitate separation between students along racial lines.

The Impact of Power Relations on Interracial Interaction

Jessica, a white student I interviewed, shared her observations about interracial interaction at Upstate University:

> I have no hesitance hanging out with anyone, but from what I can see from other people, some people that may not have been as exposed to different minorities, they are a little intimidated. I don't think that any of the black people that I've met are intimidated anyway--they'll come up and say hi to anyone. But other [white] people, they would admit it, they just don't have a feel for that.

I found her comments interesting because she identified a significant component of interracial interaction: who *approaches* whom? According to Jessica, black students will "come up and say hi to anyone." Diane, a white respondent, also addressed this issue: "I think that the black students try more to talk to the white students, than vice versa. That's what I've noticed. It just seems like they are more open to us than we are to them. I've been approached more than I've approached them." Essentially, Jessica and Diane credit black students for creating interracial interaction. Other white students I interviewed seemed to *expect* that black students join white peer groups. Some white students were critical of black students, based on the perception that they "stick together." In any case, it appears that white students believe that black students are responsible for the degree of interracial interaction that exists at Upstate University.

"Who approaches whom" is an important issue, and it is significant that some white students would not approach black students. For instance, Guy, a white student, explained: "If I wanted to go say 'Hey, what's up?' to a group of black guys, that would look real odd. This is what I'm guessing: they have to feel like they form their own little group, because maybe they feel we won't talk to them or hang out with them. But I mean, it's not like if you came up to me I wouldn't talk to you."

My view is that white students such as Guy *accept* black students into their friendship groups, but will not *approach* black students and enter into their friendship groups. Why would this be the case? I believe it pertains to an expectation that many white students, as members of a majority group, have toward black students, as members of a minority group. This expectation may be a fundamental characteristic of minority-majority relations. Keeping in mind Kanter's (1977: 210) proposition--if there are nine X's, and one O, one is likely to notice the O--I have developed an appropriate extension of the proposition pertinent to Upstate University: If there are approximately 2600 X's, and 120 O's, the O's are expected to approach the X's.

Kanter (1977) showed how males, representing the dominant culture of the workplace, made the culture clear to women, representing tokens, by stating the terms under which tokens entered relationships and by reminding women they were different people than men. Men signaled to women that they needed to acknowledge dominant cultural expressions in order for "natural" interaction to proceed. At Upstate, some white students may believe there should be a particular process that governs their relationships with black students: *you* join *our* groups, we maintain our dominant culture. Therefore, what may superficially appear as a basic approach-acceptance issue between white and black students is actually a play of power. Keep in mind that a distribution of power exists in any minority-majority relationship. The existence of a minority group implies the existence of a corresponding dominant group with higher social status and greater privileges (Simpson and Yinger 1972). Considering the structural reality that black students face--presence in a predominantly white environment, where there are approximately 2,600 white students and 120 black students--it is important to recognize that black students have less power than do white students in defining the situation at Upstate University.

Conclusion

Those white students who rely on black students to generate interracial interaction probably do not realize how serious the social stakes are for black students who befriend white students. Black individuals who join white peer groups may face rejection from other black students. This is because some black students might make the judgment that those black individuals who have joined white peer groups have not been allegiant to the black student community. As Willie (2003: 147) suggests, black students who associate with white students are vulnerable to ostracism by other black students or may encounter the accusation that they have "forgotten" who they are. At college campuses, Willie argues, black students often measure race loyalty by behavior or association. By comparison, she says, white students are allowed wider boundaries and greater freedom to express their race.

The circumstance for black students at Upstate University is both challenging and unenviable: they are expected to spark interracial interaction, but in the course of interaction with white students, they risk encountering race and gender insults. Some black students who experience insults respond in diplomatic ways, perhaps thinking it is more prudent to tolerate offenses than to return them, given their position at a predominantly white university.

Discussion and Essay Questions

1. The author maintains that Black students "fix interactions that otherwise would have broken down." Is this a two-way street? Do white students do the same?

2. Is it possible that an individual can have more power than someone else within a social interaction? How so?

References

Altbach, Philip. 1991. "The Racial Dilemma in American Higher Education." In Phillip Altbach & Kofi Lomotey (Eds.), *The Racial Crisis in American Higher Education*. New York: SUNY Press.

Anderson, Leon, and David A. Snow. 2001. "Inequality and the Self: Exploring the Connections from an Interactionist Perspective." *Symbolic Interaction* 24(4): 395 406.

Banks, Ingrid. 2000. *Hair Matters: Beauty, Power, and Black Women's Consciousness*. New York: New York University Press.

Denzin, Norman K., and Yvonna S. Lincoln. "Introduction: Entering the Field of Qualitative Research." 1994. In Denzin, Norman K., and Yvonna S. Lincoln (Eds.), *Handbook of Qualitative Research*. Thousand Oaks, CA: Sage Publications.

Fine, Gary Alan. 1992. "Agency, Structure, and Comparative Contexts: Toward a Synthetic Interactionism." *Symbolic Interaction* 15(1): 87-107.

Gates, Henry Louis. 2004. *America Behind the Color Line*. New York: Time-Warner Books.

Goffman, Erving. 1967. *Interaction Ritual*. New York: Pantheon Books.

Kanter, Rosabeth Moss. 1977. *Men and Women of the Corporation*. New York: Basic Books.

Patterson, Orlando. 1998. *Rituals of Blood: Consequences of Slavery in Two American Centuries*. New York: Basic Civitas.

Simpson, George Eaton, and J. Milton Yinger. 1972. *Racial and Cultural Minorities: An Analysis of Prejudice and Discrimination* (Fourth Edition). New York: Harper & Row.

Snow, David A. 2001. "Extending and Broadening Blumer's Conceptualization of Symbolic Interactionism." *Symbolic Interaction* 24(3): 367-377.

West, Cornel. 1994. *Race Matters*. New York: Vintage Books.

Williams, Lena. 2000. *It's the Little Things: The Everyday Interactions that Get Under the Skin of Blacks and Whites*. New York: Harcourt.

Willie, Sarah. 2003. *Acting Black: College, Identity, and the Performance of Race*. New York: Routledge.

Wilson, Midge, and Kathy Russell. 1996. *Divided Sisters: Bridging the Gap Between Black Women & White Women*. New York: Anchor Books.

Wilson, William Julius. 1996. *When Work Disappears: The World of the New Urban Poor*. New York: Vintage Books.

Chapter 10

Interracial Dating and Marriage: Fact, Fantasy and the Problem of Survey Data

Charles A. Gallagher

The U.S. Census reports that interracial marriages increased by 800 percent between 1960 and 1990.[1] This rather spectacular percent increase in the number of interracial marriages is supported by any cursory or anecdotal look at American popular culture as presented by the media. Tiger Woods "Cablinasian" mixed racial ancestry was nothing less than a media obsession when he was initially establishing himself as the world's greatest golfer. Many daytime soap operas, like the *Young and the Restless* and *All My Children* have featured at least one interracial romance subplot. Prime time television drama and situation comedies like *Dawson's Creek*, *West Wing*, *ER*, and *Sex in the City* are sprinkled with interracial relationships and plot turns. The 1990s saw a number of successful mainstream movies address various aspects of interracial romance including *Jungle Fever, Mississippi Masala* and *Bullworth*. It is practically impossible when consuming MTV not to see a cast of handsome, twenty-something, interracial hip-hoppers dancing, flirting or v-jaying. Within the world the media constructs for us it would appear that marital assimilation, the last stage of assimilation as intially outlined by Milton Gordon, has arrived. Gordon predicted as cultural differences between groups diminished a large number of individuals from different ethnic and racial backgrounds would date, fall in love and marry across the color line.[2]

The above narrative describing a society where interracial marriages are both socially accepted and becoming more common place ignores, however, a more complicated story. In 1998 interracial marriages accounted for only about 4% of all marriages in the United States even though 83% of blacks and 67% of whites approved of such pairings.[3] What individuals support in survey questions or allege they would do in the hypothetical situation offered in a survey is often quite different from what people actually do. In his now classic example of how attitudes are a poor predictor of behavior LaPiere found that restaurant and hotel owners who expressed discriminatory intent by indicating they would not serve Chinese patrons did serve them when placed in face-to-face situations with Chinese customers.[4] Given the inconsistency between thought and action it is not surprising that indication of support or willingness to enter into an interracial relationship is not matched by the actual rates of interracial marriage. This chapter attemps to draw on a number of key cultural and sociological theories to explain the disjuncture between what individuals indicate they would do and the broader patterns of interracial dating and marriage we observe in society. It will examine who marries whom and how we can explain the differences in rates of interracial marriage between groups. Finally, if racial differences in mate selection exist within and between groups to what extent do these trends reflect racial stereotypes?

Race, Ethnicity and Marriage

Within the assimilationist perspective, marriage between different ethnic and racial groups is viewed as the final stage of assimilation. As the sons and daughters of these immigrant groups gradually blend into the cultural mainstream, assimilation theory predicts their acceptance into the dominant culture and the structural mobility which that acceptance insures for future generations. Now thirty years old, Milton Gordon's predictions about marital assimilation have proven surprisingly accurate for patterns of interethnic marriage among the non-Hispanic white population. Some clarifications are needed however regarding how the meaning and salience of ethnic and racial identity has changed over time and how these changes reflect current trends in interethnic and interracial marriage. The process of assimilation and convergence of cultural differences among whites several generations removed from the immigrant experience has altered dating and marriage patterns. Two-thirds of the white children born during the 1970s had parents of mixed ancestry compared to one-third of the whites born in 1920.[5] These hybrid ethnic families create for their children social situations which involve "more ethnic heterogeneity in their social networks and may possibly lead to a diminution or dilution of ethnic identity".[6] The "unmeltable ethnics" that Robert Novak described some time ago appear to have, at least in terms of interethnic marriages, melted smoothly into the "pot" through interethnic amalgamation.[7] It often comes as a surprise to whites born after 1980 that crossing the ethnic boundaries to date or marry had social consequences in recent American ethnic history. The dating and marriage of, for example, an Italian-American and an Irish-American forty years ago not only raised eyebrows in each community but often brought disappointment and even estrangement from family members.

Gordon's theory of marital assimilation does not however, describe rates of marriage between whites and non-whites. The 1992 census found about 2% of marriages in the US were interracial.[8] Comparatively, 66% of the white families with children born in the 1970's were "interethnic." In 1970, 7/10 of one percent (.007) of all couples in the United States were interracial families. One might argue that there has been almost a 300% increase between 1970 and 1990 in the number of interracial marriages; at that rate and holding other things equal, the percent of interracial marriages would matched the current percent of interethnic marriages somewhere around the year 2065, some seventy years from now.

White and black respondents' expressed desire to enter into or avoid close interethnic and interracial relationships presents us with the interracial dating and marriage paradox; Why is it so few individuals cross the color line for romance when in surveys they say they would? A non-random purposive sample was conducted of 335 white and 105 black college students at a large urban university in 1993. The survey illuminates these questions: is dating or marrying within ones' ethnic group markedly different from dating or marrying inside ones' racial group? If there are discrepancies between the two, how should they be interpreted? Finally, what do these differences suggest about the salience of ethnic groups versus racial groups? Tables 1 and 2 examine the dating and marriage preferences of white and black respondents. See appendix "A" for the exact wording of the questions used in the survey.

The white respondents who felt it was very important to date or marry someone from their own ethnic group was quite small, about 13% and 18% respectively. The middle category "yes but would/could" can be interpreted to mean that respondents may have a preference for someone with a similar ethnic background but if they were so moved by romance, would date or marry someone from a different background. Combining columns "B" and "C" from Table 1 results in over 87% of the respondents willing to date someone from a different ethnic group, with 83% ready to consider marrying outside their ethnic group.

Table 1. Interethnic and Interracial Dating and Marriage Preferences: White Responses

	(A) Yes, Very Important To Date/Marry Within My Group	(B) Yes, But Would Date Marry Outside My Group	(C) Not Important Either Way
1. Date Same Ethnic Group:	12.8	21.5	65.7
2. Marry Same Ethnic Group:	17.1	21.0	62.0
3. Date Same Racial Group:	31.0	25.4	43.6
4. Marry Same Racial Group:	39.8	20.1	40.1

n=335

These findings are consistent with assimilation theory as it applies to interethnic marriages; respondents appear quite willing to date and marry outside of their ethnic group. Their responses should be viewed as a larger, albeit projected trend; as I mentioned previously, the 33% mixed families in the 1920's eventually grew to 66% mixed families in the 1970's. In 1980 only 25% of married couples were from the same ethnic background.[9] If student responses are to be believed, when this group reaches the typical marrying age around the year 2000, about 85% will form ethnically mixed families. As the "ethnic heterogeneity" of family networks increases predictions about the "dilution of ethnic identity" will be realized. It may be that white identities will become so diluted and Americanized through the assimilation process that young white ethnics will be culturally indistinguishable from one another, if they are not that already.

The veracity of student responses is evidenced by the ever growing pool of potential mates that are from mixed backgrounds. The sheer ethnic mixing that has taken place in the last seventy-five years supports the assertion that single ethnic identities will become an anomaly for whites as a group. If the majority of respondents come from mixed ethnic backgrounds, then the dating and marriage pool will also contain an growing population of mixed or hybrid ethnics. It will be increasingly difficult to search out a "pure" white ethnic because their pool has steadily been decreasing while that of "mixed" ethnics has been increasing exponentially. As maintenance of single ancestry becomes increasingly difficult statistically, so the majority of whites, at least in this sample, put no particular weight on the ethnic background of a potential mate.

Of course, it is possible for an individual to claim five ethnic backgrounds but identify with only one, but the literature as well as this survey suggest a watering down of ethnic salience takes place.

What is of particular note in Table 1 is the significant difference between the ethnic and racial questions on marriage. Almost 40% of the respondents replied that it was very important for them to marry someone from their own racial group. Comparatively, just over 17% answered that it was important for them to marry someone from their own ethnic group. Combining columns "B" and "C" as a measure of those that are do not care the race or the ethnicity of their potential mates, 83% of respondents would marry out of their ethnic group while just over 60% say they would marry out of their racial group. The findings among this mostly traditional age college sample is consistent with national polling data. Among whites between the 18 and 34 82.7% expressed approval of interracial marriages. Note that the question in the white college sample asked if *they would* marry someone from a different race. Given that 60.2% of whites replied that they would enter into an interracial marriage it is likely that those who would approve of such relationships would be significantly higher.

Combining columns "B" and "C" (from rows one and two) Table 2 suggest that a majority of black respondents would date (68.3%) or marry (57.7%) someone from a different ethnic background. Methodologically this questions

Table 2. Interethnic and Interracial Dating and Marriage Preferences: Black Responses

	(A) Yes, Very Important To Date/Marry Within My Group	(B) Yes, But Would Date/Marry Outside My Group	(C) Not Important Either Way
1. Date Same Ethnic Group:	31.7	37.5	30.8
2. Marry Same Ethnic Group:	42.3	30.8	26.9
3. Date Same Racial Group	41.3	33.7	25.0
4. Marry Same Racial Group:	51.9	25.0	23.1

n=105

creates a validity problem for both white and black respondents. Does this question ask, for instance, if someone who defines herself as African American would date or marry a man from Afro-Carribean from Jamaica or might it also mean the same African-American would be willing to date or marry a self-defined white Italian-American. The same understanding of ethnicity being synonymous one variation of racial identity could apply to white respondents as well. Typically within the social sciences racial groups are understood as being distinguishable on the basis of physical, ascribed characteristics. These traits are rooted in physical traits even though it is a social process that makes these arbitrary physical differences, such as skin color hair texture or eye shape important. Physical characteristics associated with racial categories are the cultural "givens" from which our everyday understanding of race is derived. Someone is "black" or "Asian," because social convention has so defined them. Members of racial groups internalize that definition, and are in turn viewed by others as being members of that racial group.[10] Ethnic groups are distinguished by sociocultural heritage or ethnic markers such as nationality, language, customs or religion but are subsumed under the larger, less mutable social category of race. For example the racial category "Asian" encompasses many Ethnicities: Korean, Filipino, Hmong, Japanese, etc., all of whom presumably share some physical race based similarities. Like race, ethnicity is socially constructed; unlike race, ethnic identity can change in response to various social pressures. Race and ethnicity are not mutually exclusive categories, nor is it difficult to find examples in which they seem to overlap or merge. The purpose of a definition which treats race and ethnicity as distinct and conceptually different facets of social identity is to suggest that individuals can construct, resurrect, ignore or abandon ethnicity, but race is generally fixed. As the saying goes, you can change your ethnicity, but you can't change your race.

An almost equal number of black respondents, slightly over 48% responded that they would date or marry someone from a different racial background. While this is somewhat lower than the whites' responses it is important to note the trend for both groups. As the questions implied more intimacy (from dating to marriage) and greater social implications (family response, the wedding, having children) the percent willing to enter into an interracial relationship and marriage decreased. The need for greater social distance appears to increase as relationships move from casual interactions to intimate relationships. However it is important to note that like the white respondents, the 48.1% of blacks who said they would marry across the color line (adding columns B and C in row number 4) stands in stark contrast to the fact that among even younger cohorts only 8.5% of black males and 3.7% of black females marry outside of their race.

Understanding the Cultural Contradictions of Race and Romance

There is a wide gulf between what respondents say and what they actually do. Respondents may think they are willing to be in white/nonwhite relationships, but find that willingness mediated by many seen and unseen social obstacles. One such obstacle is residential segregation and the resulting lack of exposure to other racial groups. If proximity and exposure to racially different groups is one possible condition for intermarriage, there is little doubt that white ethnics will increasingly be involved in relationships with other whites where it is not uncommon to find a mix of six or more Euro-ethnic ancestries.

The overwhelming majority of white respondents in the university survey described their neighborhoods as ethnically "mixed." However, and predictably, the ethnic makeup of neighborhoods stands in stark contrast to the racial makeup. Both black and white respondents described attending high schools that were primarily racially segregated. If proximity is a significant factor in mate selection, it also means that whites will be less likely to intermarry non-whites due to the high degree of racial segregation throughout the US. Almost 65% of white respondents describe living in neighborhoods that are at least 95% white. Another 24% live in neighborhoods they describe as 65% to 94% white. It is also likely that the 24% living in mixed neighborhoods live in the white section of a mixed area. Townships or even neighborhoods may have a sizable non-white population but these communities are usually quite segregated. Communities with whites and non-whites dispersed evenly from block to block and house to house are an anomaly. The metropolitan area in which this study was conducted has the dubious distinction of being ranked tenth among cities considered "hypersegregated", that is an isolated, clustered, unevenly distributed white and non-white populations.[11]

The respondents in this university study mirror larger housing trends in the United States. Census data from 1990 found that in nearly half of the counties in the United States blacks comprised less than half of 1% of the population. The suburbs are even more segregated with over 86% suburban whites living in of communities having a population of less than 1% black.[12] Racial segregation means there will be little sustained interpersonal contact with individuals from different racial backgrounds. The extent to which a racially segregated society and the resulting lack of prolonged social contact influences the likelihood of interracial dating or romance can not be overemphasized. You can not flirt, date or marry across the color line if residential and educational segregation restricts social interaction. Due to past and present patterns of discrimination in the housing market and whites' preference to live in neighborhoods that are overwhelmingly white maintains the centuries old caste like quality of US race relations and high rates of endogamy.

What makes racial residential segregation all the more suspect as a primary influence in on the low number of interracial marriages is the general liberalizing of attitudes towards interracial relationships and the percent of blacks and whites who claim close cross race friendships. A 1997 Gallup poll found that 75% of blacks had a "close" white friend and 59% of whites claimed to have a close black friend.[13] Both blacks and whites do not attach the same stigma to interracial marriages and interracial personal interaction appears to have increased. Given these two trends in the national survey data it is ponderous that we do not see more interracial marriages. Where a high number of interracial marriages occur does however tell us about the role of sharing interracial social space and the propensity to date and marry across the color line. Those individuals who serve in the military provide an important example of what happens when individuals are placed in an environment that promotes, at least in theory, a truly color blind institution. White men in the military are three times as likely to marry black women then white civilians and black men and white women seven times more likely to marry black men then women not in the military. As a total institution the military is able to de-emphasize race and promote a philosophy based egalitarianism and a camaraderie based on defending the flag.[14] The high rates of interracial marriage among the men and women in the armed services is perhaps another example of why the military is defined as the most integrated institutions in our nation.

Michael Lind points out the association between race, space and intermarriage by noting that "white men in California in 1990 were more than six times as likely as Midwestern white men to marry outside their race. Overall, interracial marriages are twice as common in California (1 in 10 new couples) as in the rest of the country (1 in 25)."[15] Whites in California now account for about 50% of the states' population. Given that Asians, Blacks and American Indians account for the other 50% it not surprising that California leads the nation in interracial marriages.

Media Mediating Marriage

The comparatively high percentage of respondents who declare themselves willing to enter an interracial relationship in the university survey may reflect an exaggerated response stemming from media exposure to non-whites. Black street culture (or more accurately the mass marketed aesthetics of black youth culture) has made significant inroads into the culture of white youths. A quick survey of fashion on campus or in the malls tells a story of many whites "dressing black." The largest consumers of rap and hip-hop music are white suburban teenagers. MTV (Music Television) once void of non-white entertainers now has a large share of videos featuring black performers. Snoop Doggy Dog, Dr. Dre and Lauryn Hill have wide appeal among young whites.

BET (Black Entertainment Television) with an all black format that no doubt taps both black and white youth markets, is part of basic cable in this metropolitan area. As Robert Staples points out "Three of the five wealthiest entertainers in America are black, the biggest box-office starts and the highest-rated TV shows have, in the past, been black, and the largest sales of a record album are by a black performer."[16] Fox network has been dubbed by some young whites I've talked with as the "black" network. In a similar way professional sports has also produced media heroes that have crossed racial lines. Seventy-four percent of the NBA and 62% of the NFL are black.[17] Magic Johnson, Michael Jordan, Emmitt Smith, Barry Bonds, to name just a few, are black sports superstars who are idealized by both blacks and whites. If Nielsen ratings, Grammies and Billboard magazines' buying charts are to be believed, then blackness, at least for a segment of young whites, may be what is considered "cool". Of course, appropriation of black culture by whites is not new but what appears different at this particular moment is the sheer magnitude of this trend. Interracial couples dancing to black entertainers and the ersatz racial harmony young whites see repeatedly on TV, especially MTV, may make interracial dating, which has historically been off limits, not only desirable, but to some degree a measure of "hipness."

If this is indeed the case then the idealized, TV constructed image of "otherness" may create a generalized willingness on the part of white respondents to be involved in an interracial marriage but only with a very specific type of racial "other". Whites may not want to be romantically involved with Snoop Doggie Dog or Sister SoulJah but Chris Tucker, Halle Berry or any of the Cosby kids might do.

Viewing the media and popular culture as interracial matchmaker, is highly speculative, however, the extent that media images are able to construct both positive and negative stereotypes of racial groups can not be ignored. Over 71% of households in the East Coast City metropolitan area have cable service. It would be difficult to argue that the 23 hours of TV 18 to 24 year olds watch a week have <u>no</u> influence on how this group constructs its social reality. [18]

Being a Certain Color Still Matters

While young whites are in large part responsible for the bulk of rap and hip-hop music sales and white Americans routinely list Colin Powell or Bill Cosby on various lists of greatest or favorite Americans, whites' fascination with black America does not, however, result in the kind of dating patterns one might expect given the huge cultural exchange which takes place between these groups. If, as trend data suggests, attitudes towards interracial marriage have become more tolerant over past decades and if the implicit assumption of this openness is that we are moving towards a color-blind society it is logical to conclude the pairings of interracial marriages would be similar between racial groups. In other words, if race has declined in social significance for a sizable part of the population then one might expect that all groups would have roughly equal rates of interracial marriage. This is however, not the case. Whites (particularly men) and African Americans (particularly women) are less likely to engage in endogamy then Asian or Latinos. What is particularly striking is how these rates vary by gender. Reynolds Farley review of marriage data of couples between 25 and 34 found that more than half, 54.5% of native born Asian American women married men that were not Asian. Native Asian American women were almost as likely to marry a white man (45.1%) as they were to marry an Asian man (45.5%) where as 96.7% of white women married white men. As a general pattern Asians, Native Americans and Latinos marry out of their group at a higher rate than blacks or whites but again important gender qualifications must be made. Within this age cohort Black men are more likely (8.5%) to marry out of their group than are black women (3.7%).[19]

How do we explain the high rates of marriage between native born Asian American women and white men and tendency for black men, when they do marry out of their own race, to marry white wives? Why are the rates of interracial marriage among blacks, particularly black women so low relative to other groups? Military service, living on the west coast and increased levels of education are strongly associated with higher rates of interracial marriage but these variables do not explain why, for example, a native born Asian American female is more likely to marry an Asian or white man rather than a black man and Asian females and black males are a rare pairing.

The answer to this question may be, at least in part, a reflection on the extent to which racial stereotypes influence mate selection at various levels. Beauty may be in the eye of the beholder but a society dominated by Euro-Americans will unsurprisingly privilege a standard of beauty and cultural styles that is a mirror image of itself, even if that image is a media distortion. Sue Chow found in her interviews of Asian men and women that a sizable minority of respondents preferred whites as potential or current mates because of their preference for "European" traits including "tallness, round eyes, "buffness" for men and "more ample breasts" for women.[20] In addition to these physical attributes Euro-Americans possess positive personality traits that, as her respondents put it, other Asian males and females lacked. If whites in this study have personality traits that are highly valued it appears that much of white America views African Americans in a much more negative light. A 1991 National Opinion Research Center study found that 78% of whites believed blacks were more likely to prefer to live off welfare, 62% believed that blacks were less hardworking, 56% believed blacks were more violent and 53% believed that blacks were less intelligent.[21] Contrast this rather disheartening list of racial stereotypes towards blacks with another; the Asian "model minority." This equally stigmatizing label of Asians who are hardworking, good at math, family centered, natural entrepreneurs, and among Asian women, demur and exotic becomes a form of marriage capital as stereotypes seep into the dominant groups' collective consciousness.

How then do we make sense of the tendency for individuals to say they would marry outside of their racial group but typically do not? The answer may in part reflect how the dominant group views race relations. The color blind narrative of contemporary, post-civil rights race relations asserts the social, economic and political playing field has been leveled. Equal opportunity for all, regardless of race, has been achieved. A 1991 poll found that whites believe that blacks now had "equal or greater opportunity" than whites in education (83%), job opportunity (60%) and "opportunity for promotion to supervisory or managerial jobs" (71%).[22]

If one embraces a color blind view of society where it is believed that individuals who delay gratification, work hard, and follow the rules will succeed, irrespective of color it becomes a contradiction to suggest that color does matter within the context of a survey question. This point is underscored by the fact that there is absolutely no social cost, no stigma from friends or family, no stares from strangers in the street by indicating you might marry across the color line. On the contrary, given the various social pressures not to appear racist in a color blind society where equal opportunity is now presented as the norm, survey responses to interracial marriage questions may reflect a socially acceptable answer rather than a response that is an actual predictor of future behavior.

Acknowledgements

I would like to express my gratitude to those who have helped shape my views on the cultural and political meaning of interracial dating and marriage. Abby Ferber's work on white supremacy discourse and sexuality Heather Dalmage's on interracial relationships has be invaluable. Charlie Jaret, Ralph LaRossa and Alexia Chororos have been a constant source encouragement and sociological insight.

Discussion Questions and Essay

1. Is interracial dating and marriage between African Americans and whites a threat to white masculinity?

2. Would perceptions of African American femininity need to change in order for a greater number of couples that are white male and African American female to occur?

3. Why is there a higher incidence of Asian Americans marrying whites proportionately than Asian Americans who marry African Americans?

4. In your opinion, why did white ethnics (Europeans from southern and eastern Europe) become de-racialized as the 20th century progressed?

5. Are whites an ethnicity?

Notes

1. Michael Lind. The Beige and the Black. *New York Times Magazine*, September 6, 1998 p 28.
2. Milton Gordon, *Assimilation in American Life: The Role of Race, Religion and National Origin* (New York: Oxford University Press, 1964). See Abby L. Ferber, *White Man Falling: Race, Gender, and White Supremacy* (New York: Rowman and Littele Field, 1998) and Heather Dalmage , *Tripping the Color Line: Blackwhite Multiracial Families in a Racially Divided World* (NJ: Rutgers University Press, 2000).
3. Howard Schuman, Charlotte Steeth, Lawrence Bobo and Maria Krysan, *Racial Attitudes in the America: Trends and Interpretations* (Cambridge MA: Harvard University Press, 1997)
4. R. T. LaPiere, "Attitudes vs. Action", Social Forces 13:230-237.
5. Richard Alba, *Ethnic Identity: The Transformation of White Identity* (New Haven, CT: Yale University Press, 1994).
6. Stanley Lieberson and Mary Waters, *From Many Strands: Ethnic and Racial Groups in Contemporary America* (New York: Russell Sage Foundation 1988).
7. Michael Novak, *The Rise of the Unmeltable Ethnics: Politics and Culture in the Seventies*, (New York: Macmillan Co., 1973).
8. Statistical Abstracts of the U.S., 1993.
9. See Alba.
10. See Michael Omi and Howard Winant, *Racial Formation in the United States: From the 1960's to the 1980's*, 2d ed. (New York: Routledge, 1994), Michael Banton, *Racial and Ethnic Competition*, (Cambridge: Cambridge University Press) and Frederik Barth, *Ethnic Groups and Boundaries*, (Boston: Little, Brown Publishing).
11. Douglas S. Massey and Nancy A. Denton, *American Apartheid: Segregation and the Making of the Underclass* (Cambridge: Harvard University Press, 1993).
12. George Lipsitz, "The Possessive Investment in Whiteness: Racialized Social Democracy and the "White" Problem in American Studies," *American_Quarterly*, Volume 47, September 1995, Number 3.
13. Cited in Orlando Paterson, *The Ordeal of Integration: Progress and Resentment in America's "Racial" Crisis* (Washington, D.C. : Civitas Press) p. 45.
14. Tim Heaton and Cardell K. Jacobson, "Intergroup Marriage: An Examination of Opportunity Structures," *Sociological Inquiry*, Vol. 70, No. 1, Winter 2000, 30-41.
15. Lind.
16. Robert Staples, "The Illusion of Racial Equality: The Black American Dilemma, " p. 229 in *Lure and Loathing: Essays on Race, Identity and the Ambivalence of Assimilation*,

Gerald Early (ed.), New York: The Penguin Press, 1993). Michael Jackson's *Thriller* is the album Staples is referring to. Some might argue that Michael Jackson has moved from being black to being racially ambiguous.
17. Staples.
18. Statistical Abstract of the United States, 1993.
19. Reynolds Farley, "Racial Issues: Recent Trends in Residential Patterns and Intermarriage" in *Diversity and Its Discontents: Cultural Conflict and Common Ground in Contemporary Society*, Neil J. Smelser and Jeffrey C. Alexander (ed.), Princeton: Princeton University Press, 1999).
20. Sue Crow, "The Significance of Race in the Private Sphere: Asian Americans and Spousal Preference," Sociological Inquiry, Vol 70, p. 2
21. New York Times, 1/10/91.
22. Jennifer Hochschild, *Facing Up to the American Dream* (Princeton, NJ: Princeton University Press 1995), p. 63.

Chapter 11

Social Distance and the "Tipping Effect" among College Students at a Northern New Jersey University

Kathleen Korgen, Gabe T. Wang, and James Mahon

If you look at the typical cafeteria on a college campus today, you will find racial segregation. Black students and white students tend not to mix in campus dining areas. Even on campuses with relatively high percentages of nonwhites, the picture remains the same. Most students claim that this separation of the races does not indicate any hostility between the two. It appears, however, to indicate a rather large degree of social distance between black and white college students. When a high degree of social distance between groups of persons exists, a lack of empathy and even possible anatagonism may exist between members of the two groups.

Previous research indicates that social distance may be influenced by several factors, including the degree of diversity in society (Goldberg and Kirschenbaum 1989; McCallister and Moore 1991; Netting 1991) and world events (Bogardus 1968; Owen et. al 1978). Social Learning Theory facilitates our understanding of how such factors can affect social distance. According to Social Learning Theory, people determine their behavior based upon what they have learned and what they believe will be the consequences of their actions (Bandura 1977). It is reasonable to expect that persons who grow up in multiracial communities will be more comfortable interacting with people of other races and more willing to do so, than those raised in monoracial settings.

The theory also helps to explain why social distance between members of different nations is high when tensions exist between the respective countries. For instance, during World War II, social distance between Americans and Japanese was great (Bogardus 1946) and in the early 1980s, shortly after the hostage crisis in Iran and in the midst of the US and Iraq war, white Americans desired a great deal of social distance from Iranians and Iraqis (Nix 1993). Today, as memories of 9/11 are still vivid and the second U.S.-Iraq war becomes increasingly bloody, there are even greater levels of social distance between white citizens in the U.S. and those who appear as though they may be from the Middle East. During periods of hostilities between nations, the citizens of each combatant country are taught to regard one another as enemies and often even as subhuman (Keene 1986).

Lack of social interaction and messages of inferiority that influence levels of social distance between members of different countries also occur among various groups within nations. The United States, with its diversity of races, provides a good example. Following the logic of Social Learning Theory and considering the history of slavery and legal segregation in the United States, it is no surprise that the greatest social distance among the various racial groups in the US exists between whites and blacks (Bobo and Zubrinsky, 1996).

This chapter examines the level of social distance between black and white students at a northern New Jersey university. As suggested above, and as much research has indicated, social distance is most likely to be overcome when physical proximity exists (Festinger, Schachter, and Back, 1950; Bersheid and Walster, 1969; Vela-McConnell 1999; Verkuyten and Kinket 2000). In most areas of the United States, blacks and whites are spatially separated, with little chance of interaction (Massey and Denton 1993; Sigelman, Bledsoe, Welch, and Combs 1996). However, at the university from which the data presented in this paper come, more than 28% of the student body describe themselves as African American, Asian, Latino/a, or Native American. African Americans comprise almost 12% of the undergraduate student population, which is similar to their proportion of the overall US population.

The university at which this study took place is well aware of the benefits of a diverse student body. A commitment to diversity is a part of this university's mission statement. All students are required to take a Racism and Sexism class and a course selected from a list of specifically Non-Western classes. The top administrators at the school believe that a diverse student body's contributions to the educational and social well-being of both white and minority students are well established (e.g. Alger, 1998; Bowen and Bok, 1998; Gurin, 1999). College students who attend schools with racially/ethnically heterogeneous populations are more open to living in diverse areas (Pascarella et al., 1996), and more likely to become better citizens (Bowen and Bok, 1999; Gurin, 1999) and have cross-racial friends after college (Gurin, 1999) than students at racially homogeneous colleges and universities.

However, as Beverly Daniel Tatum has stressed (2000), it takes more than a racially heterogeneous population to create a "healthy diverse campus." Simply adding more students of different races, without taking steps to deal with the issues that may arise from the change in campus culture, can result in increased racial animosity (Blalock, 1967; Chang, 1996; Liu, 1998). The dangers of a "tipping effect" when minorities become 20-30% of the overall population have been noted in studies of campuses (Korgen et al., 2003) as well as neighborhoods (Grodzins, 1957; Schelling, 1978; Glazer 1995).

Aside from the apparent self-segregation in the cafeteria, the overall social distance that exists between white and black students on the campus studied in this paper has been unclear. This research was undertaken to provide at least a partial answer to this query. We sought to determine 1) the degree of social distance that white students seek to maintain from their black classmates, 2) the students' perceptions of race relations on campus, 3) the actual interracial interaction among the students, and 4) the factors that contribute to the level of social distance, perceptions of race relations, and interracial interaction.

Data and Measurement

Data were collected from students through two sets of surveys at a comprehensive university in northern New Jersey in 2000. The University has approximately 10,000 students and is located in a suburban area near New York City. The first set of surveys was administered during the spring of 2000 in Social Problems and Principles of Sociology classes containing students from a variety of majors. Respondents were told that the survey was for a culture research project and their participation was voluntary. They were also told that the questionnaire was anonymous. About 97 percent of the sampled students fully completed their surveys.

Since this research specifically focused on the degree of social distance white students desire from black students, only 90 of the 127 respondents, those who identified themselves as Caucasians, were included in the data analysis. Among the selected students, 42.2% are males and 57.8% are females, and their average age is 21. The distribution among years in school are similar to those of the university students' population, 26.7% freshmen, 21.1% sophomores, 22.2% juniors, 20.0% seniors, and 10.0% graduate students. The average family income is approximately $65,000, which is typical in the Northeast coastal area but higher than the national average.

Students completing the survey were asked to provide demographic information and to respond to a question about their attitude towards the importance of understanding other cultures. In addition, five queries were used to measure white students' social distance from black students. These five items are:

1. Are you willing to sit next to a black student in a classroom?
2. Are you willing to sit next to a black student in the cafeteria?
3. Are you willing to go to a school dance with a black student?
4. Are you willing to be roommates with a black student?
5. Are you willing to date a black student on campus?

The development of the five levels of social distance measurement was based on the Bogardus social distance scale, which is a well-developed and frequently used technique for determining the willingness of people to participate in social relations with other people. The clear differences of intensity suggest a structure among the items (Babbie, 2000).

The second set of surveys was distributed during the fall of 2000 in a wide range of General Education and Sociology courses. We utilized only the 152 surveys filled out by white students for this subsample. Part of the survey consisted of the Bogardus-type questions utilized in the first survey about the white students' willingness to interact with their black classmates. Other questions asked respondents to note how many actual interactions (friendships and dating) they had with black and Hispanic persons.

The demographic makeup of the respondents to the second set of surveys was similar to those who responded to the first set. This time, however, we distinguished between residential and commuter students. Among the 152 respondents, 32.2% resided on campus and 67.8% commuted to school.

The percentage of minority residential students is rather dramatically higher than their proportion of the overall student body. As indicated in Table 2, while African Americans comprise approximately 10.8% of the entire student body, they make up 23.1% of the resident student population. The percentage of Hispanic and Asian students who live on campus are similar to their proportions in the overall student body (Hispanics = 13.6% of the entire student body and 11.5% of those who live on campus; and Asian students = 3.7% of the overall population and 3.5% of the on campus residents). In all then, over 38% of the residential undergraduates are students of color.

Table 1: Racial/Ethnic Composition of Overall Student Body

	Variables	
Race/Ethnicity	*Percentage and (Number of Students)*	*Percentage Living on Campus (Number of Students)*
Black	10.8 (1,070)	23.1 (495)
Asian American	3.5 (352)	3.5 (76)
Hispanic	12.3 (1,226)	11.4 (245)
Native American	0.2 (19)	0.1 (3)
White	69.1 (6,870)	56.7 (1,217)
Other	4.1 (408)	5.2 (111)
Total	100 (9,945)	21.6 (2,147)

Data Analysis

Simple frequency percentages were used to indicate the level of social distance and to determine the degree to which the white students are willing to associate with black students in different settings, from sitting next to them in class to dating. After considering each level of white students' willingness to associate with black students, we recoded the five levels of measurements into a comprehensive one to determine the overall willingness of the white students to associate with black students. Specifically, if a respondent marked "Yes" to answer all five questions, this respondent would have an overall value of 1. If a respondent marked "No" to answer one or more or five of the questions, this respondent would have an overall value of 3. Similarly, if a respondent checked "Uncertain" to answer one or more of the five questions, this respondent would have an overall value of 2. The last line of Table 1 reveals the results of this recoding.

We ran cross-tabulation analyses to determine if there is a relationship between 1) gender, 2) college status, 3) family income, and 4) belief in the importance of understanding other cultures and the white students' overall social distance from black students. In order to simplify the presentation of the findings, we recoded the respondents college status, family income and the variable "belief in the importance of understanding other cultures" into three categories. In recoding family income, we put those respondents whose last year's annual income was up to $30,000 in the low income group, those between $30,001 and $70,000 in the middle income group, and those more than $70,000 in the high income group. Table 3 reveals the results of this analysis.

For the second set of surveys, we used chi-square tests to determine if there is a significant difference between the residential and commuter students' perceptions of race relations on campus and their experiences with interracial friendships and romantic relationships.

Results

Table 2 presents the percentages of the white students' willingness to associate with black students on campus in different circumstances. It appears that the five questions utilized to measure social distance do form a good measurement scale. While all the white students are willing to sit next to a black student in a classroom, only 94.4% are willing to sit next to a black student in the cafeteria. This willingness continues to decrease when the association gets closer. While 76.7% are willing to be roommates of black students, 68.9% are willing to go school dance with a black student, and only 48.9% are willing to date a black student on campus.

When these five levels of measurement are combined, only 44.4% of the white students would have no problem in associating with black students in all five of the occasions. Except for sitting next to a black student in a classroom, 23.3% of the white students are uncertain whether they would be willing to associate with black students in at least one of the settings, and 32.2% are not willing to associate with black students in at least one of the proposed scenarios.

Table 3 gives white students' responses as to the level of social distance they desire from their black classmates by gender, income, college status, and belief in the importance of understanding other cultures. Chi-square tests indicate that only belief in the importance of other cultures, is statistically related to social distance (p=0.000).

Table 2: White Students Social Distance Toward Black Students

Social distance variables	Percent of students who answered Yes Cases (%)	Percent of students who answered Uncertain Cases (%)	Percent of students who answered No Cases (%)	Total percent Cases (%)
Are you willing to sit next to a black student in a classroom?	90(100)			90(100)
Are you willing to sit next to a black student in a cafeteria?	85(94.4)	1(1.1)	4(4.4)	90(100)
Are you willing to be roommates with a black student?	69(76.7)	11(12.2)	10(11.1)	90(100)
Are you willing to go to a school dance with a black student?	62(68.9)	14(15.6)	14(15.6)	90(100)
Are you willing to data a black student on campus?	44(48.9)	20(22.2)	26(28.9)	90(100)
Five levels of measurements combined	40(44.4)	21(23.3)	29(32.3)	90(100)

Table 3: Relationships Between Gender, Family Income, Importance of Understanding Other Cultures and White Students Social Distance From Black Students

Variables	Social distance variables	Percent of students who answered Yes Cases (%)	Percent of students who answered Uncertain Cases (%)	Percent of students who answered No Cases (%)	Total percent Cases (%)
Gender	Males	14 (36.8)	9 (22.7)	15 (39.5)	38 (100)
	Females	26 (50.0)	12 (23.1)	14 (26.9)	52 (100)
Family Income	Low Income	1 (20.0)	0 (0)	4 (80.0)	5 (100)
	Middle income	15 (40.5)	10 (27.0)	12 (32.4)	37 (100)
	High income	19 (50.0)	10 (26.3)	9 (23.7)	38 (100)
College Status	Fresh/Sophomore	16 (37.2)	9 (20.9)	18 (41.9)	43 (100)
	Jun/Senior	17 (44.7)	11 (28.9)	10 (26.3)	38 (100)
	Graduate	7 (77.8)	1 (11.1)	1 (11.1)	9 (100)
Import. Of understand other cultures	Not important	1 (4.8)	5 (23.8)	15 (71.4)	21 (100)
	Important	17 (46.3)	12 (30.8)	10 (25.6)	39 (100)
	Very important	22 (73.3)	4 (13.3)	4 (13.3)	30 (100)

Over 73% of respondents who believe that understanding other cultures is "very important" would be willing to interact with black students in situations ranging from sitting next to them in a classroom to dating, while only 46.3% who believe understanding cultures is merely "important" would be willing to do so. Among those respondents who believe that understanding other cultures is "not important," only 4.8% would be willing to interact with black students in all these situations.

Table 4 shows residential and commuter students' attitudes concerning campus race relations. The students who live on campus are more likely to have either positive (good/very good) or negative (bad/very bad) opinions about the state of campus race relations than are commuters. Commuters are much less likely to say race relations are bad/very bad and much more likely to say that they are fair than are residential students.

Table 4: *Perceptions of Interracial Relations by College Living Arrangements*

	On-Campus	Off-Campus
Very Good/Good	57.4%	50.0%
Fair	27.7	45.1
Bad/Very Bad	14.9	4.9
N =	47	102

The influence of place of residence on interracial friendship formation begins to emerge when students are broken down into subgroups of on-campus and off-campus students. As seen in Table 5, white residential students made fewer cross-racial friends since coming to college than did white commuters. On average, the residential students made 1.42 interracial friends while the commuter students made 1.86 interracial friends during their time in college.

Table 5: *Interracial Relations by College Living Arrangements*

	Variables	Perc./Mean
a.	One or more interracial friends since coming to college	59.9% (91)
b.	Ever dated interracially?	35.5% (54)
c.	Average # interracial friends made by campus residents since coming to college	1.42
d.	Average # interracial friends made by commuters since coming to college	1.86
e.	Campus residents who have dated interracially	32.7% (16)
f.	Commuter students who have dated Interracially	41.7% (43)

As Table 5 shows, residential students are less likely to date interracially than commuter students. The white students who have dated across racial and ethnic lines most likely have dated either (in order of likelihood) Hispanic or Asian students, rather than black students. This is despite the fact that blacks make up a disproportional percentage of the overall dating pool among residential students.

Discussion

The results indicate a traditional, Bogardus-like decrease in the comfort levels of the white respondents to increased contact with their black classmates. As noted above, while all of the students would be willing to sit next to a black student in a classroom, only 44.4% of the white students indicated that they would have no problem associating with a black student on all five of the occasions studied in this research. This lack of willingness to be a roommate or date across races seems rather high in light of such recent headlines as "Teen-age Dating Shows Racial Barriers Falling" in USA Today and the quadrupling of interracial marriages over the last three decades (Peterson 1997). Importantly, though, the increase in black and white dating and intermarriage has been slower than for other racial combinations. The taboo concerning close interracial relationships between blacks and whites, while beginning to crumble, still remains somewhat intact (Korgen 1999).

This "tipping effect" seems to be due to the relatively high number of black students who reside on campus, compared to their percentage of the overall student population. Residents are much more likely to say that race relations are bad/very bad than are commuters. These results provide support for research that reveals the danger of increased racial tension and polarization accompanying increasing numbers of racial minorities and the need to engineer diversity on college campuses (Grodzins, 1957; Schelling, 1978; Glazer 1995, Korgen et al., 2003). Those seeking the benefits of diversity on campus must ensure they put as much (or more) effort into managing that diversity as they do in recruiting a multi-racial/ethnic student body (Daniel Tatum, 2000).

The influence on social distance of belief in the importance of understanding other cultures also gives colleges the most obvious clue in the effort to determine how to combat social distance and tension between races on college campuses today. Consistently and persuasively stressing the importance of learning about cultures outside of one's own can lead to reducing levels of social distance among college students and reduce the likelihood of the occurrence of a "tipping effect." Clearly, if one is interested in increasing interaction among college students of different races, the trend over the past two decades on campuses across the U.S. to emphasize a multicultural education and respect for diversity makes sense. At the same time, higher education officials must recognize when a "tipping effect" is likely to occur and take active steps to create an environment in which racial diversity is recognized by all students as positive, rather than threatening.

Conclusion

This research, at a university in Northern New Jersey, reveals that a substantial proportion of white students desire a relatively high level of social distance from their black classmates, except for casual contact. The variables influencing the levels of desired social distance are consistent with common sense notions. Most significantly, students who maintain that understanding other cultures is important have the lowest levels of social distance. This provides evidence that the emphasis on multiculturalism on many campuses across the United States today may be an effective means of decreasing social distance among students of different races.

Another important finding in this research is the sign of a "tipping effect" due to the relatively high percentage of black students among the on-campus population. White residential students are less likely to have interracial relationships and more likely to have a negative view of race relations on campus than are commuters. The fact that they are immersed among larger percentages of blacks than are commuter students actually makes them *less*, rather than more, likely to have interracial relationships. These findings point to the need for a greater understanding of the "tipping effect" and the development of means to overcome it on college campuses, today.

Discussion and Essay Questions:

1. It would seem that the higher the percentage of African Americans, the less social contact between the two "sides." Why might this be?

2. Is an increase in feelings of social distance between African Americans and whites a result of feelings of cultural difference or a sense of increased competition between the two groups?

3. Why is the social distance between African Americans and whites greater than the social distance between whites and other minority groups?

References

Agnew, C.R., Thompson, V.D. and Gaines, S.O., Jr. (2000). Incorporating Proximal and Distal Influences on Prejudice: Testing a General Model. *Personality and Social Psychology Bulletin*. Vol. 24, 4:403-418, April.

Allport, Gordon (1954). *The Nature of Prejudice*. Reading, MA: Addison Wesley.

Alger, J.R. (1998). "The Educational Values of Diversity." <u>Academe</u>. 20, January/February.

American Association of Universities and Colleges (1998) "American Commitments: Diversity, Democracy and Liberal Learning." http://www.aacu-edu.org/Initiatives/amercommit.html

Babbie, Earl (2000). The Practice of Social Research (9th Edition). Belmont, CA: Wadsworth.

Bandura, Albert. (Ed.). (1977). *Social Learning Theory*. Englewood Cliffs, NJ: Prentice-Hall, Inc.

Blalock, Hubert (1967) *Towards a Theory of Minority-Group Relations*. New York: Wiley

Bobo, Lawrence and Camille Zubrinsky. (1996). "Attitudes on Residential Integration: Perceived Status Differences, Mere In-group Preference, Or Racial Prejudice?"

Social Forces. 74 (3):883-900.

Bogardus, Emory (1946*).* *Introduction to Social Research.* Los Angeles: Suttonhouse Ltd.

----------- (1968). "Racial Distance Changes in the United States Duringthe Past Thirty Years." *Sociology and Social Research.* 43 (2):127-135.

Bowen, W. and Bok, D. (1998) *The Shape of the River: The Long Term Consequences of Considering Race in College and University Admissions.* Princeton, NJ: Princeton University Press.

Chang (1996) Racial Diversity in Higher Education: Does a racially Mixed Student Population Affect Educational Outcomes? Unpublished Doctoral Dissertation, University of California, Los Angeles.

Festinger, L., Schacter, S., and Back, K. (1950). *Social Pressure in Informal Groups: A Study of Human Factors in Housing.* New York: Harper and Brothers.

Glazer, Nathan (1995) "Black and White after Thirty Years." *Public Interest* 121(Fall):61-71.

Goldberg, Albert and Alan Kirschenbaum. (1989). "Black Newcomers to Israel: Contact Situations and Social Distance." *Sociology and Social Research.* 74 (1):52-57.

Grodzins, Morton (1957) "Metropolitan Segregation." *Scientific American* 197(24, October):33-41.

Gurin, Patricia. (1999). Expert Report of Patricia Gurin, in *The Compelling Need for Diversity in Higher Education. Gratz et al. V. Bollinger, et al.*, No. 97-75321 (E.D. Mich.) *Grutter et al. V. Bollinger, et al.* No. 97-75928 (E.D. Mich.). Ann Arbor: University of Michigan.
http://www.umich.edu/~urel/admissions/legal/expert/gurinapb.html

Guthrie, Victoria L., Patricia King, and Carolyn Palmer (2000). "Higher Education and Reducing Prejudice: Research on Cognitive Capabilities Underlying Tolerance." Diversity Digest. http://www.inform.umd.edu/diversity web/Digest/Sp.Sm00/tolerance.html#top

Hoxter, A.L. and D. Lester (1994). "Social Distance Evaluations in White and African American Students: Gender Differences in Prejudice." *Perceptual and Motor Skills* 79:1666.

Keene, Sam. (1986). *Faces of the Enemy.* San Francisco: Harper & Row.

Korgen, K. (1999). *From Black to Biracial.* Westport: Praeger.

Korgen, K. Mahon, J. and Wang, G. (2003) "Diversity on College Campuses Today: The Growing Need to Foster Campus Environments Capable of Countering a Possible 'Tipping Effect.'" *College Student Journal.* 37, March:16-26.

Liu, G. (1998). "Affirmative Action in Higher Education: The Diversity Rationale and the Compelling Interest Test." *Harvard Civil Rights-Civil Liberties Law Review.* 33:381-442.

Massey, D.S. and Denton, N. A. (1993). *American Apartheid: Segregation and the Making of the Underclass.* Cambridge: Harvard University Press.

McAllister, Ian and Rhonda Moore. (1991). "Social Distance Among Australian Ethnic Groups." *Sociology and Social Research.* 75 (2):95 - 100.

Netting, Nancy. (1991). "Chinese Aloofness from Other Groups: Social Distance Data from a City in British Columbia." *Sociology and Social Research.* 75 (2):101-104.

Nix, Jerry Vincent (1993). "Assessing the Existence of Social Distance and Factors that Affect Its Magnitude at a Southern University." http://www.sspp.net/archive/papers/nix.htm

Owen, Carolyn, Howard Eisner, and Thomas McFaul (1977). "A Half-Century of Social Distance Research: National Replication of the Bogardus Studies." *Sociology and Social Research.* 66 (1):80-98.

Ray, J.J.and Lovejoy, F.H. (1986). "The Generality of Racial Prejudice." *Journal of Social Psychology*, 126:563-564.

Schelling, Thomas (1978) *Micromotives and Macrobehavior.* New York: Norton

Sigelman, L., Bledsoe, T., Welch, S. and Combs, M.W. (1996). *Making Contact? Black-White Social Interaction in an Urban Setting. American Journal of Sociology.* 101:1306-1032.

Southern Poverty Law Center (2000) "Hate Goes to School." *Intelligence Report.* Spring.

Tatum, Beverley Daniel (2000). "The ABC Approach to Creating Climates of Engagement on Diverse Campuses." *Liberal Education, 86 (4)*, 22-29.

Vela-McConnell, J. (1999). *Who is My Neighbor?: Social Affinity in a Modern World.* Albany, NY: State University of New York Press.

Verkuyten, M. and Kinket, B. (2000). "Social Distances in a Multi-Ethnic Society: The Ethnic Hierarchy among Dutch Preadolescents." *Social Psychology Quarterly.* Vol. 63, 1:75-85, March.

Wilson, T.C. (1985). "Urbanism and Tolerance: A Test of Some Hypotheses Drawn from Wirth and Stouffer." *American Sociological Review.* 50:117-123.

Wirth, L. (1938). "Urbanism As a Way of Life." *American Journal of Sociology.* 44:1-24.

IV

Marginality and Policy

Chapter 12

EXPLORING BLACK IDENTITY VIA MARGINALITY THEORY

Jeffrey R. Breese and G. Kathleen Grant

INTRODUCTION

While academic integration offers distinct benefits, it sometimes produces difficult, even painful encounters for students brought together from different backgrounds. Frequently college and university officials do not prepare for issues involving racial bigotry (King and Ford, 2003). When students perceive an environment as unwelcoming because of race, their desire to continue attending college diminishes and minority students are more likely then White students to report experiencing disrespect (Zea et al., 1997). Through a discussion of the concept of marginality, this paper examines issues of black identity formation and academic achievement for the African-American student population.

LITERATURE REVIEW

Marginality theory offers several advantages to studying human behavior. First, this theory stresses the sociological components of behavior. The concepts investigated in this study are *social* products. Reactions to marginality are not formed in a vacuum. They evolve over time as the individual interacts with significant social groups, such as family, peers, and social institutions. Second, this theory offers a life course perspective on behavior. Marginality theory assumes that human development is a lifelong process. As the individual encounters new experiences throughout the life course, the opportunity for change and adaptation constantly presents itself. Development does not cease at the end of childhood or adolescence, but rather occurs each time that an individual experiences a significant change in the life course. College is only one major change; career patterns, marriage, parenthood, and retirement all offer substantial opportunities for personal development. Techniques and strategies developed from earlier experiences may or may not be relevant. Marginality theory offers an additional approach to investigating success or failure in major life transitions.

The crux of this investigation is the individual's reaction to the conditions of marginality and its ramifications for successful adaption and identity development (Fordham and Ogbu 1986). This assumes that the individual who is subjected to the conditions of marginality will develop a reaction to these conditions and that, in turn, this reaction can affect one's emerging sense of identity. The model suggests that factors within the various components serve to engender a reaction to marginality. The model proposes that there is a range of reactions to and interpretations of marginality. Each of these reactions has a differential effect on the behavior of the individual. Without this range, the theory could not exist. When first conceptualized for study, the marginal situation was theorized as producing *a* personality type (Park 1928; Stonequist 1935). However, recent research reveals that this "type" is only one of several reactions possible when faced with the conditions of marginality (Rimstead 1995).

Based on standing literature, it is conceivable to identify at least six distinct reactions that could be expected from individuals in a marginal situation and used as a starting point for investigation:

1. **Affected** "Increased sensitiveness, self-consciousness, and race-consciousness, an indefinable *malaise*, inferiority and various compensatory mechanisms, are common traits in the marginal person" (Stonequist 1935, p. 6). This is the original type of reaction that directly affects personality and behavior toward others. Symptoms would include displays of internal unresolved conflict, such as delinquency, crime, mental instability, or suicide.

2. **Emulative** "To abolish marginality by psychic surgery" (Riesman, 1951, p. 122). The condition of marginality is so intolerable that people can take the stance of denial and "for them, integration is an unquestioned ideal . . ." (Riesman 1951, p. 125). Emulation and identification with the dominant culture is sought at almost any cost, including rejection of the original culture. One extreme that has been suggested is that of "passing."

3. **Defiant** "People who feel uncomfortable in the world . . . find comfort in explaining their discomfort by attributing it to an acceptable cause" (Riesman 1951, p. 114). These individuals become totally absorbed with blaming the system. Symptoms would be open hostility, acts of defiance, or angry withdrawal. The inability to resolve the situation hinders positive action for individual gains. Channelled, it can be a force for collect

4. **Emissarial** Using marginality as a social function, the marginal person sees him/herself as an emissary, an interpreter, or a go-between for both cultures. Riesman (1951) describes this reaction as carving out a specific social role and exploiting marginality for its usefulness. This type of reaction is closest to Simmel's original concept. It has a positive aspect in that the marginality of the individual is appreciated for the special skills and knowledge that the "stranger" can bring to another culture. Both cultures can use the reciprocal information to grow and avoid stagnation. This reaction is dependent on mutual respect and appreciation.

5. **Withdrawn** Complete rejection of the marginal situation can lead to total withdrawal, including moving to another country. It can also involve a retreat into the original culture and refusal to participate in activities that are not part of the sub-culture (Riesman 1951). Louis Farrakhan has voiced this position quite adamantly.

6. **Balanced** Goldberg (1941) suggests another reaction that stems from the amount of time that the sub-culture has existed within the dominant culture. Conditioned since birth to the existence of both cultures, shared experiences of dealing with both cultures during development, and presence of role models that ease the task of balancing the demands of the two cultures, create a marginal person who exists in a marginal *culture*. "For the individual concerned, however we must remember that it is not marginal, but normal" (p. 57). The conditions of marginality are not transient, but permanent, and we are likely to find a stable and normal person participating in an integrated manner in the activities of a "unitary" culture. It is implied that this person does not perceive a dichotomy, but a normal situation that relies on institutional and associational proximity.

The mechanism of differentiation identified by this study is racism. Racism, in turn, affects the social conditions as discussed by Germani (1980). The economic-social includes the availability and accessibility of funds for college. The political-social is distinguished by the ability of African-American college students to affect change with regard to institutional practices and procedures. Demographics apply to the numerical size of the minority group and its ability to create cohesion as a collective voice within the institution. In addition, sheer size can also determine the amount of consideration given to a particular minority group's needs and concerns.

Cultural dimensions are represented in this study by behavioral patterns and beliefs that are unique to African-American culture. The concern of this aspect is the amount of disparity between the African-American culture and the Anglo-American culture with special regard for the customs and norms of academic life (Grant and Breese 1997).

Key institutional factors impact this study, including: Financial aid, activities that promote cohesion, academic support services, and procedural processes. Individual factors that are identified by this study as affecting successful college performance include: Experiences with racism, exposure to the dominant culture, social support, participation in school activities, and individual attention. Standing literature addressing Black students at predominantly white institutions demonstrates that these students do not fare as well as White students in persistence rates, academic achievement, postgraduate study, and overall psychosocial adjustments (Gossett, Cuyjet and Cockriel, 1998).

The reaction to marginality emerges from the interaction of all of these factors. Marginality theory offers a concatenated approach since it is not limited to one context, but offers the opportunity to explore this concept over multiple levels of analysis and situations that would provide a chain of support for its assertions (Gossett, Cuyjet and Cockriel, 1996).

Marginality theory suggests that developmental processes as they pertain to the socialization of the individual are not the same for all members of a society. Race, in particular, continues to be a matter of significant importance in everyday life. Nonetheless, the way in which one identifies themselves racially is subjective and negotiable, and racial identity is constructed over time (Healey and O'Brien, 2004). Particularly relevant to this study is a process identified first by Cross (1971) and later researched by Parham and Helms (1985) that is unique for African-American members of American society. Incorporated into the African-American experience of socialization is the process of *nigrescense*, "the process of developing a Black identity" vis-a-vis an Anglo-American culture. Successful negotiation of the stages of this process has implications for self-esteem and academic functioning. Sedlacek (1987) explains the task of this process as follows: "In addition to the usual school pressures, a Black student must typically handle cultural biases and learn how to bridge his or her Black culture with the prevailing one at the White university" (p. 485). In contrast, development of self-concept for Anglo-Americans does not include contending with the alienating effects of racism.

Cross (1971) postulates five stages of "Negro-to-Black Conversion." The first stage (Pre-Encounter) is characterized by naivete, and individuals at this stage are programmed to have faith in the Protestant ethic. There is extreme dependency on Anglo-American leadership "and the assimilation-integration paradigm is thought to be the *only* model for cohesive race relations" (Cross 1971, p. 16). The second stage (Encounter) involves some experience or event that leads to questioning the basic assumptions of the pre-encounter stage that often generates feelings of guilt and increasing anger. The third stage (Immersion-Emersion) entails significant, if not total emersion, in the black world. "There occurs a turning inward and a withdrawal from everything perceived as being or representing the white world" (Cross 1971, p. 19). The fourth stage (Internalization) has several alternatives—disappointment and rejection, continued fixation at stage three, or internalization; whichever direction the person takes, it results in a different world view from stage one. "Generally, the self-concept modifications do make the person receptive to meaningful change in his world view" (Cross 1971, p. 22). Stage five (Internalization-Commitment) differs from stage four in that the person develops a long-term commitment and deep sense of black communalism. It is free of the anger, insecurity, and self-consciousness of earlier stages. Consequently, "attitudes toward white people become less hostile, or at least realistically contained" (Cross 1971, p. 23).

Parham and Helms (1985) have found validity for Cross' (1971) model of developing black identity:

> The data indicate that pre-encounter and immersion attitudes tend to be associated with low self-esteem. Encounter attitudes were associated with positive self-esteem, and, although not significantly related, internalization attitudes were positively associated with self-esteem. . . . Generalization that Blacks have either positive or negative self-concept seem outdated because they fail to account for any individual differences concerning attitudes or racial identity. That is, self-concept may be governed by the way the student handles the conditions of the Black experience (p. 145).

Sedlacek (1987) offers further support for this developmental task of African-Americans. A "Black who 'chooses' to confront all examples of racism may be effective in many ways, but he or she is unlikely to remain in school or get high grades" (Sedlacek 1987, p. 486). This study also offers validity for effective management of racism as a key indicator of successful college participation.

Marginality theory suggests that failure to successfully participate and complete a college program is *not* the result of inadequate skills, abilities, or values per se, but rather acquisition of these are directly affected by aversive reactions to the social conditions of the institution. Aversive reactions may well be warranted; however, the individual may not be aware of how these reactions have impacted his or her willingness to acquire the necessary skills or inhibited the knowledge of what is even needed to succeed in the social institution.

Investigation of this process of developing a black identity is important to this study for two reasons. Incorporation of marginality theory in this exploration infuses the concept of self-identity with a sociological dimension. Much of the research on racial identity focuses on the individual's reaction to the social structure without stipulating how the social structure is *perceived* by the individual and how this perception might interact with the process of racial identity. Are there distinct elements of the social system (in this case, the college or university) that give a clear indication of openness to the minority student, or conversely, a closed system that assumes homogeneity of the student population that ignores or discounts racial differences and needs? This does not refer to overt displays of discrimination per se, but rather subtle messages that convey institutional values and norms that neglect or denigrate important differences of groups and individuals who might not share these sentiments. What do these messages look like today? In other words, does discrimination manifest itself in the university system and *how* does it do this? How strong are these messages and how do these messages affect college performance? Do these messages interact with the development of racial identity? Can entry into the college system serve as the "crisis" or event that can trigger the racial identity process?

The second reason for the centrality of this process of developing a black identity is that previous research on the development of black identity has identified distinct, observable behaviors for each of the stages that can serve as a guide and comparison for this study. Investigation of the process of developing an African-American identity also raises the question of how the present social climate impacts this process. How valid is this model, formulated in the 1970s when strong, overt social forces encouraged black identity and black power, for present-day conditions? How supportive is the present social climate for stimulating this process? How relevant is this process for college performance? How significant is the interaction of this process with other factors identified as necessary and sufficient for successful college participation? Sedlacek (1987) has retained only one aspect of this process—how the minority individual handles racism, whereas Parham and Helms (1985) still utilize the full model in counseling minority individuals.

METHODS

As researchers, we both come into this study with the consciousness of being White middle-class sociologists, charged with instructing students in the areas of Minority relations and social inequality. We are both cognizant of the current racial climate in academia and are attempting to introduce both our students and colleagues to the heterogeneity of experience found among contemporary African-American students. The central educational implication to this approach is a strong awareness of white spokespeople for minority conditions (Bettis 1996; Tatum 1994). We agree with Ballantine (1995), who notes that "some of the ideals sociologists support are most successfully achieved through participatory research and application of knowledge such as challenging inequality" (219).

The data in this study was obtained by interviewing respondents using a pre-set series of questions, the interview guide. The interview guide was constructed with three goals in mind. First, the chronological order of the interview was meant to reflect the process of deciding, entering, and sustaining participation in a college program. The only exception was the first section. The section titled "Decision to Attend College" was used before, rather than after, childhood experiences in order to focus the respondent on the topic. Consequently, the order of the topics was as follows:

> Demographics
> Decision to Attend College
> Childhood
> High School Experiences
> Entering College
> Attending College
> Stay or Leave
> Goals
> Skills
> Problems and Coping
> Racism
> Self-Concept

    The second goal was to include questions that were meant to tap both institutional factors and individual factors within each topic. Each topic served as "sensitizing categories," which were the basis of data analysis. The goal was to maintain some organization of the data as it was gathered. The average time for the focused interview was two hours. Although the interview guide contained formal structure, it still allowed ample opportunities for probing and open-ended responses.

    Although the focused interview was the primary investigative tool, the study also incorporated two quantitative measures that have been used in the past to objectively assess the subjective experience of marginality and educational variables associated with positive educational outcomes. The first scale is a short version of the Racial Identity Attitude Scale (RIAS) created by Parham and Helms (1981), which is based on Cross' (1971) stage theory of Black Conversion. The RIAS was developed to provide empirical evidence that African-Americans proceed through stages in developing an African-American identity. A particular score on the RIAS is meant to identify the stage of development that an individual presently occupies. The second scale is Sedlacek's Noncognitive Questionnaire (NCQ). The NCQ was developed to ascertain the strength of non-cognitive variables on a student's academic performance. This instrument has a demonstrated adequate reliability and construct validity (Tracey and Sedlacek 1987, 1989). This questionnaire has also been shown to have good predictive validity for African-American student sub-samples. It is one of the most widely documented instruments, from 1976 to the present, on the substantive issues of this study. Inclusion of this questionnaire provides a barometer of individuals who participate in the focused qualitative interviews and presents an objective portrait of the student as underlying dimensions are explored.

The literature review provided a basis for the initial sample. Schatzman and Strauss (1973) refer to this approach as "selective sampling." A calculated decision to sample specific types of respondents is made according to a preconceived, but reasonable, set of dimensions (such as time, space, identity) that are worked out in advance. This approach is similar to that identified by Patton (2002) as purposeful sampling. Sampling procedures were also modified by procedures from grounded theory developed by Glaser and Strauss (1965, 1967). This procedure is called "theoretical sampling." Theoretical sampling dictates that the researcher constantly scrutinize data as it is collected in order to identify areas that have not been covered in the initial phase of sample selection (Patton, 2002). Restricting the sample to the selection of African-Americans is appropriate since this study examines temporal conditions of marginality, performance comparisons within the minority group, and gender comparisons *specific to* the experiential world of the minority group under investigation.

Given the theoretical objectives of this study, the selection of students from an urban, public university seems best suited to this investigation. In contrast, private and segregated schools offer only extreme cases that would not serve the objective of this study, which is to generate principles under normative conditions of marginality. The norm for the majority of African-American students is to attend a state-supported school in an urban setting close to home. In the mid 1980s, 16 percent of African-American students who attend college select a predominant African-American school (Thomas and Hill 1987). By 1999, the percentage was at 14.6%. This figure was derived by comparing total enrollment of African American students at all institutions to those at historically black colleges and universities (National Center for Education Statistics, 2003). The elite schools present financial and competitive academic standards that may offer insurmountable barriers to admission for the "average" African-American or Anglo-American student.

Two other considerations guided the sampling. The decision was made to only include full-time students (12 credits or more), since part-time students often have even more factors that impinge on college achievement and this would make a completely different study that might be useful in comparison to this study. In addition, only "traditional" students were included in this study. Traditional is defined as ages 18 to 23. There is a substantial body of literature (Breese and O'Toole 1995; Gigliotti and Huff 1995) that emphasizes that non-traditional students, again, have factors that are not relevant to the student who has made the transition to college directly from high school or a short time thereafter. The intent was to tighten the scope of this study in order to avoid extraneous factors that might confound the findings of this study.

The first respondents were initially solicited by a flyer that explained the intent of the study and requested volunteer participation. Faculty members were asked to distribute these letters to likely candidates in their introductory classes. Since only six students responded to this request, who, in turn provided two referrals, the decision was made to offer $10.00 for participating and a second flyer was distributed. This generated five volunteers, who also provided three referrals. A third approach was used to obtain participants. The flyers were then distributed at a central gathering point in the student union where African-Americans habitually congregate. This led to three additional participants.

Twenty-three students from a Midwest state university volunteered to be interviewed for this study. The mean age of this sample was 20. The average grade point average for the sample was 2.35. The average number of college credits taken during the interview semester was 12.9.

Our sample reflects the disproportionate number of female students who attend college as opposed to male students. Eight males were interviewed, as opposed to fifteen females. The sample was evenly divided between those students who worked and those who did not.

This university is very much in line with the overall percent of African-American students statewide (10 percent). The other two major universities in the same general area report 6.8 percent and 17.5 percent of the student population being African-American, with the higher percent located in a major metropolitan area.

A more telling portrait of the composition of the African-American undergraduate students (2063) at the university where this study was done illustrates the pattern of more females initially attending college and the rapid attrition of male students over the course of a college program.

FINDINGS

Reactions to Marginality

The types of reactions to marginality served as the core category, with each type as a sub-category. As Strauss and Corbin (1990) have suggested, each sub-category, or particular type, developed within the causal conditions that gave rise to it and the strategies expressed by each respondent that are used to handle, manage, and respond to the particular context of college. Institutional conditions and responses serve as intervening conditions that bear upon these strategies. Institutional factors can either facilitate or constrain strategies. However, this study demonstrates that not all individuals subjected to these conditions will react in the same way. In addition, even individuals expressing the same type of reaction to marginality will not experience the same consequences since each situation is modified by personal interpretation. Stonequist (1935) states that "the intensity of the inner conflict varies with the situation itself, the individual experience with this situation, and perhaps certain inherited traits" (p. 10).

Affected

Of the twenty-three respondents, no one demonstrated the characteristics of an Affected type. This is not to suggest that it does not exist, but that this reaction lies outside the scope of this study. A person exhibiting conflict so extreme as to induce mental instability, *malaise*, or suicidal tendencies, as described by the literature, could not cope with the demands of academic endeavors. College attendance is a voluntary act, rather than a mandatory one.

Emulative

The same can be said for the second category, Emulative. Not one respondent in this study exhibited the required characteristics of complete denial of own race, total identification with the dominant culture, or the desire "to pass" as Anglo-American. Again, college participation is filled with daily reminders for the African-American that he/she is different and will be treated differently even if the student would chose otherwise. Not one respondent expressed the desire to be Anglo-American. Each respondent was engaged in a personal struggle to cope with racism in order to pursue personal ambitions and dreams.

Defiant

Four respondents demonstrated characteristics suitable for category three, Defiant. Although this category describes an emotional reaction to marginality as defiant, angry, and challenging, it allows leeway for several behavioral responses. Case 5, on the one hand, demonstrates the kind of responses that do not serve the student well. This respondent describes herself as a loner, whose defiance of the system manifests itself in dropping any class that presents a challenge, becoming ill when the situation is threatening, and concentrating on personal problems (financial, male friends), rather than focusing on academics. The consequence of this reaction is that this respondent, although not in academic jeopardy, is not progressing through the system. She is "taking classes," but not advancing toward graduation.

Case 3, on the other hand, demonstrates how anger and defiance can be effectively channeled. The respondent has been described as "Little Malcom" by friends who have witnessed her authentic challenges to the system. A realistic perspective of situations culminates in positive actions. During the time of the interview, this respondent was actively working with Minority Affairs in resolving a situation that definitely had racist implications.

Case 17 provides a prototype for the Defiant category. This respondent had not been encouraged by the system to even consider college as a career choice. High school tracked this student away from college, so no information about college was provided. No personal friends talked about or considered college. Consequently, easier classes and lack of emphasis on academics left this student ill-prepared for the educational challenges of college-level learning. College offers little encouragement. This respondent does not understand why particular classes were advised, has found tutors to be of no help, and claimed that instructors were not clear in their expectations about what is required to pass the courses.

Emissarial

Only one respondent exhibited the characteristics of the Emissarial category. Case 22 offers a unique glimpse at middle-class African-Americans. Growing up in a predominately Anglo-American neighborhood (80 percent) and attending predominately Anglo-American schools (95 percent), this respondent is well versed in the norms of achievement in the dominant culture. These norms are used to the respondent's advantage and, although only a freshman, this individual has experienced a successful transition to college life. The ability to make friends of all races, to seek help when needed, and to maintain a strong support system all contribute to successful academic progression. Even though there have been several painful racist incidents in life before college, this student is very comfortable with Anglo-Americans (her best friend is Anglo-American). This respondent came to a large university alone and had to develop new friends for support.

Withdrawn

One case, Case 20, represents the category of Withdrawn. A strong indication of this respondent's reaction was the fact that this was the hardest interview to conduct. Although not a deliberate rejection of the dominant culture, the withdrawal from the college environment was very apparent. This respondent was very lethargic and gave few in-depth responses, even with probing. Her withdrawal took the form of not exploring sources of help, such as tutors, peer counselors, or Minority Affairs. She does not attend or participate in university activities and has made few friends at the university to support her academic efforts. The only tie to school is a relative who is attending the same college, and there is little interaction with this person. College is not a comfortable place for this respondent. The decision to attend college was made only because "there was nothing else to do."

Balanced

Nine cases exhibit the characteristics of the Balanced category. Consistently, there is a *lack* of sensitiveness, negative self-consciousness, rejection of race, anger, discomfort, or withdrawal that would suggest an internal struggle with the college environment. The most striking similarity among these respondents is that in all cases, with the exception of Case 19, either both parents or the mother hold at least a bachelor's degree and, in many cases, an advanced degree. Although his parents have had no college, Case 19 has two brothers presently enrolled in universities. The strength of these role models is that each respondent has witnessed an individual who has successfully negotiated the task of balancing the demands of two cultures.

Each respondent perceives the interface of the two cultures as a normal situation that relies on institutional and associational proximity. The key factor of the Balanced category is an awareness of two cultures and the ability to negotiate comfortably in both. There has been enough exposure to the dominant culture to learn the norms that are expected for success. It is the conscious awareness that the same norms, rules, and behavior do not apply in each culture. "I can live on both sides of the track" (Case 11). "My friends are neither black or white. If you hear me say they are my black friends or my white friends, then they are not really close friends; they are more of an acquaintance" (Case 18).

Most important, each respondent is focused on personal achievement and is absorbed with using the system for personal advancement, rather than distracted by racial incidents. There is a clear understanding of the system that does not compromise a commitment to racial identity:

> Don't get me wrong because I love being black. I wouldn't trade or anything. I just think that it is not a top focus of mine. I am trying to get some money. Whether it is white money, black money, I mean I want some green money (Case 8).

Paradoxical

Several respondents did not match the characteristics of the types of reactions to marginality established by the literature review. As a result, we conceptualized two new categories (Paradoxical and Uninvolved). These two types reinforce the idea that most (if not all) marginal individuals experience pressures from their own groups, but react differently to those pressures (Fordham and Ogbu 1986). The first new category, Paradoxical, indicates that these respondents find themselves wanting to use the system to become successful, but, at the same time, they are insulated from the dominant culture. They lack the understanding or insight about race relations that the Emissarial or Balanced types possess. In addition, these respondents feel deliberate pressure from their minority group to reject the norms and standards of the dominant group. The paradox is that they do not want to alienate their own culture, yet they desire the rewards that can be obtained by participation in the dominant culture.

Two cases provide evidence for this category. These cases share three factors that are significant for this category. First, neither parent of each respondent has attended college. The world of the university is foreign territory for them. Second, neither respondent has had a close Anglo-American friend, or anyone who could provide some understanding of the Anglo-American perspective. Their information about Anglo-Americans is primarily from media and casual interaction with Anglo-Americans. Finally, it is very significant that both respondents come from Cleveland. Several respondents from the study explained that even the African-Americans have cliques at the university. The contingency from Cleveland form one clique. The second clique are those African-Americans from the local city where the university is located. African-American students from all other areas are a third clique, although much less organized. The Cleveland clique has been characterized in less-than-favorable terms by several of the respondents. They have kept their subculture intact on campus, but often discriminate against other *African-Americans*. This can be a very insulated group. Previous research has demonstrated that it is common to have different groups in the school setting in contention over an achievement-oriented mindset (Ogbu 1978).

Uninvolved

A second new category emerged from this study. Six cases can be characterized as Uninvolved. These cases reflect a reaction to marginality that does not consider racial issues. This is not meant to indicate a denial of racial tensions and problems, but rather a personal philosophy that gives little thought to how race relations affect them personally. The major characteristics of this category is the *lack* of anger, insight, involvement, or concern for racial issues. With the exception of one case (Case 21), these respondents attended predominately African-American high schools. With the exception of one case (Case 12), the parents of these respondents have two years or less of college. With the exception of one case (Case 21), none of these respondents have had a personal racial experience. None of these respondents have actively confronted racial issues. All of these respondents come from the Cleveland area. As mentioned above, the Cleveland contingency offers social support and an insulated sub-culture to which a student can retreat after attending classes. However, these respondents did not provide evidence of the Paradoxical type. There is neither defiance or questioning about race relations nor undue pressure to reject the social system.

The data from this study offer evidence to substantiate the existence of a variety of constructed meanings of marginality as it applies to the formation of black identity for these students. These meanings can affect an individual's successful participation in collegiate endeavors. Some reactions to marginality, such as Withdrawn, have only a detrimental effect on college participation; whereas, other reactions to marginality, such as Emissarial, serve as a beneficial impetus to college participation. Finally, there are reactions to marginality (Defiant, Balanced, Paradoxical, Uninvolved) that can be mitigated by other factors and social processes. Whatever the interpretation of marginality, several factors seem to affect the student's

Developing an African-American Identity

The literature review suggested that African-Americans go through a developmental process of forming a "black identity." These stages were Pre-Encounter, Encounter, Emersion-Immersion, Internalization, and Internalization-Commitment. Three methods were used to assess each respondent's level of development: Racial Identity Attitude Scale (RIAS), Item 3 on the Noncognitive Questionnaire (NCQ), and a subjective appraisal by the interviewer at the end of the interview. The subjective appraisal is based on characteristics gleaned from Cross (1978) and Parham and Helms (1985).

The RIAS was found to be of no significance in explaining the patterns found with the respondents in this study. All respondents had similar scores in at least two separate stages of development. This reflects the caution that Parham and Helms (1981) expressed when they suggested that only respondents who are at the peak of a particular stage would have scores that differentiate a unique stage in the individual's development. In addition, the two scores often occur in stages that are non-contiguous. If this is a true measure of development, a respondent could not be in two separate stages at the same time.

A second critique of this measure is that the Pre-Encounter stage is described as a position of possessing a "Euro-American" world view and reflecting an assimilation stance. Not one respondent manifested the characteristics of the Emulative reaction to marginality, which makes a similar assumption. Consequently, if the primary assumption of this model is incorrect, the validity of this particular scale is questioned.

A third factor to consider is that this scale was developed in the 1970s. There was a *societal* sensitiveness and overt support for this model. Minority members were actively encouraged to develop attachments and loyalties to the particular groups with which they identified, such as Black Power, Brown Power, Gray Power. This mentality took the form of a social movement that was supported by media and educational institutions. As mentioned before, this is not the spirit of the 1990s. In the 1990s, any impetus for consciously developing an African-American identity is done by the individual and in isolation.

The second measurement, from the NCQ, provided little support for this factor as a critical element in academic success. Item 3 on the NCQ is labeled "Understands and deals with racism," and a high score on this variable is suppose to be a reflection of the following description:

> Understands the role of the "system" in his/her life and how it treats minority type persons, often unintentionally. Has developed a method of assessing the cultural/racial demands of the system and responding accordingly; assertively, if the gain is worth it, passively if the gain is small or the situation is ambiguous. Does not blame others for his/her problems or appear as a "Pollyanna" who does not see racism (Tracey and Sedlacek 1989, p. 173).

A low score would indicate the opposite of this description. The highest possible score is twenty-five; the lowest possible score is two. The problem is that if mid-range is interpreted as nine to seventeen, then seventeen of the twenty-three respondents, or 74 percent, fall in this range. In all fairness, this item is *not* used alone to determine the individual's chances of academic success. However, there should be some correlation between academic achievement and the respondents' scores on this particular item. Ironically, the one respondent designated as Withdrawn and not experiencing academic success (Case 20) had the second highest score on this item. The most successful respondent in regard to race relations (Case 22) only had a mid-range score of ten. The strength of this measure was that it did stress the importance of other factors in determining a student's chances of academic success.

Since the subjective assessment was initially based on the description of the stages described by Cross (1978) and Parham and Helms (1985), it suffered from the same shortcomings as the RIAS. As the study proceeded, a sixth stage was added to reflect those respondents who, although not involved in a conscious development of an African-American identity, were immersed in their own sub-culture. This group lacked the "startling event" that instigated the questioning, challenging, and conscious embracing of their own culture vis-a-vis the dominant Anglo-American culture. This type of Pre-Encounter stage was labeled Uninvolved. Twelve respondents, or 52 percent of the sample, comprised this new stage. Although this provided more correspondence between development and what the respondent was actually doing, it is still too general to be of use in quantitative or assessment studies.

At this point, the results serve to document that the development of an African-American identity does occur individually. The individual is not assisted by a societal atmosphere that encourages this type of personal evaluation and effort. The individual is dependent on personal devices to initiate development. The significant finding is that the most successful respondent has reached the stage of Internalization when measured by subjective evaluation. The findings from this study do not suggest that the concept of the development of an African-American identity should be abandoned. Rather, this concept needs to be refined to match the social factors that are currently present.

DISCUSSION

To fully understand and analyze the development of black identity, ideally, a longitudinal study that would follow students through their college careers is the optimal approach. Processes such as socialization to college, developing a "black identity," and a monitored case history of racial incidents and their effect on the individual would provide a more detailed data bank for investigation.

The concept of developing a "black identity" needs to be investigated further. This study alerts investigators to the importance of this concept and, hopefully, points out that existing measurements are either out-dated or inadequate. Turner (1988) states:

> The problem of how a given society supplies unique patterns of organization for personality, corresponding to the differentiating processes at work within that society, calls for precisely the skills of the analysis of social structure . . . it may also be the source of a major level or organization in individual personality. Because societies differentiate their populations differently, they may also provide different organizing frameworks for personality (pp. 166-67).

Introducing the construct and theoretical tradition of "marginality" is just one approach to the analysis of black identity development. This qualitative, exploratory research offers the framework for future studies on this important topic.

Discussion and Essay Questions:

1. Given what you know of marginality theory, based on what the author has written, do you believe that it is important to maintain historically Black colleges and universities?

2. How much of the relationship between African Americans and whites on college and university campuses is based on cultural differences as opposed to an overall feeling of status inequality between the two groups?

3. Do individual experiences allow the researcher to discard the concepts of African American and white when doing research today?

References

Ballantine, Jeanne. 1995. "'Teaching the Elephant to Dance': A Parable About the Scholarship of Learning." *Sociological Focus* 28: 207-221.

Bettis, Pamela J. 1996. "Urban Students, Liminality, and the Postindustrial Context." *Sociology of Education* 69: 105-125.

Breese, Jeffrey R. and Richard O'Toole. 1995. "Self Definition Among Women Students." *Journal of Research and Development in Education* 29: 27-41.

Cross, William E., Jr. 1971. "The Negro-to-Black Conversion Experience." *Black World* 20: 12-27.

Cross, William E., Jr. 1978. "The Thomas and Cross Models of Psychological Nigrescence: A Review." *The Journal of Black Psychology* 5: 13-31.

Fordham, Signithia and John Ogbu. 1986. "Black Students' School Success: Coping with the 'Burden of Acting White.'" *Urban Review* 18: 176-205.

Germani, G. 1980. *Marginality*. New Brunswick, NJ: Transaction Books.

Gigliotti, Richard J. and Heather Huff. 1995. "Role-Related Conflicts, Strains and Stresses of Older-Adult College Students." *Sociological Focus* 28: 329-342.

Giles-Gee, Helen F. 1989. "Increasing the Retention of Black Students: A Multimethod Approach." *Journal of College Student Development* 30: 196-200.

Glaser, Barney G., and Anselm L. Strauss. 1965. *Awareness of Dying*. Chicago: Aldine.

Glaser, Barney G., and Anselm L. Strauss. 1967. *The Discovery of Grounded Theory*. Chicago: Aldine.

Goldberg, M. N. 1941. "A Qualification of the Marginal Man Theory." *American Sociological Review* 6: 52-58.

Gossett, Barbara J., Michael J. Cuyjet, and Irv Cockreil. 1996. "African Americans' and Non-African Americans' Sense of Mattering and Marginality at Public, Predominantly White Institutions." *Equity and Excellence in Education* 29: 37-42.

Gossett, Barbara J., Michael J. Cuyjet, and Irv Cockreil. 1998. "African Americans' perception of Marginality in the Campus Culture." *The College Student Journal* 32: 22-32.

Grant, G. Kathleen and Breese, Jeffrey R. 1997. "Marginality Theory and The AfricanAmerican Student." *Sociology of Education* 70: 192-205.

Healey, Joseph F. and Eileen O'Brien. (eds). 2004. *Race, Ethnicity, and Gender* (2nd ed). Thousand Oaks, CA: Pine Forge.

King, Brenda T. and Ford, Thomas E. 2003. "African-American Student Perceptions of Predominately White Campuses: The Importance of Institutional Characteristics Relating to Racial Climate." Special Joint Issue of: *Journal of Applied Sociology* 20 and *Sociological Practice* 5: 65-76.

National Center for Education Statistics. 2003. Retrieved electronically.
http://nces.ed.gov.pubs/2002/digest2001/tables

Ogbu, John. 1978. *Minority Education and Caste: The American System in Crosscultural Perspective.* New York: Academic Press.

Parham, Thomas A., and Janet E. Helms. 1981. "The Influence of Black Students' Racial Identity Attitudes on Preferences for Counselor's Race." *Journal of Counseling Psychology* 28:250-57.

Parham, Thomas A. and Janet E. Helms. 1985. "Attitudes of Racial Identity and Self-Esteem of Black Students: An Exploratory Investigation." *Journal of College Student Personnel* 26: 143-147.

Park, Robert E. 1928. "Human Migration and the Marginal Man." *American Journal of Sociology* 33: 881-893.

Patton, Michael Q. 2002. *Qualitative Research and Evaluation Methods.* Thousand Oaks, CA: Sage.

Riesman, David. 1951. "Some Observations Concerning Marginality." *Phylon* 12: 113-127.

Rimstead, Roxanne. 1995. "Between Theories and Anti-Theories: Moving Toward Marginal Women's Subjectivities." *Women's Studies Quarterly* 23: 199-218.

Schatzman, L., and A. Strauss. 1973. *Field Research: Strategies for a Natural Sociology.* Englewood Cliffs, NJ: Prentice-Hall.

Sedlacek, William E. 1987. "Black Students on White Campuses: 20 Years of Research." *Journal of College Student Personnel* 28: 484-95.

Stonequist, Everett V. 1935. "The Problem of the Marginal Man." *American Journal of Sociology* 41: 1-12.

Strauss, Anselm and Juliet Corbin. 1990. *Basics of Qualitative Research.* Newbury Park, CA: Sage.

Tatum, Beverly Daniel. 1994. "Teaching White Students about Racism: The Search for White Allies and the Restoration of Hope." *Teachers College Record* 95: 462-476.

Thomas, Gail E., and Susan Hill. 1987. "Black Institutions in U.S. Higher Education: Present Roles, Contributions, Future Projections." *Journal of College Student Personnel* 28: 496-501.

Tracey, Terence J., and William E. Sedlacek. 1987. "Prediction of College Graduation Using Noncognitive Variables by Race." *Measurement and Evaluation in Counseling and Development* 19: 177-84.

Tracey, Terence J., and William E. Sedlacek. 1989. "Factor Structure of the Non-cognitive Questionnaire Revised Across Samples of Black and White college Students." *Educational and Psychological Measurement* 49: 637-48.

Turner, Jonathan H. 1988. *A Theory of Social Interaction*. Stanford, CA: Stanford University Press.

Zea, Maria Cecilia, Carol A. Reisen, Cheryl Beil, and Robert D. Caplan. 1997. "Predicting Intention to Remain in College Among Ethnic Minority and Nonminority Students." *The Journal of Social Psychology* 137: 149-160.

Chapter 13

Is Diversity Policy Inherently Contradictory? Exploring Racial and Class Year Differences in Perception of Campus Climate and Best Ways to Support A Racially Diverse Student Body

Frank M. Ridzi and Joshua G. McIntosh

Introduction

Few in today's college classroom would argue against university policies that support and encourage campus diversity. However, as is the case with most efforts to transform ideas to policy, the challenge is in the details. This paper uses an on-line survey of students in a large private northeastern university to address the possibility that supporting diversity means something significantly different for African American and white students. Divergent opinions on the current condition of campus diversity as well as on how best to support a racially diverse student body both support this possibility and pose the dilemma that a single diversity policy may be inadequate for meeting the present needs of both groups of students. As a result, future diversity policies should consider diversity's multiple meanings and may benefit from taking steps to either accommodate both simultaneously or develop a shared definition.

Increasing Racial and Ethnic Diversity and Concern Over Student Retention

Literature suggests that campus diversity policy is an issue of growing importance in America, both due to an increase in racial and ethnic tension and concerns over student retention. At colleges and universities across the country, student of color enrollment has risen substantially over the past decades. In 1976, 15% of enrolled college students were racial minorities, compared with 28% in 2000 (U.S. Department of Education, 2003). As colleges and universities have become more diverse in student population, the tensions surrounding diversity have also increased. In a survey of college deans, 62% cited diversity issues as the main cause of their campus conflict (Levine and Cureton, 1998). Racial tension on campus and the perception of discrimination can negatively effect students. Gregory (2000) reported that students of color in college and university environments encounter both institutional and overt racism. Perceptions of prejudice and discrimination have also, not surprisingly, been found to have a negative effect on both the academic and social experiences of African American students in particular (Cabrera, Nora, Terenzini, Pascarella, & Hagedorn, 1999).

Since racial minorities are grossly underrepresented in degree attainment for their enrollment percentage (U.S. Department of Education, 2003), a body of research literature has also accumulated addressing issues of campus climate for students of color. A majority of this research has examined what leads students of color to enroll in higher education and what eventually helps students persist to graduation. Analyses have generally concluded that finding a support structure and becoming involved in their institution increases their likelihood of persisting to graduation (Humphreys 1998, Tinto, 1993). Involvement in extracurricular activities, especially student organizations, and having relationships with faculty members have been found to have a positive influence on the grade point average of students of color as well (Davis and Murrell, 1993; Humphreys, 1998).

Despite campus tensions and concerns over retention, a diverse student population has been found to improve the learning environment for all students. Diverse student populations have positive effects on retention, overall college satisfaction, and college grade point averages (Chang, 1996). Similarly, multicultural classes have been found to increase students' cognitive development (Adams & Zhou-McGovern, 1994) and lead to a greater appreciation of culture in different societies (Institute for the Study of Change, 1991). These studies, however, have failed to distinguish between the perspectives of African American and white students in terms of their understandings of present circumstances and their assessments of the best ways to go about supporting a racially diverse student body in residence halls and on campus.

The research presented here uses survey data collected via an on-line survey of students in a large private northeastern university to explore the diversity-related experiences of African American and white students and to examine whether perspectives differ for first-year students as opposed to upper class students.

Data Collection and Analysis

This survey was distributed to 1,162 students who were enrolled as full-time students in campus residence halls at a large, private, northeastern US university during the Spring 2002 semester in the form of a web-based survey. Five thousand eight hundred and seventy four (n=5,874) student files were acquired from the Registrar's Office representing all University main campus residents registered for the Spring 2002 semester. Of these files, a sample of approximately 20% (n=1,162), stratified by class year, race, and gender was generated.

Electronic mailings were sent to the 1,162 students requesting that they select a web-link that was included in the body of the electronic mail (e-mail) message. Clicking on this link connected students to a university sponsored web page that briefly explained the survey and provided a web-linked button, which, upon clicking, connected students to a survey that was maintained on a university sponsored web server.

A total of 406 students responded for a response rate of 34.9%. Of these 406 completed surveys, 388 were from students living in main campus residence halls. The remaining 18 surveys were from students living either on an extended campus or off-campus. This is a result of the ever changing nature of the student records database, which was used to extrapolate the sample. Finally, of the 388 surveys, only the data from African American and white respondents was used in this analysis, leaving 330 respondents.

Results

The results are separated into three sections. The first provides the demographic information of the respondents. The second seeks to describe overall comfort levels on campus and to identify areas for potential diversity policy action by examining differences among African American and white students' involvement and comfort with campus and residence hall programming. The third examines the difficulty of responding to such differentials with a uniformed diversity policy by identifying lines of divergence between these two groups regarding how best to support diverse students in residence halls and on campus. Each of these sections provides a comparison of results for African American and white students by class year to reveal how

African American and white student experience and opinion changes with greater college experience and maturity.

Section 1: Demographic Information

Table 1
Race by Class Year

	First Year	Upper Class	Total
White	47.0% (n=155)	46.4% (n=153)	93.3% (n=308)
African American	3.3% (n=11)	3.3% (n=11)	6.7% (n=22)
Total	50.3% (n=166)	49.7% (n=164)	100% (n=330)

Despite stratifying the sample by race, the number of African American respondents was smaller than hoped for with 11 first years and 11 upper class African American students. As must be anticipated at a predominantly white university, the majority of respondents were white with 155 first year respondents and 153 upper class respondents. In total, close to 7% of the sample was African American as compared to 93% white. This, however, is reflective of the wider university composition in which African American students made up approximately 7% of the undergraduate population in the year of study. Nevertheless, the low n of African American respondents lead to small cell sizes and tests of statistical significance should be interpreted with caution.

Section 2: Overall Comfort on Campus and Student Involvement in Campus and Residence Hall Programming

Table 2
Overall Level of Comfort on Campus - Agreeing

	African American N	% Total	% 1st Year	% Upperclass	White N	% Total	% 1st Year	% Upperclass
The University is a comfortable and safe space for students of all races."	11	50.0**	45.5**	54.5	234	77.0**	81.6**	72.8

* p<.05, **p<.01 Tests of significance are Pearson chi-square for differences between African American and white.

Overall, African American students were less likely to agree that their university is a comfortable and safe space for students of all races with 50% of African Americans agreeing as opposed to 77% of whites (See Morrow, et al., 2000). This trend is consistent among both first year and upper class students. Strikingly, agreement among upper class students is lower for whites but higher for African Americans when compared to first year students.

Looking to examine student perceptions of overall diversity in campus activities, the following table (3) compares African American and white students by class year.

Table 3
Campus Programming - Agreeing

	African American N	% Total	% 1st Year	% Upperclass	White N	% Total	% 1st Year	% Upperclass
Student clubs, organizations, and activities reflect the diverse student body.	11	50.0*	45.5*	54.5	227	73.7*	78.7*	69.5
On-campus events (exhibits, plays, movies, performances, etc.) reflect the interest of diverse student groups.	14	63.6**	63.6**	63.6*	271	88.0**	90.9**	86.2*
Racially diverse students regularly participate in university activities.	12	54.5**	72.7	36.4**	243	79.0**	85.0	76.4**
Efforts are made to increase racially diverse student participation in university activities.	10	45.5**	45.5**	45.5	220	71.4**	78.6**	65.6

* $p<.05$, ** $p<.01$ Tests of significance are Pearson chi-square for differences between African American and white.

White students perceived the university to be more reflective of diversity than African American students. Whites were more likely to agree that student clubs, organizations, and activities reflect the diverse student body (73.7% as compared to 50%) and on-campus events (exhibits, plays, movies, performances, etc.) reflect the interest of diverse student groups (88% versus 63.6%, respectively). White students also agreed at a higher rate that racially diverse students regularly participate in university activities (79% as compared to 54.5%) and that efforts are made to increase racially diverse student participation in university activities (71.4% as compared to 45.5%). This suggests that whites see less of a problem when it comes to diversity on campus. Looking at class year, this trend of white students being more likely to agree persists among both first year and upper class students.

Among white students, upper class students were less likely to agree with all statements. Among African American students this was the case for the statement that racially diverse students regularly participate in university activities. For all other questions, the African American student responses stayed the same across class years with the exception of student clubs, organizations and activities in which upper class African American students were more likely to agree that they reflect the diverse student body than were first year students.

Moving beyond perceptions of student involvement, table four seeks to capture the level of student comfort in residence halls. Cabrera, Nora, & Terenzini (1999) suggest that students of color and Caucasian students are equally likely to recognize prejudice and discrimination in the classroom and on campus. This set of questions suggests that when it comes to comfort on campus, however, white and African American students' perceptions differ.

White students were more likely to agree that residents in their residence hall feel comfortable expressing diverse ideas, opinions and beliefs (85.4% as compared to 63.6% of African American students). They were also more likely to agree that their experiences in their residence hall have led them to be more understanding of diversity issues (62.3% as compared to 40.9%). This seems to be the case despite near equal participation (approximately 40%) among African American and white students in discussions related to diversity and greater participation among African American students in programs and activities related to diversity (40.9% of African American students as compared to 26.9% of white students). While African American students felt that the office of residence life was effective in marketing leadership experiences to minority students at a higher rate (68.2% versus 56.5 percent of white students), white students were more inclined to agree (64.6% as compared to 45.6%) that Hall council (a student run organization) encourages participation of minority students in its events. Both groups of students agreed at approximately 64% that their Resident Advisor encourages their participation in programs/activities related to diversity.

Looking at class year, African American and white upper class students were less likely than first year students to agree that their experiences in their Residence Halls led them to be more understanding of diversity issues. They were also less likely to agree that they participate in discussions, programs and activities related to diversity or that the office of residence life effectively markets to, and the hall council encourages participation of minority students.

Table 4
Residence Hall Programming - Agreeing

	African American N	% Total	% 1st Year	% Upperclass	White N	% Total	% 1st Year	% Upperclass
In my residence hall, residents feel comfortable expressing diverse ideas, opinions and beliefs.	14	63.6*	63.6*	63.6	263	85.4*	86.5*	84.3
My experiences in my residence hall have led me to be more understanding of diversity issues.	9	40.9	54.5	27.3	192	62.3	69	55.6
In my residence hall, I participate in discussions related to diversity.	9	40.9	54.5	27.3	125	40.6	48.4	32.7
In my residence hall, I participate in programs/activities related to diversity.	9	40.9	54.5	27.3	83	26.9	29	24.8
The Office of Residence Life is effective in marketing leadership experiences to minority students.	15	68.2	72.7	63.6	174	56.5	66.5	46.4
My Resident Advisor (RA) encourages my participation in programs/activities related to diversity.	14	63.6	63.6	63.6	200	64.9	74.8	54.9
Hall council encourages the participation of minority students in its events.	10	45.6	54.5	36.4	199	64.6	72.3	56.9

* $p<.05$, ** $p<.01$ Tests of significance are Pearson chi-square for differences between African American and white.

This suggests that upper class students (both African American and white) tend to self-segregate or withdraw from participation and to feel less encouraged to participate by peers such as hall council and in the case of whites, their Resident Advisor.

This tendency to withdraw is supported by more qualitative data that was collected in this survey. It is evident from student comments that, despite a

University wide commitment to diversity, self-segregation persists on campus. Comments like the following characterize student analysis.

> "The black students do not talk to the white students in my dorm."

> "[The University] claims to be a diverse population, which it is. However, if you walk around campus there is still a clear segregation amongst the different races."

As another student comments, this occurs despite a diversity of groups on campus and it is not just and issue for African Americans and whites:

> "Many of the students here, even in dorms where there is quite a bit of diversity, only hang out with members of their own ethnic groups and you just have groups of white guys, groups of black guys, groups of Asian guys, and groups of Latino guys. You don't see ethnically diverse cliques in residence halls that often."

Students attribute this segregation to various sources. Some blame minorities:

> "I would like to add that I feel it is horrible that students do not feel comfortable interacting with other races and I do feel there is a problem on campus with the interaction. However, I also feel this is caused by the fact that the minority groups often stick to the group and do not venture out to meet others. I feel this is a huge problem."

Others blame majority groups:

> "This campus has some serious racial issues...When minorities host events and the only people who show up are minorities (with the exception of some white people who are reporters/photographers), that's another sign."

The emphasis of this paper is not to place blame on individuals who find themselves involved in the ubiquitous complexities of race relations. Rather, our focus is on student perceptions of what can be done to improve student interaction and camaraderie across these perceived lines of race.

Section 3: Supporting A Racially Diverse Student Body

The following table presents student reaction to a list of proposed ways to support a racially diverse student body both on campus and, more specifically, in residence halls.

Table 5
Best Ways to Support A Racially Diverse Student Body - Agreeing

		\multicolumn{4}{c}{African American}	\multicolumn{4}{c}{White}
		N	% Total	% 1st Year	% Upperclass	N	% Total	% 1st Year	% Upperclass
Coffee houses with	In Residence Halls	5	22.7	18.2	27.3	59	19.1	23.9	13.7
multicultural themes	On Campus	10	45.5	45.5	45.5	117	37.9	33.5	42.5
Multicultural forums and	In Residence Halls	9	40.9*	36.4	45.5	62	20.1*	16.8	23.5
programs	On Campus	11	50.0*	45.5	54.5*	85	27.5*	31.6	23.5*
Discussion groups on	In Residence Halls	11	50.0**	54.5**	45.5**	38	12.3**	10.3**	14.4**
multicultural themes facilitated by faculty	On Campus	8	36.4	27.3	45.5*	63	20.4	21.9	19.0*
Learning communities	In Residence Halls	12	54.5	45.5	63.6	106	34.4	32.3	36.6
with multicultural themes	On Campus	3	13.6	18.2	9.1	31	10.0	10.3	9.8
Multicultural student	In Residence Halls	7	31.8*	18.2	45.5**	39	12.6*	13.5	11.8**
mentoring opportunities	On Campus	13	59.1**	54.4**	63.6**	48	15.5**	14.8**	16.3**
Multicultural newsletter	In Residence Halls	7	31.8*	27.3	36.4*	44	14.2*	14.8	13.7*
	On Campus	10	45.5*	45.5*	45.5*	74	23.9*	22.6*	25.5*
Integration of	In Residence Halls	1	4.5	0.0	9.1	18	5.8	7.7	3.9
multicultural topics in classroom discussions and assignments	On Campus	15	68.2**	81.8**	54.5	113	36.6**	34.8**	37.9
Having a more racially	In Residence Halls	10	45.5*	36.4	54.5*	67	21.7*	21.9	21.6*
diverse staff and faculty	On Campus	14	63.6**	90.9**	36.4	73	23.6**	23.9**	23.5

* $p<.05$, ** $p<.01$ Tests of significance are Pearson chi-square for differences between African American and white.

Overall, a higher percentage of African American students favored each of the suggestions, with the exception of integration of multicultural topics in classroom discussions and assignments within a residence hall setting (5.8% of white and 4.5% of African American students supported this). As seen in table 5 the most popular on campus activities among African American students are integration of multicultural topics in classroom discussions and assignments (68.2%), having more racially diverse staff and faculty members (63.6%) and student mentoring opportunities on campus (59.1%) (See Astin, 1993). For white students, the top choices for on campus activities are coffee houses with multicultural themes (37.9% as compared to 45.5% among African Americans) and integration of multicultural topics in classroom discussions and assignments (36.6% as compared to 68.2% among African Americans).

As far as in residence hall activities, learning communities with multicultural themes (supported by 54.4% of African Americans and 34.4% of whites) and discussion groups on multicultural themes facilitated by faculty (supported by 50% of African Americans and 12.3% of whites) were the top choices for African American students. Learning communities with multicultural themes (see previous sentence) and having a more racially diverse staff and faculty members (supported by 21.7% of whites and 45.4% of African Americans) were the top choices among white students.

Overall, comparing upper class to first years, support was higher among upper class African American students for 10 items (as compared to 7 items for whites). These differences between first year and upper class student support are in many cases opposite for African American and white students. In 11 of 18 cases, support for activities changed in the opposite direction when comparing class years, suggesting that student preferences for diversity support vary differently for whites and African Americans over the course of matriculation. Nevertheless, this does identify which activities are likely to receive the most support from students overall.

Table 6
Racially Integrated Residence Halls and a Diversity Course - Agreeing or Strongly Agreeing

	African American				White			
	N	% Total	% 1st Year	% Upperclass	N	% Total	% 1st Year	% Upperclass
Having first year students live in racially integrated residence halls promotes:								
Interaction	15	68.2	63.6	72.7	242	78.8	78.6	78.9
Learning	13	59.1	54.5	63.6	239	78.1	79.7	76.3
Growth	15	68.2	63.6	72.7	250	81.7	83.7	79.6
A diversity course should be a core course requirement for my school/college.	15	68.2	72.7	63.6	149	48.2	48.4	47.7

* p<.05, **p<.01   Tests of significance are Pearson chi-square for differences between African American and white.

Finally, students were asked whether they believe having first year students live in racially integrated residence halls promotes interaction, learning, and growth amongst different racial groups and whether a diversity course should be a core course requirement for their school/college (table 6).

While there are no statistically significant differences between African American and white students or between students in different class years, African American students tend to be in less agreement that having first year students live in racially integrated residence halls promotes interaction (68.2% as compared to 78.8%), learning (59.1% as compared to 79.7%) and growth (68.2% as compared to 81.7%). They are, however, more likely to support the institution of a diversity course requirement (68.2% as compared to 48.2%) (See Institute for the Student of Social Change, 1991).

Generally, among African American students, upper class African American students are more likely than first years to agree that racially integrated first year residence halls promote interaction, learning, and growth amongst different racial groups. White upper class student responses are similar to that of first years except for a lower tendency to agree that integrated halls promote growth. As for the diversity course requirement, upper class African American students are less likely to support it than are first years and white students hardly vary by class year.

Conclusion

Research has shown that a diverse campus community has benefits for all members of that community (Chang, 1996; Humphreys, 1998; Smith & Schonfeld, 2000). In a recent review of research concerning the benefits of diversity, Smith and Schonfeld (2000) report that diversity not only has positive effects on student learning, but also increases institutional effectiveness. A diverse environment creates more opportunities for students to find support, role models, and mentors. Diverse college campuses lead white students to be more open to others and they are shown to have positive effects on student cognitive development and learning (Smith & Schonfeld, 2000). Lastly, Smith and Schonfeld (2000) and Humphreys (1998) report that diversity increases students' overall satisfaction with an institution and engages the campus in a greater range of issues.

However, the present findings force us to question the underlying assumptions of this literature. African American and white students' perceptions of overall student comfort as well as diversity in campus and residence hall programming did not correspond with each other. This leads us to question the underlying meaning of diversity on which each group based its responses. If indeed diversity means different things to each "racial" group – for instance re-affirmation of being African American for African American students and exposure to African Americans for white students – then universities would seem to inherently face a challenge in balancing these two understandings. This possibility is reinforced by divergence of opinions over how best to support a racially diverse student body. African American students tended to emphasize mentoring opportunities and increasing diversity among staff and faculty. This would lead to questions such as how much does university personnel and structure need to change and can white faculty and staff serve as mentors? It would also seem to respect a need among students for re-affirmation and some related degree of self-segregation. White students, in contrast, emphasized less structural and more informal approaches such as coffee houses. Such a course of policy planning would conversely stress integration. While this paper does not offer a policy solution to these diverging approaches, it does offer that considering both together will limit the temptation to overlook diversity planning itself as a contested site of race relations in which power to influence discourse, policy, and implementation hangs in the balance.

Discussion and Essay Questions:

1. Given that diversity has increased during the past couple decades on college campuses, do you think that increased tensions on college campuses have been the result of an increase in diversity or other factors?

2. Why do African American and white students seem to have very different views about the college and university campus in regard to issues of diversity?

3. Based on the article, is it possible to conclude that as African American and white students advance through the college years, that each group actually socially separates more from each other?

4. Does it matter what percentage of the faculty and staff should be African American?

5. Can white faculty and staff be mentors to African American students?

6. Can white faculty and staff be mentors to African American faculty and staff?

References

Adams, M., & Zhou-McGovern, Y. (1994). Connecting research to practice in 'social diversity' classes: Implications of developmental findings for instructional design. Paper presented at the Annual Meeting of the American Educational Research Association, New Orleans, LA.

Astin, A. (1993). What matters in college?: Four critical years revisited. San Francisco: Jossey-Bass.

Cabrera, A. F., Nora, A., Terenzini, P. T., Pascarella, P. T. & Hagedorn, L.S. (1999). Campus racial climate and the adjustment of students to college: A comparison between White students and African American students. *Journal of Higher Education*, 70(2), 134-160.

Chang, M. J. (1996). Racial diversity in higher education: Does a racially mixed student population affect educational outcomes? Ph.D. dissertation, University of California, Los Angeles.

Davis, T. M., & Murrell, P. H. (1993). A structural model of perceived academic, personal, and vocational gains related to college student responsibility. *Research in Higher Education*, 34, 267-290.

Gregory, S. T. (2000). Selected innovations in higher education designed to enhance the racial climate for students of color in predominately white colleges and universities. Annual Meeting of the American Educational Research Association, New Orleans, LA.

Humphreys, D. (1998). The impact of diversity on college students: the latest research. Washington, DC: Association of American Colleges and Universities.

Institute for the Study of Social Change. (1991). The Diversity Project: Final Report. Berkeley, CA: University of California.

Levine, A. & Cureton, J.S. (1998). When hope and fear collide: A portrait of todays college student. San Francisco: Jossey-Bass.

Morrow, G. P., & Burris-Kitchen, D., et al. (2000). Assessing campus climate of cultural diversity: A focus on focus groups. *College Student Journal*, 34(4): 589-602.

Smith, D. G. & Schonfeld, N. B. (2000). The benefits of diversity: What the research tells us. *About Campus*, 5(5): 16-23.

Tinto, V. (1993). Leaving college: Rethinking the causes and cures of student attrition. Chicago: University of Chicago Press.

U.S. Department of Education. (2003). National Center for Education Statistics.

Chapter 14

An Old Journey in a New Direction: The Two Faces of Desegregation

F. Erik Brooks

The debate on Alabama's two historically black institutions is storied. Some argue that the maintaining of these two public historically black universities perpetuate the "separate but equal" myth set forth by the *Plessy* decision. In contrast, others argue that these institutions should not only be maintained but also enhanced to strengthen the opportunities for blacks in Alabama.

In 1903 W.E.B. Du Bois wrote in the *Souls of Black Folk*, "One ever feels his twoness-an American, a Negro; two souls two thoughts, two unreconciled strivings; two warring ideals in one dark body, whose dogged strength alone keeps it from being torn asunder." [1]

As this debate rages on, Alabama's traditionally black institutions and all black colleges are faced with a twoness, the twoness of living in a "colorblind society" while being "race conscious" in a state with a long and troubled history of segregation in higher education.

As with much of society, Alabama and many other southern states have yet to find a way to reconcile the contrasting thoughts of a "colorblind society" and "race consciousness" in higher education. The end of the Mississippi desegregation case may be followed by the conclusion of similar long-standing case across the South. The United States Supreme Court ended the Mississippi's

30-year-old court case when it refused to hear an appeal in the case. Louisiana's case could wrap up in 2005 and there is conversation that a settlement will be struck in the Alabama case by 2005.

Originally, nineteen states were originally accused in lawsuits or operating racially segregated systems of higher education decades ago. Today, there are eleven states that remain under the watchful eye of the United States Department of Education and the Office of Civil Rights. Even with years and years of litigation moving through the courts, desegregation remains an issue in states that operate public historically black colleges and universities (HBCUs).[2]

The lower federal court ruling in *United States v. Alabama* represents the problems of truly integrating educational institutions in the southern states in the modern era. The decision in the case ultimately held that vestiges of *de jure* segregation still existed in institutions of higher learning in Alabama and that the State of Alabama needed to take steps to rectify the situation. The federal district court ruling in the case mandated that the State of Alabama engage in affirmative efforts to break down the remaining vestiges of discrimination and segregation, including such affirmative actions as actively recruiting more African-American students and faculty in the historically white state schools, ensuring HBCUs within the state receive appropriate resources and funding, and ensuring that white students are recruited for HBCUs and that diversity is promoted at the state's HBCUs.

Alabama operates two publicly funded historically black universities. Alabama Agricultural and Mechanical University (AAMU) is located in Huntsville, Alabama, which is geographically located in the northern portion of the state. The university was founded in 1873. AAMU is a traditional land-grant institution, which combines professional, vocational and liberal arts pursuits. AAMU provides baccalaureate and graduate studies to all qualified, capable individuals who are interested in further developing their technical, professional, and scholastic skills and competencies. AAMU operates in the three-fold function of teaching, research, and public service, including extension.[3]

Alabama's other publicly operated black university is Alabama State University (ASU). Alabama State University is geographically located in the central portion of the state in Montgomery, Alabama, the state's capital city. ASU was founded in 1867. It provides quality undergraduate and graduate instruction, which will lead to degrees in liberal arts, the fine arts, business, the sciences, teacher education and other professions. ASU prepares students for an effective and productive role in American society as professionals and as citizens.[4] The university provides learning experiences designed to develop students' intellectual abilities, as well as their social, moral, cultural and ethical values. In so doing, ASU equips students with those skills, insights, attitudes and practical experiences which will enable them to become well-rounded and discerning citizens, fully qualified for service to humanity.[5] The university's functions are prioritized as instruction, research and public service. Both universities were founded to help educate new freed African slaves in Alabama after the Civil War.

In *United States v. Alabama,* the United States Justice Department filed suit against Alabama's higher education system. The basic contention was that vestiges of racial segregation had not been eradicated "root and branch" from public higher education in the state of Alabama and that the Court should direct the formation of a plan calculated to eliminate such vestiges.[6] Specifically, the United States charged that Alabama had required absolute segregation in all public education until the middle of the 1960's. The legislature and the executive branches actively and resolutely opposed any and all attempt to change these requirements of absolute segregation until otherwise required by federal court order.[7]

In keeping with overall policy, at the four-year level, public higher education in Alabama in 1954 was absolutely segregated with two four-year schools- Alabama A&M University and Alabama State University- limited to African American students and faculty which were substantially inferior to the four year schools established and operated for whites only.[8] The legislature and Governor as well as white schools themselves actively opposed the attendance of African-Americans at white four-year institutions until these schools were required to admit African-American students by federal order.[9]

The United States contended that Alabama had a constitutional obligation to take action to eliminate "root and branch" all vestiges of the racially dual system of public higher education which it had established.[10] Alabama had failed to take the necessary steps to compel either the disestablishment of the dual system in state higher education or to establish the conditions necessary to allow this racial duality to disappear over the course of time.[11]

They contended that the defendant universities themselves had failed to take the constitutionally necessary steps to make the transitions from white schools and black schools to just schools.[12] The white schools had affirmatively hindered historically black schools from attracting white students, primarily through course and program offerings at geographically proximate institutions.[13] The U.S. contended that the white schools had failed to hire qualified African-American faculty members and appoint qualified African-American administrators with the reciprocal effect of maintaining their own identification as white schools and cementing the identification of historically black schools.[14] They also contended the white schools had adopted admission policies, which resulted in fewer African-American students enrolling in these schools and operated their institutions so that African-American students were less likely to graduate once in attendance at white schools.[15] The historically black schools had failed to take steps to attract white students and did not appoint and retain white faculty so as to eliminate their identity as black schools and make the transition from a historically black schools.[16]

The U.S. argued that the State of Alabama had failed to disestablish its dual system of public higher education by not taking steps to make the black schools sufficiently attractive in terms of facilities to attract whites.[17] The U.S. contended Alabama had failed to dismantle its dual system of higher education by not providing sufficient funding to historically black schools to enable them to eradicate the past neglect by the state. Also it was contended that as a result of the state's failure to eliminate program duplication by continuing to operate two agricultural schools one overwhelmingly white and one overwhelmingly black at unequal funding levels.[18]

The U.S. also contended that the state had failed to disestablish its dual system by not taking steps to eliminate program duplication and by not offering unique, attractive programs at all schools so that other race students would not be discouraged from attending schools they were once absolutely precluded from attending by state action.[19] They also contended that the state and its four-year institutions of higher education had no plan, policy, or design to eliminate the racially dual structure of public higher education at the four-year level and with the exception of historically black schools and those institutions which had entered into consent decrees with the United States in the action, no current plan to foster the conditions which would allow this racially dual structure to dissipate and eventually disappear.[20] The United States and the *Knight* plaintiffs argued that they should be granted relief based on Title VI of the Civil Rights Act of 1964 and the Fourteenth Amendment to the Constitution.

Ruling

Alabama A&M University was awarded $16 million and Alabama State was awarded more than $15 million for capital expenditures to eliminate the remnants of discrimination in regards to their existing physical plants and facilities as a result of past discriminating funding practices by the state.[21] Troy State University in Montgomery was enjoined from expanding its campus's physical plant without the consent of the court. The Alabama Commission on Higher Education was ordered to change its higher education funding formula, which had heavily based appropriations on average statewide tuition and enrollment.

Alabama State University and Alabama A&M University were directed to develop and implement a recruitment policy specifically targeting white students and advertisement campaigns that focused on institutions' quality and open environment to other-race students. Also, funding for other-race scholarships were awarded to Alabama State University and Alabama A&M University to help diversify the student bodies at both universities. The scholarships would be funded annually from 1995 until 2005 and both universities would be reimbursed up to $1 million a year for diversity scholarships.[22] In addition, the two-year college system was prohibited from establishing community colleges or junior colleges in Montgomery County or Madison County, the homes of the two black colleges, so that the two historically black colleges could competitively recruit some of those students.

A trust fund for educational excellence was created at Alabama State University and Alabama A&M University to help their poor endowments. Both universities were awarded $1 million annually from 1995 until 2005 and the state was required to match contributions up to $1 million for each university's endowment annually.[23] Several high demand programs were also awarded to the two historically black universities to assist in desegregating. Alabama State University was allowed to develop programs in allied health sciences and up to two Ph. D. programs and a master's program in accounting.

Meanwhile, Alabama A&M University was permitted to establish undergraduate mechanical and electrical engineering program. The term of the consent decree was issued in 1995 and will remain in effect until July 31, 2005.[24] In essence, Judge Murphy wanted Alabama State University and Alabama A&M University to become less black. He specifically stated the state's two historically black institutions must act in a manner such that their pride in their heritage does not hinder their, the state's, or the court's efforts to reduce segregative effects on student choice. Murphy also stated that the HBCUs seemed to be motivated by a desire to please African American students and alumni rather than attract white students. The language used in the ruling angered some advocates for the HBCU's. Specifically, they argued that it was hypocritical for the government to expect black colleges to change while African Americans at predominately white institutions are expected to subdue their heritage and amalgamate with the people there and the symbols that African Americans abhor. Advocates were angered and confused by the court's ruling.

The following figures show the rate of change and the progress of desegregation over a ten-year period (fall1991- fall 2000) at Alabama State University and at Alabama A&M University.[25] Charts show statistics for undergraduate enrollment, graduate enrollment, faculty, and executive, administrative, and managerial staff. There were increases in overall demographics at the two universities, however these increases may be due to extremely low numbers at the beginning of the examined period.

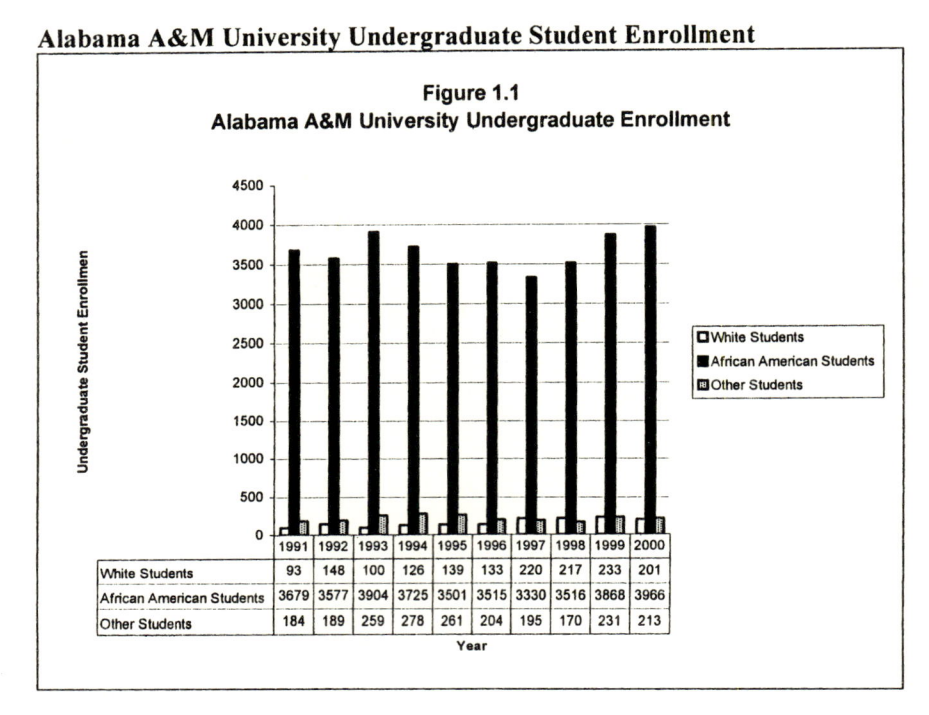

Alabama A&M University Undergraduate Student Enrollment

Figure 1.1
Alabama A&M University Undergraduate Enrollment

	1991	1992	1993	1994	1995	1996	1997	1998	1999	2000
White Students	93	148	100	126	139	133	220	217	233	201
African American Students	3679	3577	3904	3725	3501	3515	3330	3516	3868	3966
Other Students	184	189	259	278	261	204	195	170	231	213

As can be seen in Figure 1.1, there has been a steady increase of undergraduate white student enrollment at Alabama A&M University. In fall 1991, the percentage of white undergraduate students was 2.35% (93) out of a total undergraduate student enrollment of 3,956. In 1991, the percentage of African-American undergraduate student enrollment was 93.00% (3,379). The percentage of other undergraduate students was 4.86% (213). In fall 2000 the percentage of white undergraduate students rose slightly to 4.59% (201) of a total undergraduate enrollment of 4,380, while the percentage of African-American undergraduate students remained steady at 90.55% (3,966). The percentage other undergraduate students was 4.65% (184).

Alabama A&M boasted its highest percentage of white students in fall 1997, with white students, (217) or 5.56% of the 3,745 total student population. In fall 1993, the percentage of white students decreased when the figures dipped back to 2.35% (100) of a total undergraduate enrollment of 4,263. The demographics for Alabama A&M University's white undergraduate white student population doubled, but they were still significant minority as compared to the African-American student population.

Alabama State University Undergraduate Student Enrollment

Figure 1.2
Alabama State University Undergraduate Enrollment

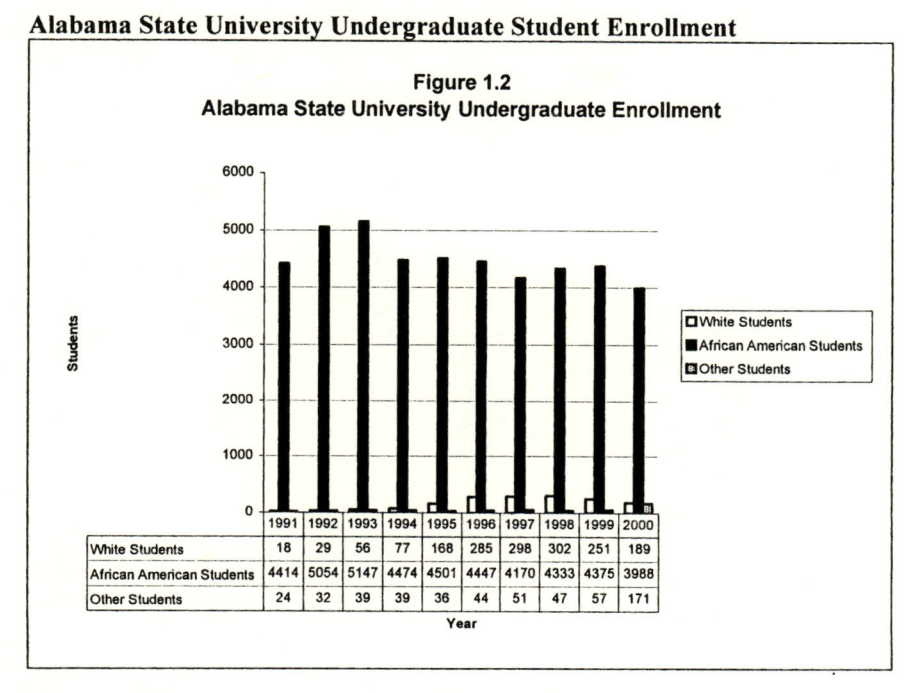

	1991	1992	1993	1994	1995	1996	1997	1998	1999	2000
White Students	18	29	56	77	168	285	298	302	251	189
African American Students	4414	5054	5147	4474	4501	4447	4170	4333	4375	3988
Other Students	24	32	39	39	36	44	51	47	57	171

There has been an increase of undergraduate white student enrollment at Alabama State University. Figure 1.2 showed that in fall 1991, the percentage of white undergraduate students was 0.40% (18) of a total undergraduate enrollment of 3,956. In 1991 the percentage of African-American undergraduate enrollment was 99.06% (4,414). The percentage other student population was 0.54% (24). By fall 2000, the percentage of white undergraduate population had risen to 4.35% (189) of a total undergraduate student enrollment of 4,348. In fall 2000, the percentage of African-American students had fallen slightly to 91.72% (3,988). The percentage of others was 3.93% (171).

In fall 1997, Alabama State University had its largest percentage of white enrollment with 6.59% (298) of the total student enrollment of 4,519. When comparing the figures for the state's two public historically black institutions there have been dramatic changes in the minority undergraduate student enrollment, but whites remain significantly under represented at Alabama's public black universities.

Alabama A&M University Graduate and Professional Student Enrollment

Figure 1.3
Alabama A&M University Gradauate and Professional Enrollment

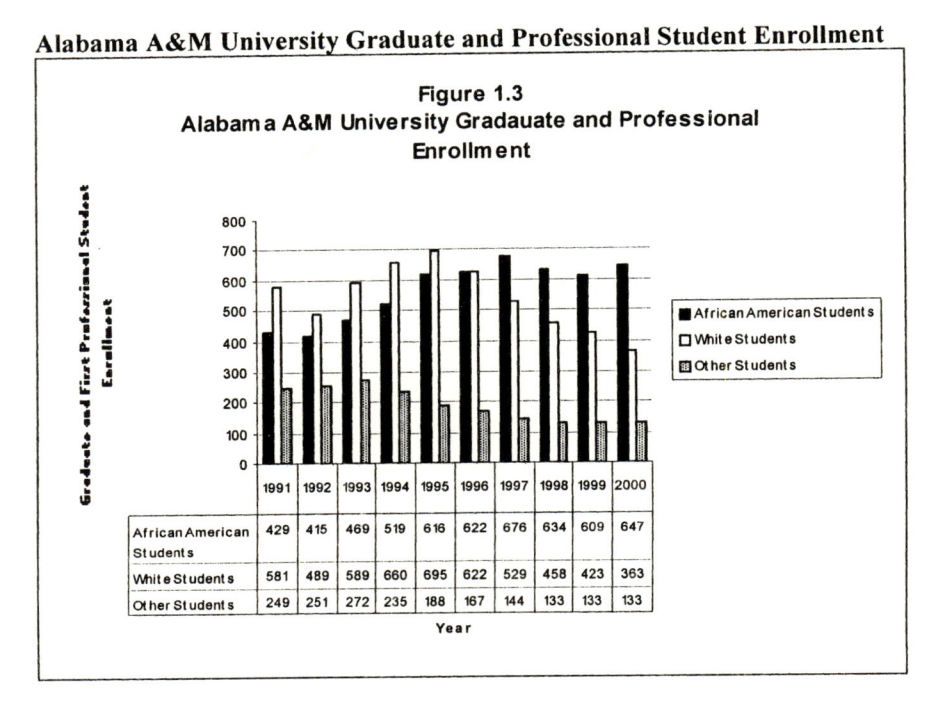

Year	1991	1992	1993	1994	1995	1996	1997	1998	1999	2000
African American Students	429	415	469	519	616	622	676	634	609	647
White Students	581	489	589	660	695	622	529	458	423	363
Other Students	249	251	272	235	188	167	144	133	133	133

Figure 1.3 showed there has been decrease in the percentage of graduate and professional students at Alabama A&M University. In fall 1991, the percentage of white graduate and professional students was 46.15% (581) of a total graduate and professional enrollment of 1,259. The percentage of African-American graduate and professional students was 34.07% (429). The percentage of other graduate and professional students was 19.78% (249). In fall 2000, the percentage of white graduate and professional students was 31.76% (363) of a total graduate and professional students of 1,143. The percentage of African-American graduate and professional students was 56.61% (647). The percentage of other graduate and professional students was 11.64% (133).

Interestingly, Alabama A&M University, a predominately black institution began the ten-year with more white graduate and professional students than African-American students. Fall 1995 was the highest percentage of white graduate and professional enrollment with 46.36% (695) of a total graduate and professional student enrollment of 1,499.

Alabama State University Graduate and Professional Student Enrollment

Figure 1.4
Alabama State University Graduate and Professional Enrollment

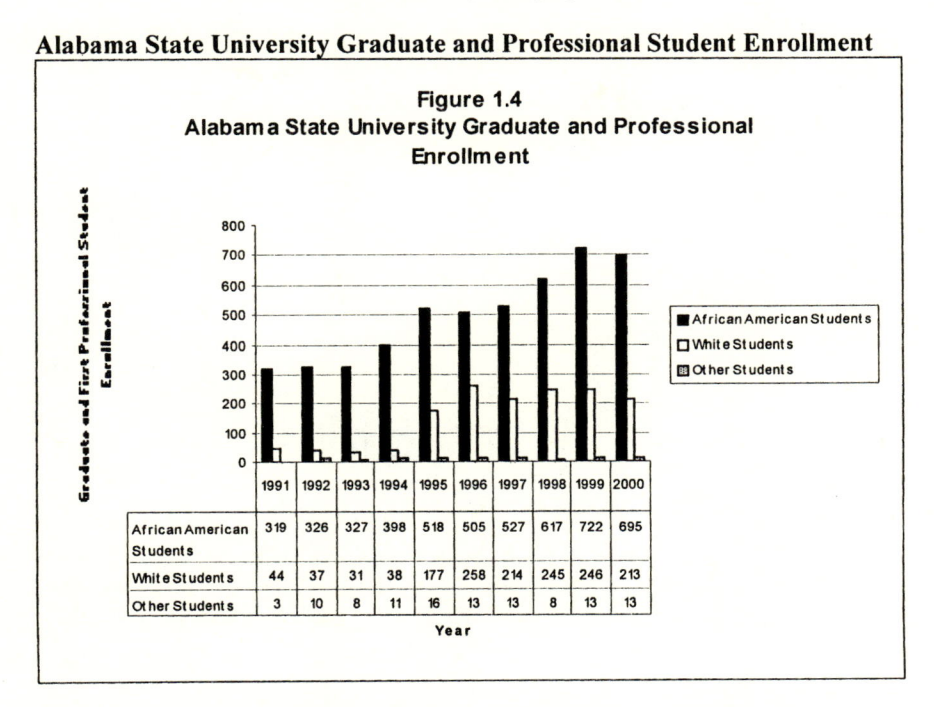

	1991	1992	1993	1994	1995	1996	1997	1998	1999	2000
African American Students	319	326	327	398	518	505	527	617	722	695
White Students	44	37	31	38	177	258	214	245	246	213
Other Students	3	10	8	11	16	13	13	8	13	13

Figure 1.4, showed an increase in the percentage of white graduate and professional students at Alabama State University for the ten-year period. In fall 1991, the percentage of white graduate and professional students was 12.02% (44), and the percentage of African-American students was 87.16% (319). The percentage of other graduate and professional students was 0.82% (3). The total graduate and professional student enrollment was 366. In fall 2000, the percentage of white graduate and professional students was 23.23% (213). The percentage of African-American graduate and professional students was 75.46% (695) of a total graduate and professional student enrollment of 921. The percentage of other graduate and professional student was 1.41% (13). From fall 1999 to fall 2000, Alabama State University's number of white graduate and professional students decreased slightly from 246 students to 213 students.

Alabama A&M University Full Time Faculty

**Figure 1.5
Alabama A&M University Full-Time Faculty**

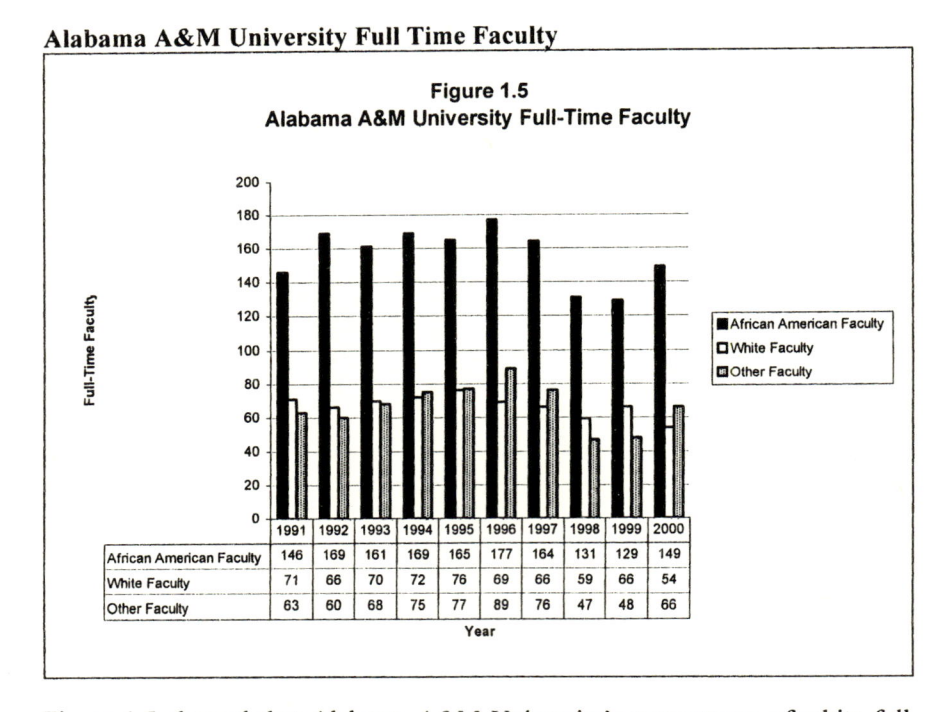

	1991	1992	1993	1994	1995	1996	1997	1998	1999	2000
African American Faculty	146	169	161	169	165	177	164	131	129	149
White Faculty	71	66	70	72	76	69	66	59	66	54
Other Faculty	63	60	68	75	77	89	76	47	48	66

Figure 1.5 showed that Alabama A&M University's percentages of white full time faculty decreased for the ten-year period. In fall 1991, the percentage of white full time faculty employment was 25.36% (71) of a total faculty of 280.

The percentage of African-American full time faculty employment was 52.14% (146) and the percentage of other full time faculty was 22.50% (63). In fall 2000, the percentage of white full time faculty employment was 20.07% (54) of a total full time faculty of 269. The percentage of African-American full time faculty employment was 55.39% (149) and the percentage of other full time faculty was 24.54% (66).

In fall 1995, the highest percentage of white full time faculty employment was recorded with 23.90% (76) of a total faculty of 318. Alabama A&M has lagged in increasing the percentage of whites on its faculty.

Alabama State University Full Time Faculty

**Figure 1.6
Alabama State Unviersity Full-Time Faculty**

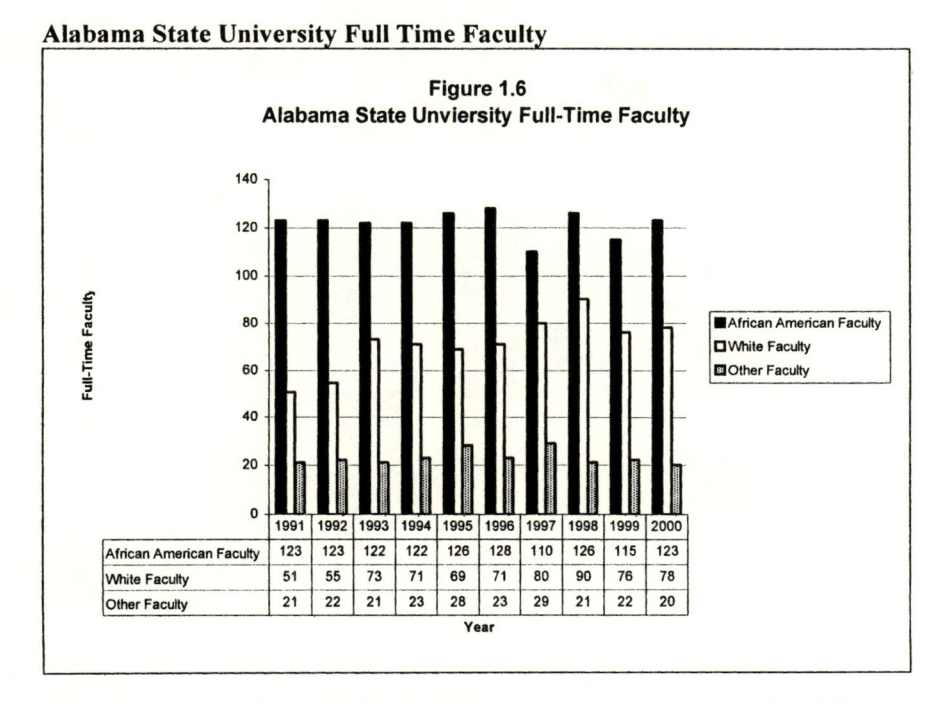

Year	1991	1992	1993	1994	1995	1996	1997	1998	1999	2000
African American Faculty	123	123	122	122	126	128	110	126	115	123
White Faculty	51	55	73	71	69	71	80	90	76	78
Other Faculty	21	22	21	23	28	23	29	21	22	20

Alabama State University slightly increased the percentage white full time faculty as seen in Figure 1.6. In fall 1991, the percentage of white full time faculty was 26.15% (51) of a total faculty of 195. The percentage of African-American full time faculty was 63.08% (123) and the percentage of other full time faculty was 10.77% (21). In fall 2000, the percentage of white full time faculty was 35.29% (78) of a total faculty of 221. The percentage of African-American full time faculty was 55.66% (123) and the percentage of other full time faculty was 9.05% (20).

Fall 1998 marked the highest percentage of white full time faculty with 37.97% (90) of a total full time faculty of 237. Although the percentage of white full time faculty increased, the demographic make up of Alabama State University's full time faculty remained predominately African-American.

Alabama A&M University Executive, Administrative, and Managerial Staff

Figure 1.7
Alabama A&M University Administrators

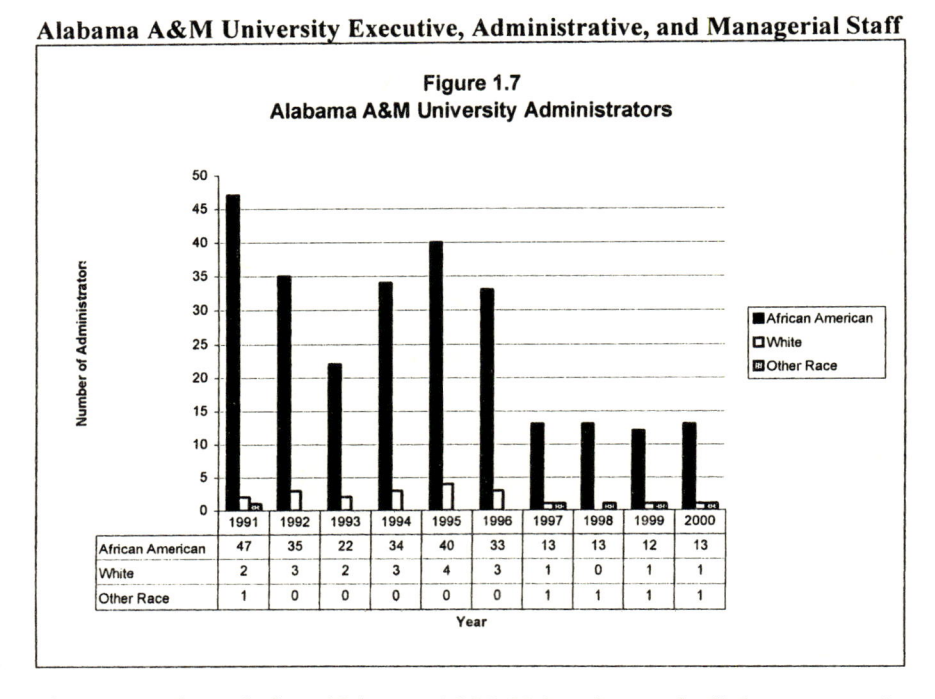

	1991	1992	1993	1994	1995	1996	1997	1998	1999	2000
African American	47	35	22	34	40	33	13	13	12	13
White	2	3	2	3	4	3	1	0	1	1
Other Race	1	0	0	0	0	0	1	1	1	1

Figure 1.7 showed that Alabama A&M University made little progress in diversifying the percentage of its white full time executive, administrative, and managerial personnel. In fall 1991, the percentage of white executives, administrators, and managers of 4.00% (2) that filled 50 full time positions. The percentage of African-Americans was 94.00% (47) that filled these positions.

The percentage of others that filled these positions was 2.00% (1). In fall 2000, the percentage of whites was 6.67% (1) that filled the 15 full time executive, administrative, and managerial positions at Alabama A&M University. The percentage of African-Americans was 86.67% (13) and the percentage of others was 6.67% (1) that filled these positions.

Interestingly, in fall 1991, Alabama A&M University began with 50 executive, administrative, and managerial positions but in fall 2000 these position had been cut to 15. The cuts in these positions caused the percentage of the others and whites increased.

Alabama State University Executive, Administrative, and Managerial Staff

**Figure 1.8
Alabama State University Administrators**

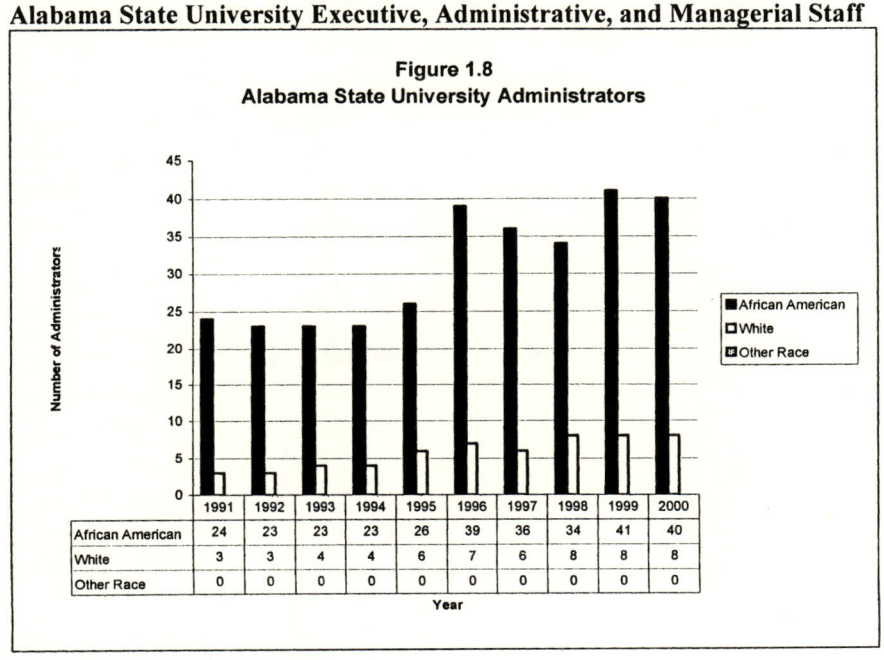

Year	1991	1992	1993	1994	1995	1996	1997	1998	1999	2000
African American	24	23	23	23	26	39	36	34	41	40
White	3	3	4	4	6	7	6	8	8	8
Other Race	0	0	0	0	0	0	0	0	0	0

Alabama State University slightly increased the percentage of whites serving in executive, administrative, and managerial positions, as can be seen in Figure 1.8. In fall 1991, the percentage of whites was 11.11% (3) that filled 27 executive, administrative, and managerial positions. The percentage of African-Americans 88.89% (24) and there were no others in these positions. In fall 2000, the percentage of whites was 16.67% (8) that filled 48 executive, administrative, and managerial positions. The percentage of African-Americans was 83.33% (40) that filled these positions. Again, there were no others in these positions.

Alabama State University had its highest percentage of whites in executive, administrative, and managerial positions in fall 1998, fall 1999, fall 2000 with 8. In contrast to Alabama A&M University, Alabama State University increased the number of executive, administrative, and managerial positions to increase the percentage of whites at the university.

Some 50 years after the landmark *Brown* decision and subsequent desegregation battles in the federal courts, many of Alabama's public universities both traditionally white and traditionally black are struggling with the same fundamental question in regards to desegregation, "How do universities in Alabama sufficiently increased the population of people who are not the majority on our campuses?"

Historically black colleges can look at having to increase its white enrollment as an opportunity to erase any myths and stereotypes about African Americans and historically black universities. By attracting more whites, black colleges can expose whites to the diversity in black culture and the richness of black history.

Discussion and Essay Questions:

1. Should the student body in historically Black colleges and universities (HBCU's) be predominantly African American?

2. Do HBCU's still fulfill a need in our society?

3. Should the faculty and administration be predominantly African American at HBCU's?

4. Are the issues the same in regard to maintaining HBCU's and maintaining historically female colleges and universities?

5. Should the number of HBCU's be expanded to areas of the country where there are few?

6. Does the existence of HBCU's promote equality or inequality in our society?

---

[1] Du Bois, W. E. B., *"Souls of Black Folks,"* A.C. McClurge & Co.; Chicago University Press John Wilson & Son, Cambridge, MA. 1903. First published in 1903, this extraordinary work recorded and explained history and helped to alter its course. Written after Du Bois had earned his Ph.D. from Harvard and studied in Berlin, this work contains both the academic language of sociology and the rich lyrics of spirituals, which Du Bois called "sorrow songs."

[2] Alabama A&M University, Huntsville, Alabama, Alabama State University, Montgomery, Alabama, Albany State University, Albany, Georgia, Alcorn State University, Lorman, Mississippi, Allen University, Columbia, South Carolina, Arkansas Baptist College, Little Rock, Arkansas, Barber Scotia College, Concord, North Carolina, Bennett College, Columbia, South Carolina, Bethune Cookman College, Daytona Beach, Florida, Bishop State Community College, Mobile, Alabama, Bluefield State College, Bluefield West, Virginia, Bowie State University, Bowie, Maryland, Central State University, Wilberforce, Ohio, Cheney State University, Cheney, Pennsylvania, Claflin University, Orangeburg, South Carolina, Clinton Junior College, Rock Hill, South Carolina, Coahoma Community College, Clarksdale, Mississippi, Concordia College, Selma, Alabama, Coppin State University, Baltimore, Maryland, Delaware State University, Dover, Delaware, Dillard University, New Orleans, Louisiana, Edward Waters College, Jacksonville, Florida, Elizabeth City State University, Elizabeth City North Carolina, Fisk University, Nashville, Tennessee, Florida A&M University,

Tallahassee, Florida, Florida Memorial College, Miami, Florida, Fort Valley State University, Fort Valley, Georgia, Grambling State University, Grambling, Louisiana, Hampton University, Hampton, Virginia, Harris Stowe State, St. Louis, Missouri, Hinds Community College, Utica, Mississippi, Howard University, Washington D.C., Huston-Tillotson, College, Austin Texas, Interdenominational Theological Seminary, Atlanta, Georgia, J.F. Drake State Technical College, Huntsville, Alabama, Jackson State University, Jackson, Mississippi, Jarvis Christian College, Hawkinsville, Texas, Johnson C, Smith, Charlotte, North Carolina, Kentucky State University, Frankfort, Kentucky, Knoxville College, Knoxville, Tennessee, Lane College, Jackson, Tennessee, Lawson State Community College, Birmingham, Alabama, LeMoyne Owen College, Memphis, Tennessee, Lincoln University, Jefferson City, Missouri, Lincoln University, Lincoln Pennsylvania, Livingstone College, Salisbury, North Carolina, Mary Holmes College, West Point, Mississippi, Meharry Medical College, Nashville, Tennessee, Mississippi Valley State University, Ita Bena, Mississippi, Morehouse college, Atlanta Georgia, Morgan State University, Baltimore, Maryland, Morris Brown College, Atlanta, Georgia, Morris College, Sumter, South Carolina, Norfolk State University, Norfolk, Virginia, North Carolina A&T University, Greensboro, North Carolina, North Carolina Central University, Durham, North Carolina, Oakwood College, Huntsville, Alabama, Paine College, Augusta Georgia, Paul Quin College, Dallas, Texas, Philander Smith College, Little Rock, Arkansas, Prairie View University, Prairie View, Texas, Rust College, Hollis Springs, Mississippi, Savannah State University, Savannah, Georgia, Selma University, Selma, Alabama, Shaw University, Raleigh, North Carolina, Shorter College, North Little Rock, Arkansas, Sojourner-Douglas College, Baltimore, Maryland, South Carolina State University, Orangeburg, South Carolina, Southern University, Baton Rouge, Louisiana, Southern University, New Orleans, Louisiana, Southern University at Shreveport, Shreveport, Louisiana, Southwestern Christian College, Terrell, Texas, Spelman College, Atlanta, Georgia, St. Augustine's College, Raleigh, North Carolina, St. Paul's College, Lawrenceville, Virginia, Stillman, Tuscaloosa, Alabama, Talladega College, Talladega Alabama, Tennessee State University, Nashville, Tennessee, Texas College, Tyler Texas, Texas Southern University, Houston Texas, Tougaloo, College, Tougaloo, Mississippi, Tuskegee University, Tuskegee, Alabama, University of Arkansas Pine Bluff, Pine Bluff, Arkansas, University of Maryland Eastern Shore, Princess Anne, Maryland, University of the District of Columbia, Washington D.C., University of the Virgin Island, Charlotte Amalie, Virgin Island, Virginia State University, Petersburg, Virginia, Virginia Union University, Richmond, Virginia, Voorhees College, Denmark, South Carolina, West Virginia State College, Institute, West Virginia, Wilberforce University, Wilberforce, Ohio, Wiley College, Marshall, Texas, Winston Salem State University, Winston Salem, North Carolina, Xavier University, New Orleans, Louisiana.

[3] http://www.aamu.edu/html/history.html
[4] http://www.alasu.edu/home/default.aspx
[5] Ibid.
[6] *United States v. Alabama*, 571 F. Supp. 958 (N.D. Ala 1983).
[7] *United States v. Alabama*, 574 F. Supp. 762 (N.D. Ala. 1983).
[8] *United States v. Alabama*, 582 F. Supp. 1197 (N.D. Ala. 1984).
[9] *United States v. Alabama*, 628 F. Supp. 1137 (N.D. Ala 1985)
[10] *United States v. Alabama*, 762 F.2d 1021 (11th Cir. 1985)

[11] Ibid.
[12] Ibid.
[13] Ibid.
[14] Ibid.
[15] Ibid.
[16] *United States v. Alabama*, 791 F.2d 1450 (11th Cir. 1986)
[17] *United States v. Alabama*, 796 F.2d 1478 (11th Cir. 1986)
[18] *United States v. Alabama*, 828 F.2d 1532 (11th Cir. 1987)
[19] *Knight v. Alabama*, 787 F. Supp. 1030 (N.D. Ala 1991)
[20] *Knight v. Alabama*, 801 F. Supp. 577 (N.D. Ala 1992)
[21] *Knight v. Alabama*, 824 F. Supp. 1022 (N.D. Ala 1993)
[22] *Knight v. Alabama*, 829 F. Supp. 1286 (N.D. Ala 1993)
[23] *Knight v. Alabama*, 14 F.3d 1534 (11th Cir. 1994)
[24] *Knight v. Alabama*, 900 F. Supp. 272 (N.D. Ala 1995)
[25] Enrollment data were provided by the Alabama Commission on Higher Education

Chapter 14

Activism Scholarship: Answering 'the Question'

Marybeth Gasman

Since pursuing research related to African American history and culture, the author has often been asked 'the question': "Why do you, a white researcher, study black history?" This essay is an exploration of the author's evolving answers to this question. The chapter examines the author's motives for conducting such research and categorizes them into three self-defined stages: rational inquiry, immersion, and activism scholarship. In addition, she compares and contrasts her ideas on this subject with the reflections of others who have studied subjects as an outsider.

> They owned all the Robeson records and all the Bessie Smith. And they had a manuscript of Countee Cullen's. They saw all the plays with or about Negroes, read all the books, and adored the Hall Johnson Singers. They had met Doctor Du Bois .... Of course they knew Harlem like their own backyard, that is, all the speakeasies and night clubs and dance halls, from themselves, down to places like the Hot Dime, where white folks couldn't get in – unless they knew the man. (And tipped heavily).
>
> -Langston Hughes in Roediger, 1998

"Why are you interested in black history?" Well, (I'm thinking ... which answer should I give this time .... I have different answers depending on the situation, the person asking, and my feelings at the time.).... Since I began doing research on the history of philanthropy and black higher education, I have been asked this question over and over. People of various backgrounds, races, and ethnicities have inquired. My answer has changed since I started this line of research in 1995. My answer changes slightly with each paper I write, with each talk I give, and many times, after a meaningful conversation. Needless to say, this question is on my mind a lot.

There are three levels of narrative: experience, telling, and interpreting. According to Donald Polkinghorne, the "(2001: 16) purpose of the telling and interpreting is to enable the reader to experience the narrative as if they lived it with the insight of the interpretation." Although I have been asked why I study black history many times, I have never thought about putting my reasons into words – about writing an autobiographical narrative. I know why I've never done it. It is one thing to let these different answers bounce around in my head but it is far different to write them down for others to read, interpret, and misunderstand.

Recently, I was invited to give a talk pertaining to philanthropy and black history at a mid-western research institution. My host, a colleague and friend, let me know in advance that someone in the audience might ask the question, "Why are you, a white person, interested in black history?" This discussion prompted me to write this essay. And, in many ways, the process has been close to the one Polkinghorne describes. In writing, I have relived my experiences, told them to you the reader, and in effect, interpreted them in various ways.

Because they think they are white, they do not dare confront the ravage and the lie of their history. Because they think they are white, they cannot allow themselves to be tormented by the suspicion that all men are brothers.
                                                    -James Baldwin in Roediger, 1998

My answer to "the question" has evolved. I have identified three distinct stages and labeled them *rational inquiry, immersion,* and *activism scholarship*. These labels are not something I spent hours thinking about – actually I asked my husband to read an earlier draft of this paper and afterward, we pulled out these themes. They seemed to fit then – they still seem to fit.

Initially, my answer to "the question" was something like, "African American culture is so rich and intertwined with United States culture as a whole – it would be difficult to explore philanthropy and higher education in this country without touching upon black culture and history." I tried (and still do) to take the lead of Patricia Coleman-Burns in her essay "The revolution within: Transforming ourselves," in which she says that when one teaches and writes from an Afrocentric perspective, blacks "(1993: 140) are viewed not as a pitiful people stripped of their humanity and without hope, but as a people who struggle to define their humanity and shape their destiny against those who would dehumanize them." Yes, I am interested in the richness of African American history and culture, but my motivation is more complex.

Occasionally, white people have asked me if I have "white guilt" or if I had something happen in my past that is the impetus for my interest in exploring black history. I have yet to identify it if it is there. Unlike Betty M. Merchant, I was not marginalized as a child. A product of a low income family, Merchant notes in her essay, "Negotiating the boundaries and sometimes missing the mark: A white researcher and a Mexican American research assistant" "(2001: 14) My decision to focus my efforts on this kind of student is directly related to the marginalization I myself experienced as a result of being labeled as culturally deprived and economically disadvantaged within the dominant school culture." I know many researchers like Merchant, who want to "make a difference" or want to "change the system." Although this is something I too would like to do, it is not my only motivation.

Sometimes, when asked, "the question," especially by other white scholars, I think, "Well, you study French literature or Chinese poetry, or Mayan ruins – what is so different about me studying African American history and culture? Is it not a valid pursuit? Is it that we as whites in the United States see black culture as something we can never appreciate, learn from, and enjoy? Is it because we see it as strange, different from our "norm?" Is it because we fail to value black contributions to society? Why do we want to limit what people can study? I have never actually given someone this answer – only contemplated it. Because it is based on the notion of the academy as a place for objective research on any topic one feels is valid, I have labeled this response *rational inquiry*. With this response, I thought of studying black history in the same way that I studied political science as an undergraduate student. It was an engaging topic – and it still is. However, I now think of it much differently. This answer, too, was not wholly adequate.

The answer to "the question" evolved further when, in 1997, I was writing my dissertation in San Antonio, Texas. My husband is a faculty member as well and asked me to move there when he took an academic position. No one wanted to offer a position in college administration to a person writing a dissertation – thus, my job search in the academic world was unsuccessful. As a result, I took a position coordinating a youth program at a local African American community center (keep in mind, I had never worked outside of academe). When I arrived, I was the sole white employee. Those on the staff were either African American or Mexican-American.[1] This experience proved to be one of the most valuable that I have had.

My supervisor, a middle-aged, African American man, taught me about *his* culture, *his* family, and *his* traditions on a daily basis. Of course, this wasn't formal teaching – it was part of our daily interactions. The community center environment and all of the possibilities it offered invigorated me. I was welcomed into the community and after a short time, I felt sincerely trusted. I had a rare, wonderful opportunity to participate in conversations that I might never have heard. My husband and I shared meals and went to weddings, baby showers, and graduations with my colleagues at the center.

"Tony," my supervisor, conveyed many memories and experiences to me. He told me about growing up in Evansville, Indiana – waiting for his mother in the dress shop as she tried on beautiful party dresses. He would eat the cookies and lemonade that the sales ladies set out for customers. Shortly after his father died, he shared stories about the significance of this man. "Tony's" father had shaped so much of his life through examples and strong support of his family. "Tony" did the same for his children.

Along with the positive stories, "Tony" shared his frustrations with San Antonio – the struggles of managing a community center literally on the "wrong" side of the tracks. He told of the extra effort it took to get politicians and potential funders to visit the facility – how the center was ignored unless he kept it in the spotlight. "Tony" also talked about his frustration with his own community – the African American population in the city. If I had developed any tendency in graduate school to boil down race to a single essence, "Tony" demolished it. Thus, in my current research on African Americans, I try to depict the nuances and diversity within the community.

Unlike my graduate school experience – one in which academics sat in the classroom discussing "this group" and "that group"— my work at the center showed me the personal side of the culture I was studying. I felt the warmth, the energy, and the frustrations of my friends. I learned "their" ways of approaching a problem, "their" ways of celebrating, and "their" ways of protesting – ideas I could never have acquired in the classroom.

> *Music! Lilting, soft and languorous,*
> *Crashing, splendid, thunderous,*
> *Music! With you, touching my finger-tips!*
> *Music! With you, soul on your parted lips!*
> *Music—is you!*
>
> Alice Dunbar-Nelson in Sondra K. Wilson, 1999

I remember attending a storytelling event in the senior area of the center. There was a strong sense of community present in the room – a mutual respect for all of those who shared in the senior program. Dressed in their Sunday best, with large fancy hats, a lot of costume jewelry, and colorful high heels, a group of seniors was singing spirituals. In between the songs, a man read from his "autobiography," which told of his experiences as a Black Panther protesting in the name of civil rights. I felt completely "filled up" by this experience – it was eerie, joyful, and profound. By its taking place at the center, it also challenged my liberal assumptions. Having taken many law classes and being a staunch supporter of the separation between church and state, I was, at first, disturbed by the inclusion of religious music at a publicly-funded community center. But, at this particular event (I had attended many before this at the center), I came to recognize that for those who were brought up in this musical tradition, spirituals were not just a religious ritual, but a cultural one as well. Of course, one can read about this experience in a book, but to fully understand its significance one must experience it first hand. Song permeated the lives of the seniors and bolstered the sense of community at the center. Singing was a way for the seniors to come together regardless of their diverse backgrounds. Their songs silenced the room.

In my role at the center, I worked closely with children every day – mostly elementary and middle school children. Along with my husband, who is an artist, I developed a fine arts program at the center, and this would also prove to be a source of information and learning. Once when I was observing the painting class, I overheard two black children – they were brothers – showing disrespect to an African American woman who taught in the center's childcare program. She caught them "acting up" in the hallway on the way to the restroom and asked them to be quiet and to return to the art studio. They snapped back at her, "We aren't letting a ghetto woman tell us what to do. We're middle class." I asked the children to apologize and I explained why what they said hurt the woman. Hearing these children and their views on class challenged my thinking. How do I think about class in the black community? How is it conveyed in my writing? What do the various sectors of the black community think about class?

In addition to expanding my worldview, the people at the center gave me something very personal – their participation in my life. Our relationship was reciprocal in nature. This community celebrated the birth of my child, supported the writing of my dissertation, and cheered when I graduated with a Ph.D. Most importantly, I heard their voices and saw their actions – and it is this voice and agency that I try to capture in my writing. I have labeled this stage *immersion*. I was as much a part of the African American community at the center as I could be. I was honored with an opportunity to participate and hear the day-to-day voices of those I study. These are the voices that I hear in my head when I think about different viewpoints within the African American community. In my writing, I try to make sure that African Americans are not "(Coleman-Burns, 1997: 140) treated as passive objects being acted upon.... [They are] subjects of and actors in their own story." My experience at the center expanded my range of viewpoints about African American culture and gave voice to those viewpoints. Thus, the African American community became much more that an object of *rational inquiry*.

*And who shall separate the dust
Which later we shall be:
Whose keen discerning eye will scan
And solve the mystery?*

-Georgia Douglas Johnson in Arna Bontemps, 1963

I eventually left San Antonio and moved to Atlanta to begin a faculty position. Recently, I was asked "the question," by one of the African American students in a class that I teach. She said, "What led you to this topic – what's your motivation? To my surprise, the answer was better developed, more methodical, and came more quickly than before: "Well, aside from finding black history to be engaging and rich, I think about my research as a form of action – a form of social justice." Being white allows me to hear many conversations that African Americans don't hear – conversations that white people don't want anyone to know they are having. How do we change these conversations? Who will educate these people as to the importance of black history and culture? Although there are plenty of African Americans partaking in this effort, I *do not* see educating whites as their responsibility – whites must also educate each other. And many whites are not enlightened enough to open up to a learning experience facilitated by an African American. I can teach whites what I have been privileged to learn. This is a long answer, but something I find myself doing a lot – educating whites about the contributions of African Americans to society, the arts, literature, science, education, etc. Cutting through vast generalizations to get at their real assumptions and questions. Showing them how African American literature, history and thought can tell us all so much about who we are. As David R. Roediger has stated, "(1998: 4) African Americans have been among the nation's keenest students of white consciousness and white behavior." It can be rather disarming when someone finds out my research topic – the reactions are usually, "Oh!" or "Really, how interesting" or "Hmm... now what makes you interested in that." – but, regardless of their initial response, most people begin to think and ask questions.

*White men's children spread over the earth
Like a rainbow of peace to the drawn-swords of birth;
Uniting the races, soft-tinted, to one—
The World-man, Cosmopolite, Everyman's Son;
Whose blood is the sum of the red and the blue
With deep comprehension transcending the two;
Unriddle this riddle, of outside—in—
White men's children, in black men's skin.*

-Georgia Douglas Johnson in Sondra K. Wilson, 1999.

I would best describe my current thinking on the subject as *activism scholarship*. For the past few years, I have been conducting research on the life of African American sociologist Charles S. Johnson (1893-1956). Previously, Johnson has been looked upon as a recipient of white philanthropy – someone who was controlled by money. However, I chose to view him as an actor – someone with agency who sought out funding from available sources and used it to implement *his* ideas. In crafting my argument, I use the voices of Johnson and his contemporaries. When we examine Johnson's actions in this way, a new story is revealed. Although I am aware that I am interpreting another's culture, I have made my motivations and approach clear (Anzaldua, 1990).

In some ways, I think of my role as that of a "mediator" (Tate, 1998).[2] Since leaving the community center, this has become more difficult. I had a sense of security within the community at the center. However, just because I was accepted into this black community did not mean I would be accepted in every black community. Each time I did an interview, each time I went to an archive at a black college, – each time, I had to gain trust. With each entry and experience, it seemed easier. I was more relaxed and it was easier to establish trust. Many African Americans are suspicious of a white person interested in their history. I don't blame them. I am suspicious of other white people who do research in this area – I want to know what their motives are as well. I agree with Gloria Anzaldua and Arlette Ingram Willis when they urge scholars of color to be "(2001: 56) suspicious of the dominant culture's interpretations of 'our' experience of the way they 'read' us."

So now I am in a new city, at a new university, and without a well-placed friend to make introductions. Once again, I have to gain entrance into the black community. I have to learn the traditions, the etiquette, who the leaders are, etc. I have to answer the question again, "Why are you studying black history?"

Although I can claim to know only very little about this vast Diaspora, through research and with the help of my work at the community center, I have gained a fair amount of knowledge about black history and culture. And, I won't claim to be able to understand the experiences that blacks have on a daily basis. However, I do understand the plight of African Americans in a historical sense and as Arlette Ingram Willis exclaims, "(2001: 45) I have found my passion." And, I will continue to convey this understanding and the "(Tate, 1998: 222) elegance of the black mind." I will also continue to answer the question, "Why do you study black history?"

Discussion and Essay Questions:

1. In what ways can whites benefit from doing research on African Americans?

2. Can the vantage points of researchers who are African American be quite different from those who are white?

3. Is "entrance" into an African American community for someone who is white different than entrance into a white community for someone who is white?

4. Is "entrance" into an African American community for someone who is white the same as entrance into a white community for someone who is African American?

References

Anzaldua, Gloria. (1990). *Making Face, Making Soul (haciendo caras): Creative and Critical Perspectives of Feminists of Color.* San Francisco: Aunt Lute Books.

_____. Quoted in Arlette Ingram Willis. (2001). An African American Female Researcher's Journey: Epistemological, Conceptual, and Methodological Concerns. In
Betty M. Merchant and Arlette Ingram Willis (Eds.) *Multiple and Intersecting Identities in Qualitative Research.* (pp. 43-59: 56). New Jersey: Lawrence Erlbaum Associates, Publishers.

Baldwin, James. (1984). On Being "White" ... and Other Lies. In David R. Roediger. (1998). (Ed.), *Black on White. Black Writers on What It Means to Be White.* (pp. 177-180: 180). New York: Schocken Books.

Coleman-Burns, Patricia. (1993). The Revolution Within: Transforming Ourselves. In Joy James and Ruth Farmer (Eds.). *Spirit, Space, & Survival. African American Women in (White) Academe.* (pp. 139-157: 140). New York: Routledge.

Dunbar-Nelson, Alice. (1925). Music. In Sondra Kathryn Wilson (1999). (Ed.). *The Opportunity Reader. Stories, Poetry, and Essays from the Urban League's Opportunity Magazine.* (p. 25) New York: The Modern Library.

Hughes, Langston. (1934). Slave on the Block. In David R. Roediger. (1998). (Ed.). *Black on White. Black Writers on What It Means to be White.* (pp. 240 – 247: 240). New York: Schocken Books.

Johnson, Georgia D. (1963). Common Dust. In Arna Bontemps. (Ed.). *American Negro Poetry.* (pp. 20-21). New York: Hill and Wang.

Johnson, Georgia D. (1925). The Riddle. In Sondra Kathryn Wilson (1999). (Ed.). *The Opportunity Reader. Stories, Poetry, and Essays from the Urban League's Opportunity Magazine.* (p. 38). New York: The Modern Library.

Merchant, Betty M. (2001). Negotiating the Boundaries and Sometimes Missing the Mark: A White Researcher and a Mexican American Research Assistant. In Betty M. Merchant and Arlette Ingram Willis. (Eds.). *Multiple and Intersecting Identities in Qualitative Research.* (1-18: 14) New Jersey: Lawrence Erlbaum Associates, Publishers.

Polkinghorne, Donald (1988) quoted in Robert V. Bullough, Jr. and Stefinee Pinnegar. (2001). Guidelines for Quality in Autobiographical Forms of Self-Study Research. *Educational Researcher.* 30 (3), 13-21:16.

Roediger, David R. (1998). (Ed.). *Black on White. Black Writers on What It Means to be White.* (p. 4). New York: Schocken Books, 1998.

Tate, Greg. (1992). Guerrilla Scholar on the Loose. In David R. Roediger. (1998). (Ed.). *Black on White. Black Writers on What It Means to be White.* (pp. 218-224). New York: Schocken Books.

---

[1] In the city of San Antonio, among the professional population that I worked with, the term Mexican American was used as a way to describe race and ethnicity.
[2] Greg Tate, a writer for Vibe Magazine, used the term "mediator" in conjunction with race to describe Robert Farris Thompson, the white Yale University historian of African art.

About the Contributors

Tim Baylor is an Assistant Professor of Sociology at Lock Haven University of Pennsylvania. Besides Introductory Sociology he teaches Race and Ethnicity and Marriage and Family. His interest include issues tied to creating and maintaining identity, Native American culture,, the role of religion, and various forms of inequality."

Kianda Bell was a Ph.D. student and Graduate Fellow in sociology at The American University. It is with great sadness that his untimely death in December of 2005 is acknowledged.

Jeffrey R. Breese is the new Associate Dean of the School of Education and Human Services at Marymount University in Arlington, VA. His areas of interest and research in sociology are in the fields of applied sociology, race/ethnicity, and social psychology. He is a past president of the Society for Applied Sociology.

F. Erik Brooks is a Montgomery, Alabama native. He holds a Bachelor of Science in Journalism and Art from Troy State University. He holds a Master of Science in Counseling and Human Development from Troy State University. He also holds a Master of Public Administration from Auburn University at Montgomery and he holds a Master of Education from Alabama State University. He holds a Ph.D. from the L. Douglas Wilder School of Government at Virginia Commonwealth University in Public Policy and Administration. Currently, Dr. Brooks serves as the Director of the Master of Public Administration Program and an Assistant Professor of Political Science at Georgia Southern University.

Erica Chito Childs is an Assistant Professor of Sociology at Hunter College in New York City. She is the author of *Navigating Interracial Borders: Black-White Couples and Their Social Worlds* (Rutgers University Press 2005), which looks at contemporary views on interracial dating and marriage. Her areas of research are race and ethnic relations, multiracial issues, family diversity and media/popular culture images. She currently lives in New York City with her two children Christopher and Jada.

Bette J. Dickerson is Associate Professor of Sociology at American University and a past President of the Association of Black Sociologists. She has a master's degree in education from the University of Louisville and a PhD. in sociology from Washington State University. She has authored several book chapters and her most recent book is *African American Single Mothers: Understanding Their Lives and Families*. Her work primarily involves the socio-historical analysis of race, gender, and identity development among African American women.

Marybeth Gasman is an Assistant Professor of Higher Education at the University of Pennsylvania. She is an historian and her work focuses on historically Black colleges and universities and philanthropy. Dr. Gasman's is currently working on a history of the United Negro College Fund.

Charles A. Gallagher is an associate professor in the department of sociology and the race and urban studies concentration director at Georgia State University. His research focuses on racial and social inequality and the ways in which the media, the state and popular culture shape representations of race. He has published articles on the sociological functions of colorblind political narratives, how racial categories expand and contract within the context of interracial marriages, race theory, racial innumeracy and how one's ethnic history shapes perceptions of privilege.

G. Kathleen Grant is an associate professor of sociology at Findlay University in Findlay, OH. Her areas of concentration are in the fields of race/ethnicity, gerontology, and social psychology.

Larry J. Griffin is the John Shelton Reed Distinguished Professor of Sociology and History and Adjunct Professor of American Studies at the Univesity of North Carolina at Chapel Hill. He hails from Mississippi, and, except for Ph.D., received all of his education in the state's public schools. His teaching and research interests include the American South, race and ethnic relations, social inequality, and collective memory.

Contributors

Kathleen Korgen is Associate Professor of Sociology at William Paterson University in Wayne, NJ. Her research areas include race relations, racial identity, and civic engagement.

James Mahon is Associate Professor of Sociology at William Paterson University. Professor Mahon has conducted research in such areas as geographical migration and changes in church affiliation and diversity on college campuses.

Andrea Malkin Brenner is an Assistant Professor of Sociology at American University in Washington, DC. Her research interests include the sociology of education, race and identity politics and diverse family structures. Her latest publications include Understanding Social Location, The Symbolic Basis of Culture and Stereotyping and Labeling by Pine Forge Press. She was recently named Professor of the Year at American University.

Stephanie M. McClure is a doctoral student at the University of Georgia. Her interests include minority student access and success in higher education, the college student experience, education for social justice, and exploring and identifying the complications associated with the intersection of race, class, and gender identities.

Eunice Matthews-Armstead is an associate professor of sociology and social work at Eastern Connecticut State University. Her areas of research are racial identity, educational attainment, and women's development.

Joshua McIntosh earned his Bachelor of Science in Biology from Elon University, Master of Arts in College Student Development from Appalachian State University, and is currently a Ph.D. candidate in the School of Education at Syracuse University. He has served as an administrator in residence life, fraternity and sorority affairs, and student activities. He is currently the Director of Housing at Harvard University.

Robert M. Moore III is an Associate Professor of Sociology at Frostburg State University. He edited, *The Hidden America: Social Problems in Rural America for the Twenty-first Century*, published in 2001 by Susquehanna University Press. He edited in 2002, *The Quality and Quantity of Contact: African Americans and Whites on College Campuses*, published by University Press of America. He is the recipient of two university faculty achievement awards, teaching and service. He was recently nominated for a University System of Maryland Board of Regents' Award for teaching.

Frank Ridzi is an Assistant Professor of Sociology in the Department of Sociology at Le Moyne College, where he is also Director of Urban and Regional Studies and Director of the Urban and Regional Center. He earned a Ph.D. and a Master of Public Administration from Syracuse University's Maxwell School of Citizenship and Public Affairs.

Zandria Robinson is completing her Master's degree is Sociology at the University of Memphis and preparing to enter a Ph.D. program in Sociology.

Joe Ruane is Professor of Sociology and Health Policy at University of the Sciences in Philadelphia (formerly Philadelphia College of Pharmacy and Science), received his M.A. from Temple University, and Ph.D. from University of Delaware. He has a Certificate in Intercultural Communication from the Universidad de Catolica, Ponce, Puerto Rico. He holds a citation from the Chapel of Four Chaplains for the interracial work in the North Philadelphia community, and another citation from the Black Academic Achievement Society at PCPS. Joe is a past president of the Pennsylvania Sociological Society (1989-90), and of the National Council of State Sociological Societies of the American Sociological Society (2000). He is presently Chair of the Board of the West Philadelphia Partnership, and Chair of Health Services Group, Inc. He is past President and Board Chair of the Federation of Christian Ministries, and is listed in *Who's Who in America* and is also undergraduate dean of Global Ministries University. He is the Faculty Athletic Representative to the National Collegiate Athletic Association (NCAA) for USP, and a member of USP Institution Review Board, and Strategic Planning Committee Community Task Force. He is married to Nancy DiPasquale, MN,RN, and they have a married daughter Krista.

Wanda Rushing is Associate Professor of Sociology at the University of Memphis whose research interests include social inequality and the U.S. South. Currently, she is writing a book about Memphis.

Todd Schoepflin received his B.A. from SUNY Fredonia in 1994 and attended graduate school at Stony Brook University. In 2004 he completed his dissertation at Stony Brook, entitled "A Sociological Analysis of Interracial Interaction at a Predominantly White University." He is currently an Assistant Professor in the department of Criminal Justice at Niagara University.

Gabe T. Wang is Chair of the Department of Sociology at William Paterson University. Professor Wang's research interests include cross-cultural comparative studies, population and development, and adolescent deviant behavior in both the United States and China.